IMAGE DATABASES AND MULTI-MEDIA SEARCH

SERIES ON SOFTWARE ENGINEERING AND KNOWLEDGE ENGINEERING

Series Editor-in-Chief
S K CHANG (*University of Pittsburgh, USA*)

Vol. 1 Knowledge-Based Software Development for Real-Time Distributed Systems
        Jeffrey J.-P. Tsai and Thomas J. Weigert (Univ. Illinois at Chicago)

Vol. 2 Advances in Software Engineering and Knowledge Engineering
        edited by Vincenzo Ambriola (Univ. Pisa) *and Genoveffa Tortora* (Univ. Salerno)

Vol. 3 The Impact of CASE Technology on Software Processes
        edited by Daniel E. Cooke (Univ. Texas)

Vol. 4 Software Engineering and Knowledge Engineering: Trends for the Next Decade
        edited by W. D. Hurley (Univ. Pittsburgh)

Vol. 5 Intelligent Image Database Systems
        edited by S. K. Chang (Univ. Pittsburgh), *E. Jungert* (Swedish Defence Res.
        Establishment) *and G. Tortora* (Univ. Salerno)

Vol. 6 Object-Oriented Software: Design and Maintenance
        edited by Luiz F. Capretz and Miriam A. M. Capretz (Univ. Aizu, Japan)

Vol. 7 Software Visualisation
        edited by P. Eades (Univ. Newcastle) *and K. Zhang* (Macquarie Univ.)

Vol. 8 Image Databases and Multi-Media Search
        edited by Arnold W. M. Smeulders (Univ. Amsterdam) *and*
        Ramesh Jain (Univ. California)

Forthcoming titles:

Acquisition of Software Engineering Knowledge
edited by Robert G. Reynolds (Wayne State Univ.)

Monitoring, Debugging, and Analysis of Distributed Real-Time Systems
Jeffrey J.-P. Tsai, Steve J. H. Yong, R. Smith and Y. D. Bi (Univ. Illinois at Chicago)

Series on
Software
Engineering
and
Knowledge
Engineering

Vol. 8

Series Editor

S K Chang

IMAGE DATABASES AND MULTI-MEDIA SEARCH

editors

Arnold W M Smeulders
University of Amsterdam

Ramesh Jain
University of California

World Scientific
Singapore • New Jersey • London • Hong Kong

Published by

World Scientific Publishing Co. Pte. Ltd.

P O Box 128, Farrer Road, Singapore 912805

USA office: Suite 1B, 1060 Main Street, River Edge, NJ 07661

UK office: 57 Shelton Street, Covent Garden, London WC2H 9HE

British Library Cataloguing-in-Publication Data
A catalogue record for this book is available from the British Library.

IMAGE DATABASES AND MULTI-MEDIA SEARCH

ISBN 981-02-3327-2

This book is printed on acid-free paper.

Printed in Singapore by Uto-Print

PREFACE

The Web and Internet are signs that things will be different in the future. And, what is so striking about this future, is that it comes so incredibly fast and is so incredibly overwhelming. Anyone who surfs the Web will exclaim at one point or the other that there is so much information available, so much to search, so much to keep up with.

Where Lycos and Altavista are already accepted tools for textual information, image databases and multi-media search engines are the natural answers in the quest for pictorial information. This book provides the state of the art description of this field. It contains the proceedings of a valuable workshop in Amsterdam, where people gathered to openly discuss the progress in the field: how to search for pictures, to define pictorial clues, to store them in databases by indexes, and, to access the information.

The strange thing with image databases and pictorial search is that the topic received only marginal attention in the computer vision world, where much attention is focussed on the finding of the general solution for scene segmentation first. Most authors in this book take a reverse approach: to solve the indexing and searching first and, if still needed, then the segmentation of the scene.

Applications of pictorial search are many: identification of trade marks, identification of stolen goods, searching for an exact copy, pictorial encyclopedia in manufacturing, agriculture, product handling. The purpose of this book is to identify computational methods to achieve the search.

The editors of this book would like to thank cordially the people who made the workshop happen, Dr. Marcel Worring for very efficient local organisation, Dr. Theo Gevers for persistent handling of electronic submission and, Dr. Carel van den Berg, the secret force behind the scenes.

The editors also thank the reviewers of the papers: S.K. Chang (University of Pittsburg, USA), M.M. Chanowski (University of Amsterdam, the Netherlands), A. del Bimbo (University of Florence, Italy), W.I. Grosky (Wayne State University, USA), A. Hsu (Siemens Corporate Research, USA), H. Ip (City University, Hong Kong), J.K. Wu (NUS, Singapore), T. Kato (ETL Tsukuba, Japan), R. Kasturi (Penn State University, USA), M.L. Kersten (Centre of Mathematics and Computer Science, the Netherlands), C. Leung (Victoria University of Technology, Australia), R. Pickard (MIT, USA), D. Petkovic (IBM Almaden, USA), S.W. Smoliar (FXPAL, USA), H. Tagare (Yale University, USA).

Arnold Smeulders
Ramesh Jain

CONTENTS

Multi-Media Search

Multi-Media Search: An Authoring Perspective

Stephen W. Smoliar
James D. Baker
Takehiro Nakayama
Lynn Wilcox
FX Palo Alto Laboratory, Inc.
3400 Hillview Avenue, Building 4
Palo Alto, CA 94304
Telephone: +1-415-813-6703 (Smoliar)
Fax: +1-415-813-7081
Email: {smoliar, baker, nakayama, wilcox}@pal.xerox.com

1. The Nature of Authoring

If we are to achieve a world in which hypermedia has become the basis of the documents we exchange, then that world will require that we first achieve the goal of authoring software that makes hypermedia documents as easy to create as text documents are through current word processing environments. However, we can only succeed in inventing authoring technology if we also invent the relation of that technology to the human behaviors of both writing and reading (Baker *et al.*, 1996). We already tend to identify authoring with writing, but it is often overlooked that the role of the reader is just as important to effective communication as that of the writer.

While we may all have learned to read from printed books, our appreciation of other media allows us to generalize those intuitions we have formed about reading. When we talk about "reading" a film, a painting, or even a personality evoked by a stage actor, there may be some argument as to whether or not we are using the verb "read" in a literal or metaphorical sense. We feel it is important that this view of reading *not* be taken as 'mere metaphor. Rather, adopting the terminology of Ferdinand de Saussure (1986), we wish to view the objects we encounter in printed books, films, paintings, and even the personalities evoked by actors as instances of a single collective called *signs*. Saussure proposed a new science, to be called *semiology*, "which studies the role of signs as part of social life." Semiology is thus concerned with both the nature of signs and how we "read" them as a fundamental aspect of our human behavior.

The attempt to characterize the nature of signs began with those that seemed the most straightforward, the linguistic signs (de Saussure, 1986):

> A linguistic sign is not a link between a thing and a name, but between a concept and a sound pattern. The sound pattern is not actually a sound; for a sound is something physical. A sound pattern is the hearer's psychological impression of a sound, as given to him by the evidence of his senses. This sound pattern may be called a 'material' element only in that it is the representation of our sensory impressions. The sound pattern may thus be distinguished from the other element associated with it in a linguistic sign. This other element is generally of a more abstract kind: the concept.

This approach is a useful one because it can be generalized to signs in other media that must be founded on not only a concept but also some set of sensory impressions that are perceived as a pattern. Saussure then assigned names to designate these two elements of a single sign. The pattern of sensory impressions was called the *signifier*, and the concept associated with that pattern was called the *signified*. Louis Hjelmslev then introduced the idea of "planes" for distinguishing the respective domains of signifiers and signifieds, described by Roland Barthes (1973) as follows: "The plane of the signifiers constitutes the *plane of expression* and that of the signifieds the *plane of content.*"

What does this have to do with reading and writing signs? First of all, it is necessary to put aside any view of reading as a relatively passive task: A passive approach to reading is one in which the reader is not paying attention! An alternative approach, which has been introduced by Umberto Eco (1979), is that reading is an *activity* in which the reader, negotiating between signifiers and signifieds, *reconstructs* the material being read, transforming one body of signs into another. This approach is based on the hypothesis that a reader has understood a document when he is capable of recounting its content (and perhaps its expression) back to himself (or to anyone else). This reconstructive process frequently takes place in the reader's head, but if it is translated to some concrete medium, then, for all intents and purposes, it is another writing task. In other words an authoring technology that supports writing in a manner both efficient and unobtrusive may be equally valuable in the support of reading.

2. Where Does Search Fit Into the Processes of Reading and Writing?

Where does search fit into this story? While hypermedia existed before the rise of the World Wide Web, we now tend to think of the Web as the most significant repository of hypermedia documents. More important, however, is that, as that repository grows, it will become the *primary information resource* for authors preparing the documents it contains. In other words the Web is a potential paradigm shift of authors' attitudes towards libraries. After all, most authors still tend to consult a variety of resources as part of the normal course of a writing task. If those resources are now going to be available through Web pages, what will be the effect on the resulting writing behavior?

The nature of writing behavior itself has been an object of study for many research projects that we have reviewed elsewhere (Baker *et al.*, 1996). In an attempt to generalize the results of these projects from text to hypermedia, we have developed our own model of reading and writing illustrated in Fig. 1. For the purposes of this discussion, we shall not dwell on the generation of outlines and the rendition of a hypermedia document, concentrating instead on the role of search in the first two stages of this model.

When we think of a writer researching material in a conventional library, we usually envisage a process that begins by accumulating a pile of books and articles. Then, as each of those items is read, the writer tends to make note of specific *points*, traditionally assigning each point to the proverbial index card (Baker *et al.*, 1996).

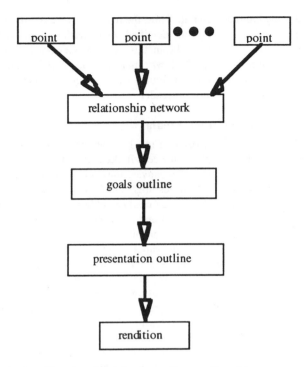

Fig. 1. Model of reading and writing

This need to *extract* such points from "the literature" will be just as important if that literature is on the Web as it would be in any other library. Sometimes, however, the writer has a specific point in mind that needs to be validated by consulting available sources. In this case that point becomes an *object of search*: The writer needs to associate it with a source document in order to establish a confirming citation or to help find additional material relating to the point being developed.

However, a writer does more than cull points from large quantities of reading matter. The actual *synthetic* side of writing begins with the hypothesizing of *relationships* among those points. One of the most important of these relationships is the organizing of points into groups, and such grouping leads to another approach to search. Once a group has been defined, one often wishes to add further points to it, seeking out additional confirming evidence. Thus, one point may serve to drive the search for other points, provided the nature of the grouping relationship can be suitably articulated.

Furthermore, extracting points and searching for related points can be just as important to reading as they are to writing. Eco's reconstructive approach to reading comprehension is often driven by the reader's ability to relate the content of a new document to already familiar material. Thus, the reader may be as likely to undertake a "search-by-relationship" on a point identified while reading as a writer would be while engaged in a literature search. From this point of view, search may be one of the most fundamental activities for both writing and reading. If its significance tends to be overlooked, it is because so much of it frequently takes place in the subconscious of both the writer and the reader.

3.   Implications for Different Media

The whole point of the model in Fig. 1, however, is that "points" need not necessarily be restricted to simple sentences of declarative text. Art historians see such "points" as particular regions of a canvas, musicologists hear them in melodic, harmonic, rhythmic, or even timbred gestures, and film theorists may make a point out of an entire *mise en scène*. We are currently working on a hypermedia authoring environment that supports the collection and management of points in any of these media, as well as the definition of relationships among those points (Baker *et al.*, 1996). However, this environment must support not only the accumulation of those points but also search processes through which they may be encountered and extracted.

From a semiological point of view, the target of a search is always a *sign*. However, the terminology of semiology allows us to be more specific. A search operation is usually confined to only one of Hjelmslev's planes, and explicitly identifying that plane may facilitate expressing the search target more clearly. This distinction may be found in the data model for the Visual Information Management System (VIMSYS) (Gupta, Weymouth, and Jain, 1991) developed under the InfoScope project at the University of Michigan. That model partitioned information into planes of its own (not to be confused with Hjelmslev's planes) that distinguished data derived from *images* (Hjelmslev's plane of expression) from those derived from *domain objects* being represented by those images (Hjelmslev's plane of content). Bearing this distinction in mind, let us now examine the nature of search with respect to the media of text, images, audio, and video.

3.1   Text

When one has a specific pointer (URL) to the target text, the World Wide Web works very well. However, this is not always the case. When one doesn't have a pointer but specific text in mind, he might want to use the current keyword search technology. There are some search engines available on the Web (e.g., http://www.altavista.digital.com/); but there is no guarantee that their search space includes the target text. They can search only a limited part of the Web, because it is impossible to take a snapshot of a structure that may be changing at any place at any moment. Furthermore, it is often a difficult task to compose a set of keywords that selectively represents the target of the user's search.

Following the model shown in Fig. 1, writers need to try to relate as many relevant combinations of text as possible when they want to accumulate points and organize them into a relationship network. Fortunately, because the text on the Web is machine-readable, we can use it not only as targets of search but also for assistance in formulating queries. In other words one uses information from the plane of expression of one document as cues for searching the plane of expression of other documents; and, as we learn more about which features on the plane of expression tend to yield the best search results, we may use those features as a basis for indexing, rather than the conventional keyword-based approach. However, because we are searching on the plane of expression, rather than the plane of content, we must be satisfied with only a list of potential candidates, many of which may have nothing to do with the target the user had in mind. Nevertheless, by beginning the search on the plane of expression, analysis on the plane of content, which is far less susceptible to automation, may be concentrated on the candidate set, rather than the entire search space.

3.2 Images

The better part of this decade has seen considerable effort towards advancing technology in "content-based image retrieval" (Furht, Smoliar, and Zhang, 1995). Unfortunately, none of this work really has anything to do with content in Hjelmslev's sense of the word. A humbler awareness of history and a more generous acknowledgment of Hjelmslev's perspective would rightfully call this technology *expression*-based retrieval.

From a Saussurean point of view, expression-based retrieval would be driven by sound patterns. However, if we are interested in images rather than language, we may assume that signifiers consist in patterns of visual, rather than auditory, stimuli. If such patterns are to drive our abilities to perform search operations, then we need to understand their nature before we understand how we may exploit them. What, after all, *are* patterns of visual stimuli?

One fruitful way to approach this question is to consider the research of Gerald Edelman (1987). For over a decade Edelman has been investigating the construction of automata that not only are capable of general visual perception but also have designs that reflect our knowledge of the neural architectures that support *biological* perception. Edelman's model takes a two-stage approach to the perception of visual patterns. The first stage is the recognition and classification of *image features*, while the second stage identifies patterns in terms of relationships among those features.

From this point of view, even expression-based retrieval still comes up short, because almost all technological advances have addressed the detection and representation of image features. It *is* true that this technology can now provide mathematical models for a variety of these features, including color, texture, object shape, and edge relationships of the sort one might encounter in a hand-drawn sketch (Furht, Smoliar, and Zhang, 1995). However, while the technology for representing an object's shape is promising, the segmentation technology that identifies an object in the first place is far weaker. As Edelman (1987) has demonstrated, that technology requires building beyond the recognition of features to the more sophisticated identification of actual patterns. Consequently, even the representation of features such as color and texture still cannot be readily associated with objects, but only with either the entire image or some isolated region of that image (determined *a priori*).

This means that, if we wish to include the search for image signs in the course of either writing or reading, we shall have to reduce our expectations of what such a search is likely to retrieve. First of all, we need to provide support in expressing our query in a form that has only to do with image features, rather than patterns of those features, let alone any properties on Hjelmslev's plane of content. Thus, if we wish to formulate such a query based on a specific source image, we must first reduce that image to its features and then decide which of those features will be incorporated in the query (and how they will be incorporated). Finally, we have to accept that searching on such a query can only be viable if it yields a set of candidates, some (if not many) of which may have nothing to do with the content we had in mind and many of which may only be valuable to the extent that they can help us formulate a more accurate query (Furht, Smoliar, and Zhang, 1995). Clearly, this is not the best of situations; but, on the basis of some experiences with such feature-based retrieval systems (Seybold, 1994), it *does* seem to be better than nothing.

3.3 Audio

In some cases, the author of a hypermedia document may want to create textual links to audio. For example, in an educational document on various types of musical instruments, the author may want to provide links from the instrument names to their pictures as well as to sound samples produced by each instrument. While it is reasonable to do this for a small number of examples, it is not feasible to label manually large collections of music by the instrument being played. However, using techniques similar to speaker identification and segmentation (Wilcox *et al.*, 1994), it may be possible to search arbitrary collections of music for examples of a particular instrument. This capability would not only provide the author with an easier means to locate musical examples, but also allow the reader to enrich the document by locating examples on his own.

Also, in a hypermedia document analyzing a particular piece of music, the author may want to point out to the reader a particular melodic theme. While the author might highlight the melody line in the musical score, it would also be informative to highlight the melody in the music itself. This requires first that the melody be found within the context of the entire musical piece, and second that the melodic line be segmented from the accompaniment. Locating the melody within the piece could be performed using techniques for wordspotting in speech (Wilcox and Bush, 1992). Segmentation of the melodic line, however, requires partial transcription of music.

Finally, it is important to recognize that there is more to audio than speech and music. There is a broad variety of other sound objects that may be targets of search operations. Classifying these sounds is no easy matter (Smoliar, 1993). Various descriptive ontologies have been proposed, but none have been particularly effective. Indeed, in the case of film and video, the evidence strongly suggests that the classification of a sound is tightly coupled to what the audience sees while the sound is heard (Metz, 1985). Thus, while feature-based search may be the only viable approach, there is a significant danger that its performance for audio will be far weaker than is currently achieved with images.

3.4 Video

For all intents and purposes all problems concerned with searching video are subsumed by problems concerned with searching both images and audio. Thus, as is the case with images, we cannot really expect video search to rise above the level of stimuli features, let alone accommodate any technique that is truly content-based. The best we can hope for is that a repository of video source material be indexed with respect to one or more *abstractions* of that content.

The simplest technique is to formulate abstractions in text and reduce the problem to search in the text domain. While useful results based on free text are feasible, search may be facilitated by constraining the text according to different "styles of discourse." One such style is stratification, where text is constrained to account for a time table of events (Aguierre Smith, 1992). Another style is that of object-oriented frames (Smoliar, Zhang, and Wu, 1994). In this case the "text" is basically constrained to forms similar to that of a propositional calculus, and search may require supplementing conventional matching with inference on those propositional forms. Yet another style is that of the database record, and a variety of different approaches to data modeling for video databases have been proposed (Furht, Smoliar, and Zhang, 1995).

Alternatives to text styles have not yet been explored very extensively, but several have been investigated (Furht, Smoliar, and Zhang, 1995). One possibility is to reduce the problem strictly to one of image search. This is achieved by first reducing the video to a collection of static images. If these images are *key frames* extracted from the individual camera shots, this approach becomes feasible with respect to the amount of data that must be stored and subjected to search. However, the method also inherits all of the shortcomings of the current state of the art of image search. Another possibility is to abstract a video strictly into its camera movements. These movements may be regarded as features at the video level, rather than the image level. They are characteristically unique to video and film data. The problem is that it tends to be difficult to formulate useful queries based on these features. Finally, there are features concerned with movement in the entire image frame, rather than just movement due to the camera. These features (or some approximation of them) are often explicitly detected and recorded as part of a compressed representation of a video source. If the video is stored in that compressed form, then searching based on those features does not require that the images first be reconstructed. Again, however, the key problem is one of being able to formulate useful queries in terms of those features.

4. Bibliography

Aguierre Smith, T. G., If You Could See What I Mean ... Descriptions of Video in an Anthropologist's Video Notebook, Master's thesis, Massachusetts Institute of Technology, Cambridge, September 1992.

Baker, J. D. *et al.* Reinventing Reading and Writing in the Context of Hypermedia, submitted to the International Working Conference on Integration of Enterprise Information and Processes (November 1996).

Barthes, R.   *Elements of Semiology*, translated by A. Lavers and C. Smith, New York: Noonday, 1973.

Eco, U.   Introduction: The Role of the Reader, *The Role of the Reader: Explorations in the Semiotics of Texts*, Bloomington: Indiana University Press, 1979, pp. 3–43.

Edelman, G. M. *Neural Darwinism: The Theory of Neuronal Group Selection*, New York: Basic Books, 1987.

Furht, B., Smoliar, S. W., and Zhang, H.-J.   *Video and Image Processing in Multimedia Systems*, Boston: Kluwer Academic Publishers, 1995.

Gupta, A., Weymouth, T., and Jain, R.   Semantic Queries with Pictures: The VIMSYS Model, Proceedings of the 17th International Conference on Very Large Data Bases (September 1991), pp. 69–79.

Metz, C. Aural Objects, *Film Sound: Theory and Practice*, edited by E. Weis and J. Belton, New York: Columbia University Press, 1985, pp. 154–161.

de Saussure, F. *Course in General Linguistics*, edited by C. Bally and A. Sechehaye with the collaboration of A. Riedlinger, translated and annotated by R. Harris, La Salle: Open Court, 1986.

Seybold, IBM Unleashes QBIC Image-Content Search, Seybold Report on Desktop Publishing, Vol. 9, No. 1 (September 1994).

Smoliar, S. W.   Classifying Everyday Sounds in Video Annotation, *Multimedia Modeling*, edited by T.-S. Chua and T. L. Kunii, Singapore: World Scientific, 1993, pp. 309–313.

Smoliar, S. W., Zhang, H.-J., and Wu, J.-H.   Using Frame Technology to Manage Video, Proceedings: Second Singapore International Conference on Intelligent Systems (November 1994), pp. B189–B194.

Wilcox, L., and Bush, M.   Training and Search Algorithms for an Interactive Wordspotting System, Proceedings: International Conference on Acoustics, Speech and Signal Processing (March 1992), pp. 97–100.

Wilcox, L. *et al.* Segmentation of Speech Using Speaker Identification, Proceedings: International Conference on Acoustics, Speech and Signal Processing (April 1994), pp. 161–164.

Picture Indexing

Painting Retrieval Based on Color Semantics

J. M. Corridoni, A. Del Bimbo, E. Vicario

Dipartimento di Sistemi e Informatica, Università degli Studi di Firenze
Via S. Marta 3 50139 Firenze, Italy
E-mail: {corridon|delbimbo|vicario}@aguirre.ing.unifi.it

Abstract. The availability of large image databases is emphasizing the relevance of *visual filters*, which permit to focus search on a small subset of data with characterizing visual features. Visual specification of such filters provides a natural way to express content–oriented queries. An original visual language is proposed for the symbolic representation of the semantics induced by the color quality and arrangement over a painting. The proposed language is based on the theory of color semantics introduced by artists in the twentieth century and is developed so as to permit visual querying. The grammar and the visual representation of the language are presented, and its implementation is discussed with reference to a prototype system supporting retrieval by color contents of artistic paintings.

1 Introduction

In the access to image databases, the expression of queries plays a critical role shaping which part of information stored is actually accessible to users. Conventional techniques based on textual captions often result to be inadequate, as they require users to cast their visual knowledge into a textual form, not directly related with the appearing, physical contents of searched data. Textual labels become even more inadequate to express the *meta-language* conveyed by images, which mostly deals with the impressions induced by color, light and mass distribution on the image. While visual querying systems have been proposed to express queries in terms of *objective* low-level visual features, few attempts have been made to formalize the hidden semantics associated with images belonging to a specific context and to interpret the visual features in terms of sensations and emotions induced on the observer. This hidden semantics assumes a major relevance in retrieval based on color features.

First image retrieval techniques based on color have been proposed by Swain and Ballard in [11]. There, image contents are described by color histograms and queries are expressed by means of example images. Retrieval is performed by evaluating the similarity of color histograms in examples and stored images. In doing so, image similarity does not account for the spatial arrangement and coupling of colors over the image, which actually plays a major role in the user's perception of image chromatic contents. This limit is partially overcome in [12], by partitioning images into blocks, each associated with a localized own histogram. In this case, similarity matching also considers adjacency conditions among blocks with similar histograms. However, blocks are created according to a static partitioning of the image which prevents spatial arrangement conditions from reflecting the native patching of the image. In the QBIC database system [10], [2], perhaps the most notable example of querying by color, queries are expressed in terms of properties of color histograms, so as to support retrieval of images featuring a given color in a given proportion. Again, these properties neglect color localization and rather refer to low level image attributes which do not have a sound counterpart in the user's perception of chromatic contents. Recently, an image database system has been proposed by A. K. Jain [6], which exploits both color and shape features. In this system the query is formulated through an example image and retrieval is accomplished by a similarity evaluation measure computed on the basis of global color histogram and of edges.

A common trait of all these experience is the fact that they base retrieval on low-level properties of the image which can be automatically extracted through pattern recognition techniques, and which do no require high level interpretation. This largely reduces the archiving effort and ensures objective descriptions which avoid mismatches between the archiving and querying stages. However, the implementation of a low-level querying expressiveness forces the user to cast the high-level knowledge of searched data into a machine-oriented model.

The role of high-level semantics of color arrangements is explicitly tackled in [8], by exploiting textual annotations capturing sensations that images induce. While permitting the expression of high-level semantic concepts, this approach does not maintain any objective relation with the actual contents of the image. Annotation reflects definitely subjective factors such as culture, sensitivity, and even on the particular mood of people fronting the painting. This easily yields mismatches in the perception of painting contents at storage and retrieval time.

In this paper, we propose a new approach for bridging the "semantic gap" between visual features that can be automatically derived at the archiving time and visual properties that correspond to the *user-task model* [7] of retrieval. To this end, we resort to a theory of color perception, which was developed by Johannes Itten after the experience of the Bauhaus movement, and which permits to interpret high-level perceptual concepts on the basis of low-level image features. While breaking the limits of low-level descriptions, this approach overcomes the problems of users' subjectivity provided that the system is employed by a user community which agrees on the interpretation theory.

The rest of the paper is organized as follows. In Sect.2, we briefly recall Itten's theory of color semantics. Sect.3 addresses the definition of a visual querying language which mirrors this theory to capture properties about the spatial arrangement of chromatic regions. A prototype system implementing retrieval based on the querying language is discussed in Sect.4 through a few operation examples.

2   A High-Level Semantics for Image Retrieval by Color

Starting from the observation of the effects and sensations induced by colors on humans (harmony, disharmony, calmness, excitement), in 1960 Johannes Itten [5] formulated a theory of artistic color usage and of the semantics that this induces. The basis of Itten's theory is the creation of a color taxonomy that maps color space onto a discrete space of 180 fundamental colors characterized by their geographical coordinates. Twelve pure hues are identified as the fundamental elements for color semantics (see the circle of Fig. 1). The fundamental colors are then distinguished through variation of luminance and saturation and arranged into a chromatic sphere (*Runge–Itten sphere*), whose equatorial circle encompasses the 12 pure colors. By imposing 5 levels of luminance and 3 levels of saturation for each color, Itten identifies 180 reference colors, to which every color in the spectrum is assimilated. This formal taxonomy is especially intended to discriminate among the psychophysic effects that colors have on human perception. The analysis of the way color couplings on the paintings are mapped into geometrical relations over the sphere is exploited to derive high level assertions on the meaning and on the sensations induced. The absolute position of one color on the sphere triggers its level of *warmth*, or the sensation of temperature which it has been proven to be intrinsic with it, according to psychophysic experiments [9]. Specifically, pure colors are divided into the categories of *warm* colors (red-orange area) *cold* colors (green-blue area) and *mid–level* colors. The spheric arrangement of principal colors allows to define a connection between the sensations induced by chromatic compositions and the geometrical relations among the positions that colors forming the combination occupy on the sphere. Such a connection is expressed through chromatic operators such as the *contrast* operator. Two colors have contrasting qualities (wrt. hue or warmth) if these occupy (quasi–) opposite positions in Itten's sphere. The degree and the type of contrasts or assonance generates emotions like, for instance, anguish (dark cold colors), excitement (warm pure colors), ... In this application context, these sensations can be translated in terms of low–level chromatic and geometric properties of color regions in the image. One typical high level quality of paintings is *harmony* (or *disharmony*), which is defined in terms of combination and spatial arrangement of color masses over a painting. *Harmony*, is a rhythmic combination of chromatic elements, creating a stability effect onto human eye. The combination of chromatic elements is called *accordance of colors*, which is an ordered sequence of n colors, chosen in Itten's sphere, by defining a regular polygon over one of its circles. Fig. 1 shows how to create a color accordance and displays an example of a three–chromatic one. If color patches create a gravitational equilibrium on the painting and form a chromatic accordance, then the painting is said to be harmonic.

3 Querying Images by Color Arrangements

The rules of Itten's theory have been cast into a color description language supporting expression about the spatial arrangement of chromatic contents of images.

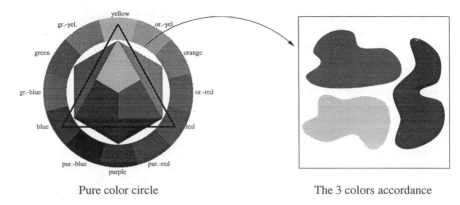

Pure color circle   The 3 colors accordance

Fig. 1. Creation of a color accordance. Example of 3-chromatic accordance

3.1   Chromatic Regions

The basic element of the language is the concept of region with homogeneous chromatic attributes. Such regions are identified over the image at archiving time through a segmentation process, and they are labeled with their histograms of *hue, luminance* and *saturation*, and with a representation of their spatial adjacencies and absolute positioning.

A thorough description of the segmentation process can be found in [4]. Briefly described, this segmentation is carried out by looking for clusters in the space of image colors obtained by replacing each image pixel with its characterization in terms of a color value. Segmentation is achieved by back–projecting cluster centroids in the feature space onto the image. Segmentation validity is obtained through an appropriate selection of the color space so that small feature distances correspond to similar colors in the perceptual domain. This condition, which is not exhibited by the standard RGB space, has been accomplished with the adoption of the CIE $L^*u^*v^*$ (*extended chromaticity*) space, where L^* is luminance, u^* is redness-greenness and v^* is approximately blueness-yellowness. Conversion between RGB to $L^*u^*v^*$ requires a non linear transformation which is surveyed in [1]. The selection of $M = 180$ Itten reference colors $c_i = (L_i, u_i, v_i)$ induces a quantization transform $Q^M : (L, u, v) \rightarrow m \in [1, M]$, that approximates every color with its closest reference point. The sampling operation produces minimal perceptual shift, which guaranteed by the uniformity properties of the $L^*u^*v^*$ space. The average radius of tessels induced by the Q^M transform determines the sampling imprecision δ with which a generic color c is mapped onto its nearest reference color point c_i.

3.2   Region and Picture Formulae

At querying time, searched image contents are qualified in terms of *region formulae* (ϕ) capturing chromatic properties of individual regions, and *picture formulae*

(Φ) capturing the spatial arrangement of regions over the image.

Region and picture formulae are expressed according to the following syntax:

$$\Phi := \exists\phi \mid \phi_1 \wedge \phi_2 \mid \phi_1 \vee \phi_2 \tag{1}$$

$$\phi := hue = \lambda_h \mid lum = \lambda_l \mid sat = \lambda_s \mid warmth = \lambda_w \mid$$
$$\mid size = \lambda_S \mid position = \lambda_p \mid \mathfrak{U}\phi_1 \mid \subseteq \phi_1 \mid \overset{\gamma}{\rightleftharpoons} \phi_1 \mid \tag{2}$$
$$\mid \phi_1 \wedge \phi_2 \mid \phi_1 \vee \phi_2.$$

where λ_γ is an evaluation for the measure of $\gamma \in \{h, l, s, w, S, p\}$ which denotes the attributes of hue, luminance, saturation, warmth, size, and position, respectively.

Region formulae are interpreted over the set of regions identified at archiving time according to a *satisfaction relation* $\models$, which returns the degree of truth ξ by a region R satisfies a formula ϕ. The satisfaction relation is defined through the following set of inductive clauses:

- $R \models_\xi \gamma = \lambda_\gamma$ for $\gamma = hue|luminance|saturation$ iff λ_γ represents the attribute γ of region R with degree of truth not lower than ξ, i.e. iff

$$\int_{\lambda_\gamma - \frac{\delta_h}{2}}^{\lambda_\gamma + \frac{\delta_\gamma}{2}} \mathcal{H}_\gamma(x)dx \geq \xi$$

  where $\mathcal{H}_\gamma(x)$ is histogram of γ-values of region R, and δ_γ is the maximal difference in the attribute γ between two adjacent *reference colors*.
- $R \models_\xi size = \lambda_S$, where $\lambda_S \in \{small, medium, large\}$, iff the actual size of R can be cast in the qualifier λ_S with membership not lower than ξ.
- $R \models_\xi warmth = \lambda_w$ with $\lambda_w \in \{very\ warm, warm, neutral, cold, very\ cold\}$ iff the the weighted sum of warmth measures of the colors of region R is not lower than ξ, i.e. iff

$$\int\int\int \mu_{\lambda_w}(\varrho, \vartheta, \varphi)\mathcal{H}(\varrho, \vartheta, \varphi)d\varrho d\vartheta d\varphi \geq \xi$$

  where: $\mu_{\lambda_w}(\varrho, \vartheta, \varphi)$ is the three-dimensional membership function which associates the truth degree with which a color having polar coordinates $(\varrho, \vartheta, \varphi)$ on Itten-Runge sphere can be defined as having the warmth level λ_w; and $\mathcal{H}(\varrho, \vartheta, \varphi)$ is the histogram function of region R, computed on the polar coordinates of the pixel colors.
- $R \models_\xi \mathfrak{U}\phi_1$ iff R is adjacent to a region R_1 which satisfies ϕ_1 with degree of truth not lower than ξ;
- $R \models_\xi \overset{\gamma}{\rightleftharpoons} \phi_1$ iff there exists a region R_1 which satisfies ϕ_1 with degree of truth not lower than ξ and which is contrasted in the attribute γ with respect to region R with a dgeree of truth not lower than ξ. To this end, the attributes γ of two regions R and R_1 are said to be contrasted with confidence ξ_2 if the average value of their colors are located (in Itten's sphere) in antipodal positions with respect to the pseudo–coordinate γ, within an angle displacement δ;

- $R \models_\xi \subseteq \phi_1$ iff R contains a region R_1 satisfying ϕ_1 with degree of truth not lower than ξ;
- $R \models_\xi \phi_1 \wedge \phi_2$ iff R satisfies both ϕ_1 and ϕ_2 with degree of truth not lower than ξ.
- $R \models_\xi \phi_1 \vee \phi_2$ iff R satisfies ϕ_1 or ϕ_2 with degree of truth not lower than ξ.

Once region formulae have been interpreted on the regions identified by the segmentation process, the following clauses which define a *satisfaction relation* $\models$ returning the degree of truth by which an overall image satisfies a picture formula:

- $\mathcal{I} \models_\xi \exists \phi$ iff the image I contains a region R which satisfies the region formula ϕ with degree of truth not lower than ξ;
- $\mathcal{I} \models_\xi \Phi_1 \wedge \Phi_2$ iff the image I satisfies both Φ_1 and Φ_2 with degree of truth not lower than ξ;
- $\mathcal{I} \models_\xi \Phi_1 \vee \Phi_2$ iff the image I satisfies Φ_1 or Φ_2 with degree of truth not lower than ξ;

Semantic clauses of both region and picture formulae have been directly translated into a model checking engine based on Unix tools Lex and Yacc. The engine decides about satisfaction of a legal formula Φ over an image description $\mathcal{I}_n$ with a two step process. First, the formula Φ is recursively decomposed in sub-formulae in a top-down manner. Afterwards, regions in the image description are labeled with the sub-formulae that they satisfy in a bottom-up approach: The satisfaction of region formulae is decided by directly referring to the chromatic and geometric descriptors associated with the region in the index; this first labeling level is then exploited to decide the satisfaction of composition formulae.

4   The Prototype System

The querying language described in Sect.3 has been employed as internal formal engine of a prototype system supporting visual retrieval by color content from a database of artistic paintings. [1].

In order to provide the user with a feedback about the meaninig of querying sentences, the system embodies the syntax of Sect. 3 onto a set of icon symbols and composition patterns [3]. The user builds region formulae by modifying the view of a *multi–aspect icon* according to the attributes by which the region is specialized. The relevant quality by which a region is characterized in the query (f.e. hue, warmth,...) is associated with a constant visual feature of the icon. The quantification of such quality tunes such feature accordingly. Fig. 2 displays

---

[1] The system manages a databases of more than 1000 paintings dating from the Renaissance to nowadays and presently runs under IRIX 5.3 operating system on an SGI Indy. Interfacing is based on OpenGL graphic libraries.

an example of progressive tuning of an icon quality characterized by warmth. The quality *warmth* is visualized on the background, while the actual degree of warmth contribution (amount of warmth, region dimension, ..) are visually expressed through progressive specialization of the icon foreground, which create a hierarchical chain of n levels. The number of levels is proportional to the degree of specification of the region: A high value of n implies a strict constraint on region features. Icon chains, can be composed through the chromatic and spatial operators introduced in Sect. 3 and boolean connectives.

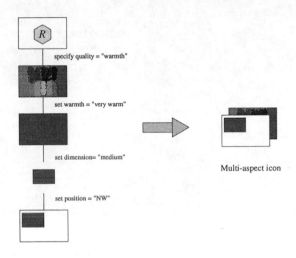

Fig. 2. Visualization of the concept of *multi-aspect icon*. Region qualification by warmth quality.

Fig. 3 shows the visual interface of the sentence editor, where icon chains are composed by the user querying the system. The main clipboard shows the regions characterized by region formulae (ϕ) appearing in the statement. The lower part of the screen displays the iconic representation of qualifying features: hue, luminance, saturation, and warmth. Two high-level shortcuts of harmony and focus of attention are also at user's disposal. The construction of visual regions in the main clipboard is performed by selecting and specializing icons through the tools in the right part of the interface. Tools are made visible in dependence on the current state of the formula, so to drive user attention on the attributes that can be legally updated. Once region formulae have been instantiated, they can be combined into composition formulae (Φ) by dragging region icons into the lower clipboard.

Completed visual arrangements are passed to a parsing engine, which checks for syntactic correctness and generates a search string for the retrieval engine. Matching images are ranked according to the degree of truth by which they

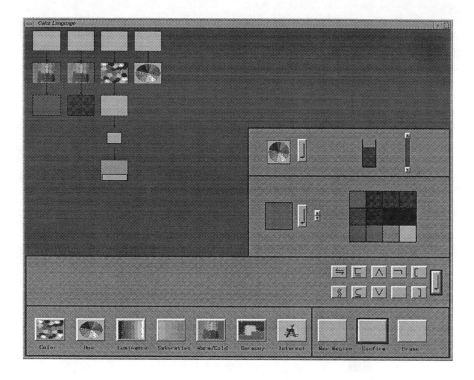

Fig. 3. The user interface for color–based querying with multi–aspect icons.

satisfy the query, and they are presented to the user in decreasing order.

Figg.4 and 5 report two operation examples.

Fig.4 addresses a query with higher level semantics: the query searches those paintings that are characterized by regions having sharply different levels of luminance. Arrangement of such regions in the form of planes ("planes of luminance") is often used to induce the sense of depth in the observer (light⇒far; dark⇒near). Fig. 4a shows the visual expression of the query on paintings, where those with three planes of luminance are sought. To perform the query, three regions R_1, R_2 and R_3, characterized by luminance are instantiated. The three are specialized as having a high, medium and low level of luminance, respectively. The query is then expressed by the visual assertion in the *Sentence Editor*, whose translation is $\phi = R_1 \land R_2 \land R_3$. The first three retrieved paintings are shown in Fig. 4b, where the planes of luminance have been manually evidenced.

Fig. 5 addresses a query searching for paintings which include regions with a contrast in warmth. Fig. 5a shows the expression of the query and Fig. 5b displays the result. The first two paintings are clear examples of what we mean as contrasted paintings in terms of warmth qualities. The orange–red color of the fishes in Klee's painting is opposed to the cold sensation expressed by water

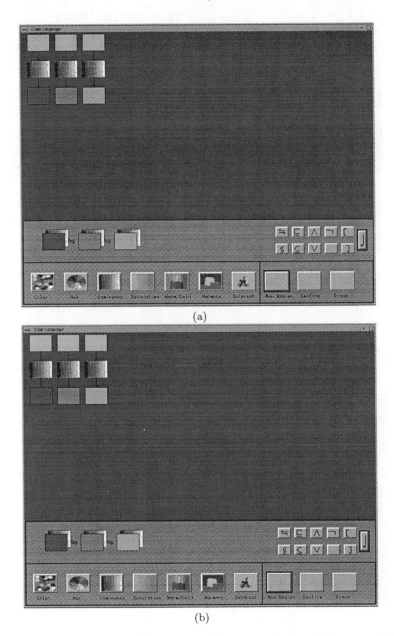

Fig. 4. Visual query on luminance planes. (a) The formulation of the query. (b) The retrieved paintings.

Fig. 5. Visual query on warm/cold contrast. (a) The formulation of the query. (b) The retrieved paintings.

color. The same notations can be done for the Monet, where the sun in the dark environment excites the contrast of color "temperatures".

References

1. R.C. Carter and E.C. Carter. CIELUV color difference equations for self-luminous displays. *Color Res. & Appl.*, (8)4:252–553, 1983.
2. W. Cody. Querying multimedia data for multiple repositories by content: the GARLIC project. *Visual Data Base Systems III.*
3. J.M. Corridoni, A. Del Bimbo, S. De Magistris and E. Vicario. A Visual Language for Color–Based Painting Retrieval. *IEEE Int. Symp. on Visual Languages VL '96*, Boulder, CO, USA, September 1996.
4. J.M. Corridoni, A. Del Bimbo, and E. Vicario. Image Retrieval by Color Semantics with Incomplete Knowledge. to appear in the *Journal of the American Society for Information Systems.*
5. P. Itten. *Kunst der Farbe.* Otto Maier Verlag, Ravensburg, 1961.
6. A. K. Jain and A. Vailaya. Image retrieval using color and shape. *Pattern Recognition*, 29(8):1233–1244, Aug. 1996.
7. D. R. Gentner and J. Grudin. Design models for computer-human interface. *IEEE Computer*, (29)6:28–36, June 1996.
8. T. Kato, T. Kurita, and H. Shimogaki. Multimedia interaction with image database systems. *SIGCHI Bullettin*, 22(1):52–54, July 1990.
9. Luscher. *Test dei Colori (Test on Colors).* ed. Astrolabio, Roma, Italy, 1976.
10. W. Niblack and al. The QBIC project: Querying images by content using color, texture and shape. In *SPIE Storage and Retrieval for Image and Video Databases*, volume 1908, February 1993.
11. M. Swain and D. Ballard. Color indexing. *International Journal of Computer Vision*, 7(1):11–32, January 1993.
12. A. Nagasaka and Y. Tanaka. Automatic video indexing and full video search for object appearances. *IFIP Trans., Visual Database Systems II*, pages 113-127, Knuth, Wegner (Eds.), 1992. Elsevier.

PicToSeek: A Color Image Invariant Retrieval System

T. Gevers and A.W.M. Smeulders

Department of WINS, University of Amsterdam
Kruislaan 403, 1098 SJ Amsterdam, The Netherlands
email: gevers@wins.uva.nl
PicToSeek is available on-line at:
http://www.wins.uva.nl/research/isis/zomax/

Abstract

In this paper, our goal is to analyze and evaluate various color features to be used for the purpose of image retrieval by color-metric histogram matching independent of varying imaging conditions.

In theory, we will examine the effect of a change in camera viewpoint, object surface orientation, illumination intensity, and illumination color for the various color features under a simple reflection model.

To evaluate photometric color invariance in practice, experiments have been carried out on a database consisting of 500 images taken from multicolored man-made objects in real world scenes. Images in the database show a considerable amount of noise, shadows, shading and specularities resulting in a good representation of views from everyday life as it appears in home video and consumer photography in general.

Finally, using the color invariant models, we describe an image search system by which visual information is automatically collected, indexed and cataloged entirely on the basis of the pictorial content. The system allows for fast on-line image search by combining: (1) visual browsing through the precomputed image catalogue; (2) query by pictorial example; (3) query by image features. The system shows high image retrieval accuracy and fast image search.

1 Introduction

A promising approach to image retrieval is image retrieval by content [2], [3], for example. The search is carried out from a pictorial specification defined by an example picture image given by the user on input. Image retrieval is then the problem of identifying the query image as (a part of) target images in the image database.

A simple and effective retrieval scheme is to represent and match images on the basis of color-metric histograms [4]. In this regard, images are retrieved that have similar color information distribution with respect to the color information distribution of the query image.

In this paper, our aim is to analyze and evaluate various color features to be used for the purpose of image retrieval by color-metric histogram matching according to the following criteria:

- Invariant to a change in viewpoint of the camera.
- Invariant to a change in position and orientation of the object in view.
- Invariant to a change in the direction and intensity of the illumination.
- Invariant to a change in the color of the illumination.
- High discrimination power to allow for color image retrieval of large image databases.
- Robust to noise in the images or model deviations in the object.
- Easy to compute to allow for fast image retrieval.

The general application is considered of matching and retrieving images taken from 2-D and 3-D multicolored objects in real-world 3-D scenes which is representative for applications such as the retrieval of postal stamps, museum objects, textile patterns, supermarket objects and 2-D and 3-D multicolored objects in general.

Further, we propose an image search engine, called PicToSeek, for cataloging and searching images on the Web entirely on the basis of the pictorial content. In the first stage, PicToSeek collects images on the Web by means of autonomous Web-crawlers. Then, the collected images are automatically cataloged by image analysis methods into various image styles and types: JFIF-GIF, grey-color, photograph-synthetic, size, date of creation, and color depth. After cataloging images, the invariant color image features are extracted from the images. The color invariant features are properly integrated to produce a high-dimensional image index independent of the accidental imaging conditions. When images are automatically collected, cataloged and indexed, PicToSeek allows for fast on-line image search by combining: (1) visual browsing through the precomputed image catalogue; (2) query by pictorial example; (3) query by image features.

This paper is organized as follows. In Section 2, basic color features are defined and a simple reflection model is discussed. The reflection model is used to analyze color features with respect to the first four above mentioned criteria. In Section 3, image retrieval by color-metric histogram matching is discussed. The performance of the various color features is evaluated on the image database in Section 4. Finally, in Section 5 the color image invariant retrieval system PicToSeek is described.

PicToSeek is available on-line at http://www.wins.uva.nl/research/isis/zomax/.

2   Photometric Invariant Color Models

Commonly used well-known color spaces include: RGB, YIQ, XYZ, $I_1I_2I_3$, rgb, xyz, $U^*V^*W^*$, $L^*a^*b^*$, Luv and ISH. However, a number of these color features are related to intensity I (L^*, W^*), or they are linear combinations of RGB (YIQ, XYZ and $I_1I_2I_3$) or normalized with respect to intensity rgb (xyz, U^*V^*, a^*b^*, uv). Therefore, in this paper, we concentrate on the following well-known standard, **essentially different**, color features: RGB, I, rgb, H, S. We define these color features in Section 2.1. Further, in Section 2.2, we study the effect of varying imaging conditions on the various color features for the Lambertian reflection model. The effect of highlights is studied in Section 2.3. Because all color features depend on the illumination color, a color constant color model is proposed in Section 2.4.

2.1 Basic Color Definitions

Let R, G and B, obtained from a color camera, represent the tri-stimulus components defining a mapping from image space to a 3-D sensor space:

$$C = \int_\lambda E(\lambda)U_C(\lambda)d\lambda \tag{1}$$

for tri-stimulus values $C \in (R, G, B)$, where $E(\lambda)$ is the radiance spectrum and U_C are the three color filter transmission functions.

To represent the RGB-color space, a cube can be defined on the R, G, and B axes. The axis connecting the black and white corners defines the intensity:

$$I(R, G, B) = R + G + B \tag{2}$$

The projection of RGB points on the chromaticity triangle is defined by:

$$r(R,G,B) = \frac{R}{R+G+B}, \; g(R,G,B) = \frac{G}{R+G+B}, \; b(R,G,B) = \frac{B}{R+G+B} \tag{3}$$

yielding the rgb color space.

The transformation from RGB used here to describe the hue H is given by:

$$H(R,G,B) = \arctan\Big(\frac{\sqrt{3}(G-B)}{(R-G)+(R-B)}\Big) \tag{4}$$

and S measuring the relative white content of a color as having a particular hue by:

$$S(R,G,B) = 1 - \frac{\min(R,G,B)}{R+G+B} \tag{5}$$

In this way, all color features can be calculated from the original R, G, B values from the corresponding red, green, and blue images provided by the color camera.

2.2 Body Reflection Invariance

In this paper, body (diffuse) reflection is assumed to be Lambertian:

$$L_C = \alpha I_C k_C (\mathbf{n} \cdot \mathbf{s}) \tag{6}$$

for $C \in \{R, G, B\}$ giving the Cth sensor response. I_C is the intensity of a point light source and k_C is the diffuse reflection coefficient of the surface. The surface normal is denoted by $\mathbf{n}$ and illumination direction by $\mathbf{s}$. Furthermore, $\alpha = \frac{1}{a+h}$ where a is the distance from the viewpoint to the surface and h is a constant. Lambertian reflection models dull, matte surfaces. For the moment, we assume that the illumination color is white (i.e. $I = I_R = I_G = I_B$).

According to the body reflection model, the color depends only on the surface albedo k_C and the brightness on factor $\alpha I(\mathbf{n} \cdot \mathbf{s})$. As a consequence, a homogeneously painted surface (i.e. with fixed k_C) may give rise to a broad variance of RGB values due to the varying circumstances induced by the radiometric process. The same argument holds for intensity I.

Opposed to RGB and I, other color features are invariant under the given body reflection model.

rgb is an invariant for the set of matte, dull surfaces mathematically specified by:

$$r(L_R, L_G, L_B) = \frac{\alpha I(\mathbf{n} \cdot \mathbf{s}) k_R}{\alpha I(\mathbf{n} \cdot \mathbf{s})(k_R + k_G + k_B)} = \frac{k_R}{k_R + k_G + k_B} \tag{7}$$

where $I = I_R = I_G = I_B$. Equal argument holds for g and b.

In fact, the scalar multiplier $\alpha I(\mathbf{n} \cdot \mathbf{s})$ is factored out resulting in an expression of (normalized) surface albedos independent of the viewpoint, surface orientation and illumination direction and intensity.

S is also an invariant for the set of matte, dull surfaces:

$$S(L_R, L_G, L_B) = 1 - \frac{\min(\alpha I(\mathbf{n} \cdot \mathbf{s}) k_R, \alpha I(\mathbf{n} \cdot \mathbf{s}) k_G, \alpha I(\mathbf{n} \cdot \mathbf{s}) k_B)}{\alpha I(\mathbf{n} \cdot \mathbf{s})(k_R + k_G + k_B)} =$$

$$1 - \frac{\min(k_R, k_G, k_B)}{(k_R + k_G + k_B)} \tag{8}$$

Similarly, H is an invariant:

$$H(L_R, L_G, L_B) = \arctan\left(\frac{\sqrt{3}\alpha I(\mathbf{n} \cdot \mathbf{s})(k_G - k_B)}{\alpha I(\mathbf{n} \cdot \mathbf{s})((k_R - k_G) + (k_R - k_B))}\right) =$$

$$\arctan\left(\frac{\sqrt{3}(k_G - k_B)}{(k_R - k_G) + (k_R - k_B)}\right) \tag{9}$$

The effect of surface reflection is discussed in following section.

2.3 Body and Surface Reflection Invariance

In this paper, the reflection from composite materials is approximated by the sum of the Lambertian body reflection component L_C and a surface reflection component S_C. This is the Torrance-Sparrow model:

$$M_C = L_C + S_C \tag{10}$$

where $C \in \{R, G, B\}$.

We use the modified Torrance-Sparrow specular reflection term:

$$S_C = \left(\frac{FPG}{\mathbf{n} \cdot \mathbf{v}}\right) I_C \tag{11}$$

where $\mathbf{v}$ is a unit vector in the direction of the viewer and F is the Fresnel coefficient describing the percentage of the light reflected at the interface. Because the Fresnel coefficient is weakly dependent on incident angle and wavelength we will assume that it is a constant for a given material. P models the surface roughness and G is the geometric attenuation factor. Under the given conditions, the color of highlights is not related to the color of the surface on which they appear, but only on the color of the light source.

By filling in $L_C + S_C$ in the hue equation, we can see that all possible colors of the same shiny homogeneously colored surface, illuminated by a white light source, have to be of the same hue mathematically specified as:

$$H(M_R, M_G, M_B) = \arctan\left(\frac{\sqrt{3}(k_G - k_B)}{(k_R - k_G) + (k_R - k_B)}\right) \tag{12}$$

where illumination and geometric components are factored out resulting in an expression of surface albedos.

Unfortunately, all above mentioned color models depend on the illumination color [2]. Therefore, in the next section, a color constant color model is proposed.

2.4 Color Constant Color Model

[1] proposes a simple and effective illumination-independent color feature for the purpose of image retrieval. The method fails, however, when images are contaminated by shadows, shading and highlights.

To that end, we propose a color constant feature not only independent of the illumination color but also discounting shadowing and shading cues.

The color feature is defined by:

$$m(C_1^{\mathbf{x}_1}, C_1^{\mathbf{x}_2}, C_2^{\mathbf{x}_1}, C_2^{\mathbf{x}_2}) = \frac{C_1^{\mathbf{x}_1} C_2^{\mathbf{x}_2}}{C_1^{\mathbf{x}_2} C_2^{\mathbf{x}_1}} \tag{13}$$

expressing the color ratio between two neighboring image locations, for $C_1, C_2 \in \{R, G, B\}$ and $C_1 \neq C_2$ where $\mathbf{x}_1$ and $\mathbf{x}_2$ denote the image locations of the two neighboring pixels.

Having three color components of two locations, color ratios obtained from a RGB-color image are:

$$m_1(R^{x_1}, R^{x_2}, G^{x_1}, G^{x_2}) = \frac{R^{x_1} G^{x_2}}{R^{x_2} G^{x_1}} \qquad (14)$$

$$m_2(R^{x_1}, R^{x_2}, B^{x_1}, B^{x_2}) = \frac{R^{x_1} B^{x_2}}{R^{x_2} B^{x_1}} \qquad (15)$$

$$m_3(G^{x_1}, G^{x_2}, B^{x_1}, B^{x_2}) = \frac{G^{x_1} B^{x_2}}{G^{x_2} B^{x_1}} \qquad (16)$$

For the ease of exposition, we concentrate on m_1 based on RG in the following discussion. Without loss of generality, all results derived for m_1 will also hold for m_2 and m_3.

Assuming Lambertian surface reflection, the color ratio is independent of a change in surface orientation, viewpoint and direction of the illumination as follows from:

$$m_1(L_R^{y_1}, L_R^{y_2}, L_G^{y_1}, L_G^{y_2}) = \frac{\alpha^{y_1} I_R k_R^{y_1}(n^{y_1} \cdot s) \alpha^{y_2} I_G k_G^{y_2}(n^{y_2} \cdot s)}{\alpha^{y_2} I_R k_R^{y_2}(n^{y_2} \cdot s) \alpha^{y_1} I_G k_G^{y_1}(n^{y_1} \cdot s)} = \frac{k_R^{y_1} k_G^{y_2}}{k_R^{y_2} k_G^{y_1}} \qquad (17)$$

where y_1 and y_2 are two neighboring locations on the object's surface not necessarily of the same orientation. Further, $\alpha^y = \frac{1}{r^y + k}$ depends on r^y denoting the relative distance of the perspective viewpoint to object's surface location y.

In theory, when y_1 and y_2 are neighboring locations on the same homogeneously painted surface, the color ratio will be 1. Except along color edges, assuming that the neighboring locations are at either side of the color edge, the value of the color ratio will deviate from 1. Thus, in theory, the number of distinct color ratio values is a measure for the amount of distinct color edges.

If we assume that the color of the illumination is locally constant (at least over the two neighboring locations from which ratio is computed), the color ratio is also independent of the illumination color:

$$m_1(L_R^{y_1}, L_R^{y_2}, L_G^{y_1}, L_G^{y_2}) = m_1(\beta_1 L_R^{y_1}, \beta_1 L_R^{y_2}, \beta_2 L_G^{y_1}, \beta_2 L_G^{y_2}) =$$

$$\frac{\alpha^{y_1} \beta_1 I_R k_R^{y_1}(n^{y_1} \cdot s) \alpha^{y_2} \beta_2 I_G k_G^{y_2}(n^{y_2} \cdot s)}{\alpha^{y_2} \beta_1 I_R k_R^{y_2}(n^{y_2} \cdot s) \alpha^{y_1} \beta_2 I_G k_G^{y_1}(n^{y_1} \cdot s)} = \frac{k_R^{y_1} k_G^{y_2}}{k_R^{y_2} k_G^{y_1}} \qquad (18)$$

where we assume that the change in illumination color is equal to the multiplication of each I_R, I_G and I_B by an independent scalar factor $\beta_1, \beta_2, \beta_3 \in [0, 1]$. Hence, color ratio m is independent of a change in viewpoint, surface orientation, illumination intensity, and illumination spectral color composition.

Taking logarithms of both sides of equation 13 results for m_1 in:

$$\ln m_1(R^{x_1}, R^{x_2}, G^{x_1}, G^{x_2}) = \ln R^{x_1} + \ln G^{x_2} - \ln R^{x_2} - \ln G^{x_1} \qquad (19)$$

The color ratios can be seen as differences at two neighboring locations x_1 and x_2 in the image domain:

$$d_{m_1}(\mathbf{x}_1, \mathbf{x}_2) = \ln R^{\mathbf{x}_1} + \ln G^{\mathbf{x}_2} - \ln R^{\mathbf{x}_2} - \ln G^{\mathbf{x}_1} \qquad (20)$$

When these differences are taken between neighboring pixels in a particular direction, they correspond to finite-difference differentiation. To find color ratio edges in images we use the edge detection proposed in [2] which is currently of the Sobel type.

The results obtained so far for m_1 hold also for m_2 and m_3, yielding a 3-tuple $(\mathcal{G}_{m_1}(\mathbf{x}), \mathcal{G}_{m_2}(\mathbf{x}), \mathcal{G}_{m_3}(\mathbf{x}))$ denoting the gradient magnitude for every neighborhood centered at $\mathbf{x}$ in the image.

For pixels on a uniformly painted region, in theory, all three components will be zero whereas at least one the three components will be non-zero for pixels on locations where two regions of distinct color meet.

3   Image Retrieval

Color-metric histograms are created on the basis of each color feature defined in Section 2 for each image in the image database by counting the number of times a discrete color feature occurs in the image. The color-metric histogram from the query image is created in a similar way. Then, image retrieval is reduced to the problem to what extent histogram $\mathcal{H}^Q$ derived from the query image Q is similar to a histogram $\mathcal{H}^{I_k}$ constructed for each image I_k in the image database. A similarity function $\mathcal{D}(\mathcal{H}^Q, \mathcal{H}^{I_k})$ is required returning a numerical measure of similarity between $\mathcal{H}^Q$ and $\mathcal{H}^{I_k}$.

For comparison reasons in the literature, in this paper, $\mathcal{D}$ is expressed by histogram intersection [4]:

$$\mathcal{D}_a(\mathcal{H}^Q, \mathcal{H}^{I_i}) = \frac{\sum_{\mathbf{k}=1}^{N_d} \min\{\mathcal{H}^Q(\mathbf{k}), \mathcal{H}^{I_i}(\mathbf{k})\}}{N_d} \qquad (21)$$

where $\mathbf{k}$ denote the bin index and N_d the number of non zero bins.

4   Experiments

To evaluate the various color models, the criteria 1-7 of Section 1 will be addressed.

The data sets on which the experiments will be conducted are described in Section 4.1. The error measures and histogram formation are given in 4.2 and 4.3 respectively.

4.1   Datasets

The database consists of $N_1 = 500$ images of 2-D and 3-D domestic objects, tools, toys, food cans, art artifacts etc., all taken from two households. Objects were recorded in isolation (one per image) with the aid of the SONY XC-003P CCD color camera (3 chips) and the Matrox Magic Color frame grabber. The digitization was done in 8 bits per color. Objects were recorded against a white cardboard background. Two light sources of average day-light color are used to illuminate the objects in the scene. Objects were recorded at a pace of a few shots a minute. There was no attempt to individually control focus or illumination. Images show a considerable amount of noise, shadows, shading and highlights. As a result, recordings are best characterized as snap shot quality, a good representation of views from everyday life as it appears in home video, the news, and consumer photography in general.

A second, independent set (the query set) of recordings was made of randomly chosen objects already in the database. These objects, $N_2 = 70$ in number, were recorded again (one per image) with a new, arbitrary position and orientation with respect to the camera (some recorded upside down, some rotated, some at different scale).

In the experiments, all pixels in a color image are discarded with a local saturation smaller then 5 percent of the total range (this number was empirically determined by visual inspection); otherwise calculation of H, S, rgb and m becomes unstable. Consequently, the white cardboard background as well as the grey, white, dark or nearly colorless parts of objects as recorded in the color image will not be considered in the matching process.

4.2   Error measures

For a measure of match quality, let rank r^{Q_i} denote the position of the correct match for query image Q_i, $i = 1, ..., N_2$, in the ordered list of N_1 match values. The rank r^{Q_i} ranges from $r = 1$ from a perfect match to $r = N_1$ for the worst possible match.

Then, for one experiment, the average ranking percentile is defined by:

$$\bar{r} = (\frac{1}{N_2} \sum_{i=1}^{N_2} \frac{N_1 - r^{Q_i}}{N_1 - 1})100\% \tag{22}$$

The cumulative percentile of query images producing a rank smaller or equal to j is defined as:

$$\mathcal{X}(j) = (\frac{1}{N_2} \sum_{k=1}^{j} \eta(r^{Q_i} == k))100\% \tag{23}$$

where η reads as the number of query images having rank k.

4.3   Histogram Formation

Histograms are constructed on the basis of different color features representing the distribution of discrete color feature values in a n-dimensional color feature space, where $n = 3$ for RGB, rgb and m, and $n = 1$ for I, S and H.

Except for m, see [2], histogram axes are partitioned uniformly with fixed intervals. The resolution on the axes follows from the amount of noise and computational efficiency considerations. We determined the appropriate bin size for our application empirically. This has been achieved by varying the same number of bins on the axes over $q \in \{2, 4, 8, 16, 32, 64, 128, 256\}$ and chose the smallest q for which the number of bins is kept small for computational efficiency and large for retrieval accuracy. The results show (not presented here) that the number of bins was of little influence on the retrieval accuracy when the number of bins ranges from $q = 32$ to $q = 256$ for all color spaces. Therefore, the histogram bin size used during histogram formation is $q = 32$ in the following.

4.4 Discriminative Power

In this subsection, we report on the image retrieval accuracy of the matching process for $N_2 = 70$ query images and $N_1 = 500$ target images for the various color features. As stated, white lighting is used during the recording of the images in the image database and the independent query set. However, the objects were recorded with a new, arbitrary position and orientation with respect to camera. In Fig. 1.a accumulated ranking is shown for similarity function based on histogram intersection.

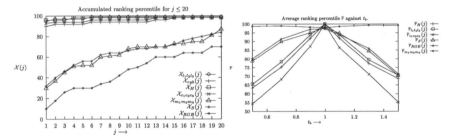

Fig. 1. *a. The accumulated ranking percentile. b. The discriminative power plotted against the change β in the color composition of the illumination spectrum.*

From the results of Fig. 1.a we can observe that the discrimination power of rgb and H is higher then the other color features. Saturation S and color ratio m provide slightly worse image retrieval accuracy. As expected, the discrimination power of RGB has the worst performance due to its sensitivity to varying imaging conditions.

Hence, for image retrieval purposes under white lighting, color features rgb and H are most appropriate achieving a probability of respectively 98 and 92 perfect matches out of 100.

4.5 The Effect of a Change in the Illumination Color

The effect of multiple light sources of different color distributions and a change in the illumination color is equal to the multiplication of each RGB image by an independent scalar factor. To measure the sensitivity of the various color feature in practice with respect to a change in the color of the illumination, the R, G and B-images of the query set are multiplied by a factor $\beta_1 = \beta$, $\beta_2 = 1$ and $\beta_3 = 2 - \beta$ respectively (i.e. $\beta_1 R$, $\beta_2 G$ and $\beta_3 B$) by varying β over $\{0.5, 0.7, 0.8, 0.9, 1.0, 1.1, 1.2, 1.3, 1.5\}$. The discrimination power of the histogram matching process differentiated for the various color features plotted against the illumination color is shown in Fig. 1.b.

As expected, only the color ratio m is insensitive to a change in illumination color. From Fig. 1.b we can observe that color features H and rgb, which achieved best retrieval accuracy under white illumination, see Fig. 1.a, are highly sensitive to a change in illumination color followed by S. Even for a slight change in the illumination color, their retrieval potential degrades drastically.

5   PicToSeek: A Content-Based Image Search System

With the growth and popularity of the Web, a tremendous amount of information is made accessible publicly. Although the Web allows for storage of great amounts of multimedia information, computational methods are needed to explore and locate specific information. Currently, a large number of text-based search engines are available which explore the Web for text documents. The textual content of the documents are analyzed and condense into concise searchable indexes. The problem of locating documents on the Web shifts to fast index-searching. To explore visual information, text-based search engines assume that textual descriptions of the visual data are available. However, people are reluctant in categorizing visual information on the Web. Moreover, pictorial data is very hard to be described by verbal descriptions. Often no textual description of the pictorial information is present at all. Hence, the capabilities of current text-based search engines for cataloging visual information is very limited. Therefore, we concentrate on the use of pictorial information for cataloging and exploring visual data on the Web.

We have implemented content-based image search system, called PicToSeek, for exploring visual information on the World Wide Web. PicToSeek collects images on the Web by means of autonomous Web-crawlers. Collected images are automatically cataloged by image analysis methods into various image styles and types: JFIF-GIF, grey-color, photograph-synthetic, size, date of creation, and color depth. After cataloging images, the proposed color invariant image features are extracted from the images to produce a high-dimensional image index independent of the accidental imaging conditions. When images are automatically collected, indexed and cataloged, PicToSeek allows for fast on-line image search.

There are many ways in which images can be retrieved. To that end, in Section 5.1, the retrieval methods used by PicToSeek are discussed. In Section 5.2, the query capability of the system is illustrated.

PicToSeek is on-line at http://www.wins.uva.nl/research/isis/zomax/.

5.1 Image Retrieval Methods Supported by PicToSeek

PicToSeek allows the following retrieval methods:

visual browsing through the precomputed image catalogue: In the first stage, the specific image class is selected. For example, the user can select the image class of small, photographical color images. Then, PicToSeek allows visual browsing through the collection of images of the same image class.

query by external pictorial example: The pictorial example can be provided to the PicToSeek by an external source. This means that a user can bring in its own image by means of a URL-address.

query by internal pictorial example: When no external image example is available, the user can select a query image from the available image classes.

query by image features: PicToSeek allows the user to specify image features. For example, a user can specify "dark and reddish" images by setting the image feature parameters.

5.2 Query Scenario

All queries follow the same scenario:

Step 0 **Image Domain Selection:** Visual browsing through the precomputed image catalogue;

Step 1 **Image selection:** select an image from the catalogue or capture the query image from an object by giving an URL-address.

Step 2 **Query image:** the query image is defined as an user-specified interesting part of the selected image.

Step 3 **Invariance selection:** the required invariance is selected from the list of available color invariant indices. They have been computed and stored in separate (histogram) tables for each image when it entered the database.

Step 4 **Search:** the same color invariant indices are computed from the query and matched with those stored in the database (histogram) tables.

Step 5 **Display:** an ordered list of most similar images is shown.

Step 6 **Image selection:** if the right image is found, the imag e can be displayed at full resolution.

Step 7 **Rerun:** if the right image is not found the query image is adjusted (go to step 1) or the most similar image is used to refine query definition (go to step 3).

To illustrate the query capability of the system, the typical application is considered of retrieving images containing an instance of a given object. To that end, the query is specified by an example image taken from the object at hand. A typical query specification is shown in Figure 2.

PicToSeek enables the user to select and display the image of the object at hand by a Url-address. At run time, the user specifies the preferred invariance. Then, the required color invariants are extracted from the query and matched with those of the target images in the database.

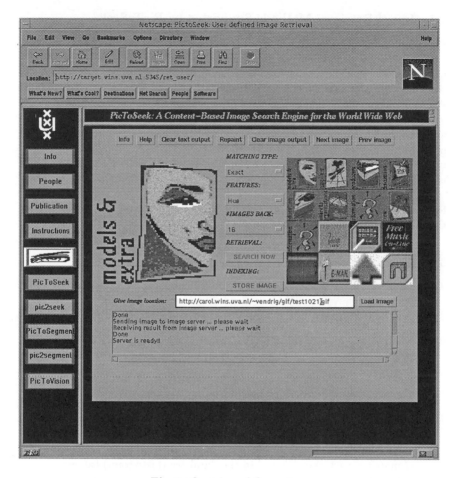

Fig. 2. *Overview of the system.*

After matching, images are ordered with respect to the query according to their similarity measure and displayed in the retrieval unit one by one through image browsing or as an as an ordered set according to the user preferences.

6   Implementation

The graphical-user interface of PicToSeek has been implemented in Java. The Web-crawler, image analysis and feature extraction methods have been implemented in C++. A database is used to store the images and indexes. The server runs on a SPARCstation 5 with 110 Mhz.

7 Conclusion

In this chapter, various color features have been analyzed and evaluated for the purpose of image retrieval by color-metric histogram matching under varying illumination circumstances.

On the basis of the above reported theory and experiments, it is concluded that H and rgb are most appropriate to be used for image retrieval by color-metric histogram matching under the constraint of a white illumination source. When no constraints are imposed on the imaging conditions (i.e. the most general case), the proposed color ratio m is most appropriate discounting the disturbing influences of shadows, shading, illumination intensity and illumination color.

Finally, we described a content-based image search system for exploring visual information on the World Wide Web. PicToSeek collects images on the Web by means of autonomous Web-crawlers. Collected images are automatically cataloged by image analysis methods into various image styles and types: JFIF-GIF, grey-color, photograph-synthetic, size, date of creation, and color depth. After cataloging images, invariant color image features are extracted from the images to produce a high-dimensional image index independent of the accidental imaging conditions. PicToSeek allows for fast on-line image search by combining: (1) visual browsing through the precomputed image catalogue; (2) query by pictorial example; (3) query by image features.

References

1. B. V. Funt and G. D. Finlayson, *Color constant color indexing*, IEEE PAMI, 17(5), pp. 522-529, 1995.
2. Gevers, T., *Color Image Invariant Segmentation and Retrieval*, PhD Thesis, ISBN 90-74795-51-X, University of Amsterdam, The Netherlands, 1996.
3. W. Niblack, R. Barber, W. Equitz, M. Flickner, E. Glasman, D. Petkovic and P. Yanker, *The QBIC project: querying images by content using color, texture, and shape*, Proc. storage and retrieval for image and video databases, SPIE, 1993
4. M. J. Swain and D. H. Ballard, *Color indexing*, Int'l, J. Comput. Vision, 7(1), pp. 11-32, 1991.

Content Based Image Retrieval:
Optimal Keys, Texture, Projections, or Templates

Michael S. Lew   D.P. (Nies) Huijsmans
Department of Computer Science
Leiden University, Postbus 9512
2300 RA Leiden, The Netherlands
{mlew huijsman} @wi.leidenuniv.nl

Dee Denteneer
Philips Research Laboratory
Prof. Holstlaan 4
5656 AA Eindhoven
dentenee@natlab.research.philips.com

Topics: content based image retrieval, Fisher's linear discriminant, Karhunen-Loeve, LBP, texture, optimal keys, template, projections,

Abstract. Two significant problems in content based retrieval methods are (1) *Accuracy*: most of the current content based image retrieval methods have not been quantitatively compared nor benchmarked with respect to accuracy and (2) *Efficiency*: image database search methods must be analyzed for their computational efficiency and interrelationships. We assert that the accuracy problem is due to the generality of the applications involved. In the current systems, the goal of the user is not clear, which results in difficulties in creating ground truth. In this paper, we quantitatively compare and evaluate four fundamentally different methods for image copy location, namely, optimal keys, texture, projection, and template methods in a large portrait database. We discuss some important theoretical interrelationships, computational efficiency, and accuracy with respect to real noise experiments.

1 Introduction

There has been vigorous recent interest in searching large image databases. For an overview, see Gudivada and Raghavan [3]. As libraries, museums, etc. become digitized, we will need tools to search through terrabyte databases for semantically meaningful information. However, most current methods have not been quantitatively compared nor benchmarked.

In content based image retrieval, there are several different problem spaces. These are locating (1) exact copies; (2) copies with artificial noise; (3) copies with real noise; and (4) finding similar images, which we refer to as *image association*. In problem spaces (1), (2), and (3), we can define the ground truth because the goal is clear. In problem space (4), it is difficult to define the ground truth because different users may have different preferences for what a "similar image" is. Thus, systems such as QBIC [1], etc. have not been quantitatively compared with respect to performance accuracy.

There are a wide variety of sources for real noise. We examined print-scanner noise, and general image degradation. In print-scanner noise, the image is printed to plain paper and then scanned in. This test is indicative of the performance of an algorithm for finding copies of scanned in newspaper or magazine pictures. For the general image degradation, the copies of the original image have been subjected to decades of different handling and treatment by their owners.

In this paper, we compare optimal keys, texture, projections, and template methods for the purpose of noisy image copy location (problem spaces (2) and (3)) in the Leiden 19th century portrait database (LCPD). Section 2 describes the image database and ground truth. Section 3 discusses the relationship between optimal keys, the Karhunen Loeve Transform (KLT) and Fisher's linear discriminant. Section 4 describes the implementations of the different methods, and in Section 5, we test the methods on the full noise database. Conclusions are given in Section 6.

2   Image Database and Ground Truth

The LCPD (see Figure 1) is currently composed of 5570 images taken during the 19th century, and it will be continually expanded until at least 50,000 images are in the database. Some images are copies of each other, however, due to different storage conditions, the copies have varying kinds and differing amounts of degradation. The degradation varies from light and moisture damage to scratches and writing on the images.

Figure 1. Sample images from the Leiden 19th Century Portrait Database.

3   Optimal Keys, KLT, and Fisher's Approach

Both the Karhunen-Loeve transform (KLT or Hotelling transform) and Fisher's linear discriminant method are well documented in the pattern recognition and statistics literature [2,4,5]. The KLT determines the optimal (in a truncation sense) linear features for describing a data set. Fisher's approach focuses on determining the optimal linear discriminant features for classification. Since Fisher's approach minimizes the classification error, it seems to be the appropriate measure. However, it is often difficult to accurately model real world noise, which is a requirement for optimality of Fisher's method. In the rest of this section we derive the theoretical mathematical relationship between optimal keys, KLT, and Fisher's linear discriminant.

With respect to large image database, it is also of significant importance to develop computationally efficient algorithms. Instead of comparing the raw images, we could compare keys: functions or algorithms which map images onto one or more feature values. Thus instead of computing

$$d_i = \|X - \Xi_i\|^2 = \sum \left(x^{(kl)} - \xi^{(kl)} \right)^2 \qquad (1)$$

for $i = 1,...,N$, we need only compute $k(X)$ and compare it with $k(\Xi_i)$, $i = 1,...,N$. Here X denotes an input image, Ξ_i, $i = 1,...,N$ denote the images in the database, and k denotes the key. Moreover, for the comparison of these key values efficient data structures and algorithms are readily available. This approach using keys to index the database may also be combined hierarchically with a more sophisticated matching algorithm. In such a hierarchical approach, a small subset of the database is selected very efficiently using the key values, and then this subset is searched using another key index.

From a mathematical-statistical viewpoint, there are two stochastic processes of relevance. The first process is denoted the image process and the exact images within the database are considered to be realizations of this process. The second process is called the noise process. Input images are assumed to result from a combination of the image process and the noise process. Formally, denote the probability distribution of the image and noise process by F_Ξ and F_E, respectively. Then the *optimal key* algorithm is that k such that

$$\Pr\{ |k(\Xi+E) - k(\Xi)| < |k(\Xi+E) - k(\Phi)| \} \qquad (2)$$

is maximized. Here Ξ and Φ are distributed according to F_Ξ and E is distributed according to F_E and Ξ, Φ, and E are independent. Thus equation (2) states that *optimal keys maximize the probability that the key computed from a corrupted image is closer to the key computed from its original than to the key computed from another image.* In short, the optimal key criterion in (2) results in maximizing the probability of finding the correct image. However, in practice, it is difficult to model F_Ξ and F_E so that the optimization of equation (2) is not realistic. Thus, we simplify equation (2) by restricting the space of keys to linear keys, such that $k(\Xi+E) = k(\Xi) + k(E)$. This means that $k(E)$ must be small and that $k(\Xi)$ - $k(\Phi)$ must be large. Furthermore, we implement the magnitude of a stochastic variable through the magnitude of its variance. Assuming that F_Ξ has covariance matrix Σ_B and that F_E has covariance matrix Σ_W, then the requirement that $k(E)$ be small and $k(\Xi)$ - $k(\Phi)$ be large amounts to

$$\text{maximize} \quad \frac{k^t \Sigma_B k}{k^t \Sigma_W k} \qquad (3)$$

or, equivalently,

$$\text{maximize} \quad k^t \Sigma_B k \qquad (4)$$
$$\text{subject to} \quad k^t \Sigma_B k = 1 \qquad (5)$$

Criterion (3) is the criterion used in Fisher's linear discriminant. Furthermore, if we ignore the noise process then equations (4) and (5) become

$$\text{maximize } k^t \Sigma_B k \tag{6}$$
$$\text{subject to } k^t k = 1 \tag{7}$$

which is the Karhunen-Loeve transform.

4   Description of Methods

In the previous section, we discussed the theoretical interrelationships between optimal keys, the KLT and Fisher's linear discriminant. Optimal keys were defined as functions on the images which maximized the probability of finding the correct copy of image. It was found that when the noise could be accurately modeled, the optimal key method is similar to Fisher's linear discriminant. When the noise is ignored, the optimal key method reduces to the Karhunen-Loeve transform. Thus, in the experiments, we use Fisher's linear discriminant for the print-scanner problem, and the KLT for the general image degradation.

There are a vast number of texture methods in the research literature[6]. In a recent comprehensive survey [6], the method of linear binary patterns (LBP) [7] had the lowest error rate for the first image set. On this basis, we chose to use the LBP as our representative texture method. In the surveyed LBP method [6], a texture unit is a two-level 3x3 pattern where the threshold is the center pixel. This gives 2^8 or 256 possible texture units. The texture spectrum is the distribution of the 256 patterns. In our copy location problem space, we calculate the texture spectrum for each image, and then rank by feature vector distance.

Projections have been used for many different classification problems, and most recently applied to image copy location [8]. The projections method refers to comparing the horizontal and vertical projections of the images (compute the row and columns sums), whereas the template method (image differencing) refers to comparing the images pixel by pixel based on spatial location. The ranking error is defined for our test as the average rank at which a copy of the input image was found in the database. Thus, the best possible score would be 1.0, which would mean that the copy in the database was always the best matching image. For the template and projection methods, both intensity and gradient were used as features. For all methods, the metric was the average absolute difference.

5   Experiments: KLT, Projections, and Template

In this section, we performed two experiments to compare the ranking error for three different methods, KLT/Fisher, projections, and template. The experiments are intended to duplicate real noise applications. In the print-scanner experiments, the original image is printed to plain paper using a laser printer and then scanned in. An example of the noise is shown in Figures 2.

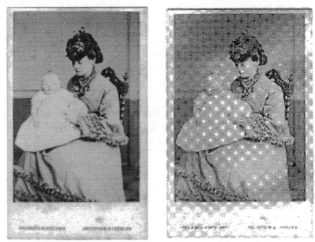

Figure 2. Image 140 and print-scanner degraded copy

In the general image degradation experiments, the copies of the original were subjected to decades of general noise which includes scratches, writing, environmental exposure, etc. An example of the copies is shown in Figure 3. Note that these copies have different contrast and markings.

Figure 3. Two copies (c000409 and c000412) subjected to general noise.

5.1 Print-Scanner Noise

In this experiment, 25 images were printed to plain paper, and then scanned in. Fisher's method was used instead of the KLT since the print-scanner noise can be statistically modeled. Table 1 and Figure 4 show the distribution of the rank of the print-scanner experiments. Note that for the sake of visual clarity, we only graphed the top 3 methods. The column labeled *Best* refers to the number of times in which the copy in the database was in the first rank. The other columns show the distribution as the copy in the database was found in positions 2 - 6, 7 - 16, and 17 - 36. Column *Worst* shows the number of times that the database copy was not among the first 36.

Table 1. Distribution of Position of Print-Scanner Degraded Image

Method	Best	Top 5	Top 10	Top 20	Worst
Template - intensity	1	1	1	0	22
Template - gradient	17	2	0	0	6
Projection - intensity	1	1	1	1	21
Projection - gradient	17	2	1	1	4
LBP	17	3	1	1	3
Fisher - 10 features	8	8	4	3	2
Fisher - 25 features	22	1	0	0	2

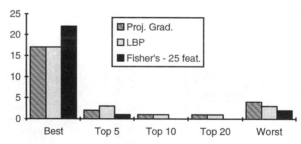

Figure 4. Chart of the rank distribution for the print-scanner degraded image

In this experiment, the Fisher method with 25 features had higher performance relative to the other methods.

5.2 General Image Degradation

Since the image degradation is general, the noise could not be modeled accurately. Thus the KLT was chosen as the optimal key method for this experiment. In Table 2, and Figure 5, the distribution of the rank error for the general degradation is shown.

The projection and template methods using intensity as the feature class performed the worst for our database with average ranking errors of 14.33 and 14.42, respectively. When the gradient images were used for the projection and template methods, the average ranking errors decreased to 5.92 and 5.5, respectively. The KLT with 10 features had the least average ranking error of 4.33.

Table 2. Distribution of Position of General Degraded Image

Method	Best	Top 5	Top 10	Top 20	Worst
Template - intensity	12	0	2	0	9
Template - gradient	8	3	5	0	7
Projection - intensity	12	0	1	0	10
Projection - gradient	14	1	2	0	6
LBP	6	5	1	3	8
KLT - 5 features	8	3	0	4	8
KLT - 10 features	8	3	2	5	5

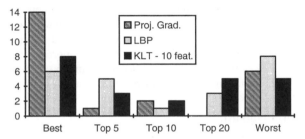

Figure 5. Chart of the rank distribution for the general noise degradation

Regarding computational efficiency, Table 3 shows the number of features used by each method

Table 3. Number of Features Used by Each Method

Method	Number of Features
Template - intensity	47250
Template - gradient	47250
Projection - intensity	440
Projection - gradient	440
LBP	256
KLT - 5 features	5
KLT - 10 features	10
Fisher - 10 features	10
Fisher - 25 features	25

Overall, the methods which were based on the optimal key selection, KLT and Fisher's approach, not only had greater accuracy than the other methods, but also required only 10% of the features as the LBP or Projection methods.

6   Conclusions

In this paper we applied the Karhunen-Loeve transform and the Fisher linear discriminant to a large portrait database. Regarding the general degradation (light, moisture, physical scratches, etc.) noise, the Fisher linear discriminant is not appropriate until an accurate noise model can be found. For images which have been printed and then scanned in, Fisher's method and the projection method using the gradient had the least ranking error. In the case of the real noise from decades of exposure to different environments and scanner noise, the KLT had the least ranking error with respect to the projection and template methods. Overall, the optimal key methods performed significantly better than the texture, projection and template methods when the noise could be modeled accurately, and slightly better in the case of general noise.

With respect to computational efficiency, it was shown that optimal key selection techniques are directly related to principal component methods. Key selection techniques require fewer features for similar accuracy, which results in less computation. In the experiments, the methods based on the optimal key selection techniques, namely, the KLT and Fisher's approach were shown to require less than 10% of the features relative to the texture, projection and template methods, while still achieving equivalent or better accuracy.

WWW Demo Program

The method described here can be evaluated directly via our WWW image database retrieval demo.
See *http://ind156b.wi.leidenuniv.nl:2000*

Acknowledgments

This research was supported by the Advanced School for Computing and Imaging, Delft, and the Netherlands Computer Science Research Foundation.

References

1. Faloutsos, C., R. Barber, M. Flickner, J. Hafner, W. Niblack, D. Petkovic, W. Equitz, "Efficient and Effective Querying by Image Content," Journal of Intelligent Information Systems, pp. 231-262, 1994.
2. Fisher, R.A., "The Use of Multiple Measurements in Taxonomic Problems," Annals of Eugenetics (London) 7, pp. 700-725, 1936.
3. Gudivada, V. N., and V. V. Raghavan, "Finding the Right Image, Content-Based Image Retrieval Systems," Computer, IEEE Computer Society, pp. 18-62, Sept. 1995.
4. Hotelling, H., "Analysis of a Complex of Statistical Variables into Principal Components," Journal of Educ. Psychol., vol. 24, pp. 417-441, 498-520, 1933.

5. Therrien, C. W., Decision Estimation and Classification, John Wiley & Sons, Inc., New York, 1989
6. Ojala, T., M. Pietikainen and D. Harwood, "A Comparative Study of Texture Measures with Classification Based on Feature Distributions," Pattern Recognition, vol. 29, no. 1, pp. 51-59, 1996
7. Wang, L. and D. C. He, "Texture Classification Using Texture Spectrum," Pattern Recognition 23, pp. 905-910, 1990
8. Huijsmans, D. P. and M. S. Lew, "Efficient Content-Based Image Retrieval in Digital Picture Collections Using Projections: (Near)-Copy Location," Proc. International Conference on Pattern Recognition, Vienna, Austria, August, pp. 104-108, 1996..

Multi-Scale Shape Indexing

Efficient and Robust Retrieval by Shape Content through Curvature Scale Space

Farzin Mokhtarian, Sadegh Abbasi and Josef Kittler

Vision Speech and Signal Processing Group
Department of Electronic & Electrical Engineering,
University of Surrey
Guildford, Surrey GU2 5XH
England
Email F.Mokhtarian@ee.surrey.ac.uk
Tel +44-1483-300800 extension 2288
Fax +44-1483-34139

Abstract. We introduce a very fast and reliable method for shape similarity retrieval in large image databases which is robust with respect to noise, scale and orientation changes of the objects. The maxima of curvature zero_crossing contours of Curvature Scale Space (CSS) image are used to represent the shapes of object boundary contours. While a complex boundary is represented by about five pairs of integer values, an effective indexing method based on the aspect ratio of the CSS image, eccentricity and circularity is used to narrow down the range of searching. Since the matching algorithm has been designed to use global information, it is sensitive to major occlusion, but some minor occlusion will not cause any problems.

We have tested and evaluated our method on a prototype database of 450 images of marine animals with a vast variety of shapes with very good results. The method can either be used in real applications or produce a reliable shape description for more complicated images when other features such as color and texture should also be considered.

Since shape similarity is a subjective issue, in order to evaluate the method, we asked a number of volunteers to perform similarity retrieval based on shape on a randomly selected small database. We then compared the results of this experiment to the outputs of our system to the same queries and on the same database. The comparison indicated a promising performance of the system.

1 Introduction

Shape representation is one of the most challenging aspects of computer vision. The problem has proven to be difficult [8][9], because shapes are often more complex than color and texture. While color and texture can be quantified by a few parameters, common shapes need hundreds of parameters to be represented explicitly.

The problem remains difficult in similarity retrieval applications in image databases. For example in [7], the authors have noted lack of reliability of their shape feature measurements. Because of the complexity and the huge variety of shapes, the problem of user interface in shape similarity retrieval has its own difficulties. While the user can specify the desired image texture or color using a menu, it is difficult to represent the same menu for shape representation.

Most proposed content based database systems aim to retrieve a small set of candidate images which include the desired image. The successful retrieval of the best candidate then relies on the final user judgement. In [1], the authors have used Polygonal approximation, while a set of features like boundary/perimeter, elongation (major axis/ minor axis), number of holes, etc, have been used in [2] for shape similarity retrieval. The authors in [3] have used a combination of heuristic shape features such as area, circularity, eccentricity, major axis orientation and a set of algebraic moment invariants. They have also used other features such as color, texture, and even sketch features.

We use a modified version of Curvature Scale Space image matching [5] for comparing shapes of objects in an image database. Our prototype database includes more than 450 colored images of marine animals, with every image containing one animal. The preprocessing step (consisting of gray-level morphology, thresholding and binary morphology) extracts the boundaries of objects. Other techniques such as active contours can also be incorporated at this stage if necessary. We compute the CSS image of every boundary and then find the maxima of CSS contours which are used as a shape descriptor to compare objects. The coordinates of these points together with the *aspect ratio* of the CSS image (number of rows / number of columns), eccentricity [10], circularity, and the name of the original image constitute a record which represents the object.

To retrieve similar images from the database, the user can either input an image and ask the system to find all images similar to it or sketch a boundary of his/her desired object using a painting package such as *xpaint*. The system computes the CSS image of the input and finds its maxima, and after comparison, assigns a matching value to every image *candidate* in the database which is similar to the input and shows the first n matched images with best values where n is determined by the user. The *candidates* are those images which their aspect ratio, eccentricity, and circularity, fall in the certain interval of the input ones. The acceptable interval can be selected by the user.

2   Curvature Scale Space image

Let Γ be a closed planar curve, and let u be the normalized arc length parameter on Γ:

$$\Gamma = \left\{ \, \big(x(u), y(u) \big) \mid u \in [0,1] \, \right\}$$

If each coordinate function of Γ is convolved with a 1-D Gaussian kernel of width σ , the resulting curve, Γ_σ, will be smoother than Γ . The locations of curvature zero crossings of Γ_σ can then be found [4]. As σ increases, Γ_σ becomes smoother and the number of zero crossings on it decreases. When σ becomes sufficiently high, Γ_σ will be a convex curve with no curvature zero crossings (see figure 1). The process can be terminated at this stage and the resulting points can be mapped to the (u, σ) plane. The result of this process will be a binary image called Curvature Scale Space image of the curve (see figure 2). The horizontal axis in this image represents the normalized arc length u, and the vertical axis represents σ, the width of the Gaussian kernel. The intersection of every horizontal line with the contours in this image indicates the locations of curvature zero crossings on the corresponding evolved curve Γ_σ.

Every object in our database is represented by the x and y coordinates of its boundary points. The number of these points varies from 400 to 1200 for these images. To normalize the arc length, we re-sample the boundary and represent it by 200 equally distant points. Therefore, the perimeter of all boundaries will be the same and every point on the boundary has a correspondence in the horizontal axis of the CSS image (figure 2).

Every CSS contour corresponds to a concavity or a convexity on the original boundary. For example in the first row of figure 2, there are six main contours in the CSS image, and there are six concavities or convexities in the relevant boundary. This correspondence is shown by numbering the contours on the CSS image and the regions on the boundary.

The boundary will finally be represented by the locations of the six maxima of its CSS image contours, shown in the third column of figure 2.

Also note that every re-sampled point on the boundary can be considered as the starting point. A change in the starting point only causes a circular shift in the CSS image. This can be observed by comparing the second and the third rows of figure 2.

3 CSS matching

As mentioned before, every object in the database is represented by the locations of the maxima of its CSS image. In this section we explain the basic concepts of our matching algorithm which compares two sets of maxima and assigns a matching value to them which represents the similarity between the actual boundaries of objects. For a more complete description of the CSS matching algorithm, see [6].

Consider the objects in figure 2. The regions 6 and 1 of the first object must be matched with the regions 7 and 8 of the second object respectively. Looking at the locations of the relevant maxima on the first and second row of this figure, we realize that they are in quite different positions. This is due to different starting points. If we change the starting point properly, then the locations of corresponding maxima on CSS images will be near each other. This can be observed on the third row of figure 2.

Therefore, the first step in CSS matching is to shift one of the two sets of maxima so that the effect of randomly selected starting point is compensated. Since the exact value of required shift is not available, we choose several values for it and then find the best match among them. The best choice is a value that shifts one CSS image so that its major maximum covers the major maximum of the other CSS image. Other possible choices are those values which accomplish the same with the second and possibly the third major maxima. For the two sets of maxima shown in figure 2, four choices are shown in figure 3.

Considering this figure, one can quickly realize that the first one is the best. Every maximum of the first CSS image is matched with a maximum of the second one, and two maxima remain unmatched. The matching value will be the summation of the the straight line distances between the matched pairs plus the vertical coordinates of the unmatched maxima.

4   Results and discussion and evaluation

We tested the proposed method on a database of 450 images of marine animals. Each image consisted of just one object on a uniform background. The system software was developed using the C language under Unix operating system. The response rate of the system was less than one second for every user query.

In this section we represent some of our experimental results through several examples. In these examples the inputs are images which already exist in the database. The first output of the system is always identical with the input image, with a zero match value.

In the example shown in figure 4a there is a difference in the view angle between the input and the fourth output and in figure 4b, the outputs are in different scales. This examples show that the system is robust with respect to scale and orientation changes of the objects. Other examples in this figure and figure 5 show the variety of shapes of objects in our database.

The evaluation of the performance of the system is a difficult task, because shape similarity is a subjective matter. We selected 50 images from our prototype database randomly and created a small database. We then selected 20 inputs from this database and asked a number of volunteers to find the shapes similar to every input from the database. The results of the subjective test indicated that human judgements of shape similarity noticeably differ. Interestingly though, the ranking produced by our system always agreed quite closely with, at least, a subset of the human evaluators. The short lists of the top five shapes generated by the different judges almost always included the "closest" machine selected shape. These findings indicate that the proposed approach is promising.

Four examples which can be used to compare the human judgements and the performance of the system are shown in figures 6 and 7 respectively.

We intend to test our method on another application involving a database of about 3000 varieties of chrysanthemum leaves. Each variety is represented by a sample of 10 leaves. The task is to check whether new varieties of the plant produced every year differ from all existing varieties. We believe that our method can be used to select varieties from the collection that have similarly shaped leaves to an unknown leaf and ease the process of testing a potential new variety.

Acknowledgements Sadegh Abbasi is grateful to the Ministry of Culture and Higher Education of Iran for its financial support during his research studies.

References

1. E. Gary and R. Mehrorta, " Shape similarity-based retrieval in image databases " in SPIE, Vol. 1662, 1992.
2. P. Eggleston, " Content based feature indexing and retrieval for image databases " in SPIE, Vol. 1819, 1992.
3. W. Niblack *et al* , " The QBIC project; querying images by content using color , texture and shape " in SPIE, VOL. 1908, 1993.
4. Mokhtarian, F. and Mackworth, A. K. " A theory of multiscale, curvature-based shape representation for planar curves " in IEEE Trans. on Pattern Anal. Mach. Intell. , VOL. PAMI-14, No. 8, August 1992 pp789-805.
5. Mokhtarian, F. " Silhouette-based isolated object recognition through curvature scale space " in IEEE Transactions on Pattern Analysis and Machine Intelligence, May 1995, Vol.17, No.5, pp.539-544
6. Mokhtarian, F., Abbasi S. and Kittler J. " Robust and Efficient Shape Indexing through Curvature Scale Space " in Proceedings of the 1996 British Machine and Vision Conference BMVC'96, September 1996, Edinburgh, Scotland.
7. Y. Gong, H. Zhang H.C. Chuan and M. Sakauchi , " An image database system with content capturing and fast image indexing abilities " in Proceedings of the International Conference on Multimedia Computing and Systems, 1994, pp.121-130.
8. Mumford, D. " Mathematical theories of shape: Do they model perception? " in Geometric Methods in Computer Vision, VOL. 1570, pages 2-10, SPIE, 1991.
9. Mumford, D. " The problem of robust shape descriptions " in First International Conference on Computer Vision, pages 602-606, London, England, June 1987. IEEE.
10. Heijden, F. " Image based measurement systems ", John Wiley & Sons, 1995.

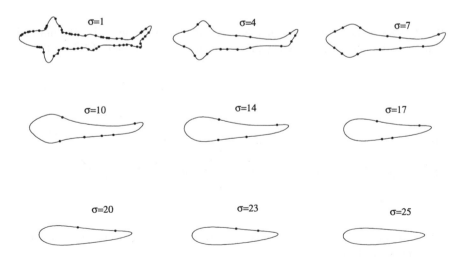

Fig. 1. Curve evolution.

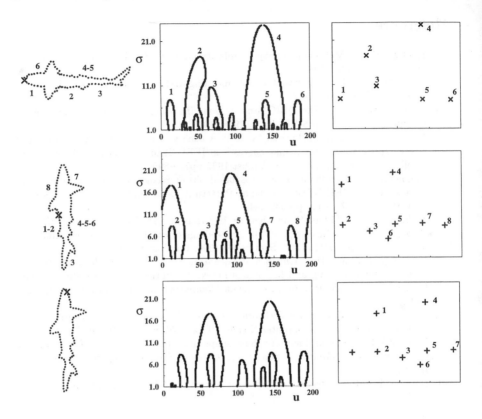

Fig. 2. CSS image and its maxima, left: re-sampled boundary with the marked starting point, middle: CSS image, right: normalized maxima of CSS images.

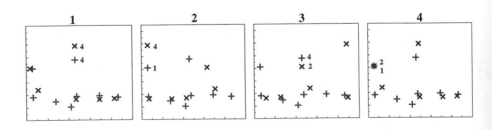

Fig. 3. Four possible choices for matching of the two sets of maxima related to first and second rows of figure 2.

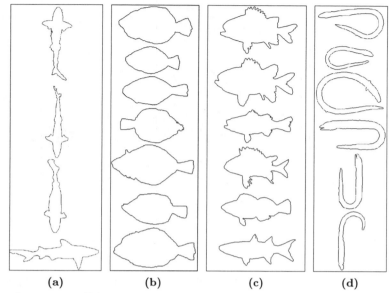

Fig. 4. query results

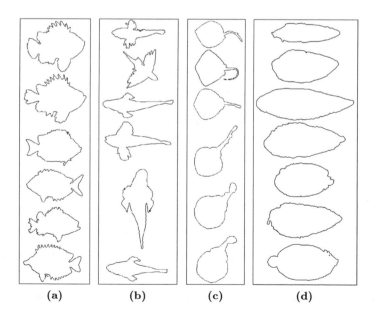

Fig. 5. query results

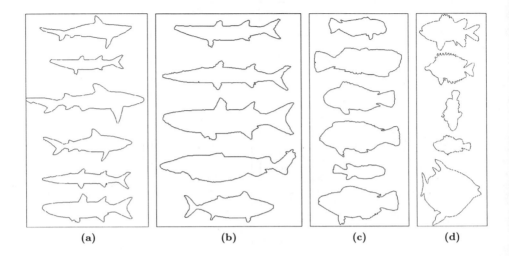

Fig. 6. Results of evaluation, human judgements. The first image is the input and the others are the most similar shapes found by volunteers.

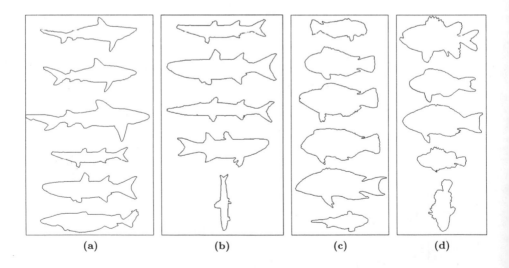

Fig. 7. Results of evaluation, system response to the same queries as above.

Shape Indexing by Multi-scale Representation

A. Del Bimbo and P. Pala

Dipartimento di Sistemi e Informatica, Università di Firenze, 50139 Firenze, Italy

Abstract. The availability of large image databases and retrieval by content has imposed the requirement for indexing procedures to allow a fast pruning of the database items. Indexing of shapes is particularly challenging owing to the difficulty to derive a similarity measure that supports clustering of shapes according to human perceptual similarity. In this paper, we present a technique which exploits a multi–scale analysis of shapes, to derive a hierarchical shape representation in which shape details are progressively filtered out while shape characterizing elements are preserved. To provide the necessary degree of robustness with respect to shape variability, fuzzy sets have been used to describe the visual appearance of shape parts. A graph–like index structure is derived by clustering shapes sharing similar part descriptions. Results of indexing for a sample database are reported, with efficiency and effectiveness measures.

1 Introduction

The ever increasing rate at which images are being generated in many application areas, gives rise to the need of content-based image retrieval systems to provide an effective and efficient access to databases of images, on the basis of their visual content. Since visual information is difficult to be described using words, image attributes by themselves, instead of their textual representations, have to be used to access the database. The problem is complicated by the fact that in large image databases indexing procedures need to be developed to provide an efficient retrieval. In fact, indexing allows to roughly filter out non interesting images and to reduce the number of images to be processed through fine matching procedures. Several image properties and structures can be exploited to this end, such as colors, textures, shapes, and spatial relationships among image objects. Differently from colors and textures, shape based image retrieval is particularly challenging owing to the lack of a complete mathematical model of how humans perceive shapes and similarities among different shapes.

The traditional approach to shape description is to extract a suitable number of features from the shape, and represent it as a point in a multi-dimensional feature space. Moment invariants have been used as a set of features representing shape attributes which are invariant under translation, rotation, and scale [14], [15], [5]. Boundary features such as chain codes of contour segments or high–curvature points, whose saliency is demonstrated in [1] [2], have been used as well [11], [9], [10], [12]. In [3] it is suggested to break curves at points of negative minima of curvature. The portions of the curve lying between these points are known as *codons*. The curvature maxima and zeroes are then used to classify each codon as one of six possible types [17]. Another approach is proposed in [4] where shapes are interpreted as the result of various processes of growth, pushing, pulling and resistance, that act on a circular shape deforming its aspect. Limitations of feature based approaches are related to the fact that the similarity between two shapes must be computed as a distance in the feature space, but for most of the features, there is no guarantee that close distances in the feature space correspond to perceptually similar shapes.

In recent works [13], [16], elastic approaches have been used to provide an effective measure of perceptual similarity between shapes, avoiding the need to evaluate shape features. According to these approaches, the amount of deformation which leads two shapes to overlap is described by an appropriate energy functional. Similarity between two shapes is computed on the basis of the energy spent in the deformation.

Feature based approaches to shape description have been coupled with traditional hierarchical index structures by a few authors [5], [11], [9], [10], [12], to provide efficient access to image databases, avoiding the sequential scanning of the entire set. Since features are points in a multi-dimensional feature space, multi-dimensional point-access methods are used to perform indexing. In [5], a combination of heuristic shape features (area, circularity, major axis orientation) and a set of algebraic moment invariants, are embedded in an $R^* -$ tree index structure. Since the index size grows exponentially with the dimensionality of the feature vector, distance preserving transformations are needed to map feature vectors in a lower dimensional space. In [11], [9], [10], [12] a K-D-B tree index scheme is used to arrange feature vectors, each leaf of the index including a shape boundary feature and a list of shapes associated with the feature. Retrieval is performed by matching chain codes of object contours.

Clustering of shapes through the index is made by evaluating distances among shape features. Since there is no guarantee that close distances in the feature space correspond to perceptually similar shapes, clusters may include non perceptually similar shapes.

Elastic based approaches have proven to be a more robust technique for measuring the similarity between shapes. However, they cannot be directly coupled with traditional index structures. It follows that with these techniques, searching for a desired shape, requires to sequentially match it against every shape stored in the database.

To overcome these limitations, an efficient shape representation model should be designed, retaining both the advantages of an indexed hierarchical structure and the robustness to shape distortion of elastic approaches. The notion of similarity between two shapes is strongly related to our capabilities to partition the shapes in structural sub–parts, and to find close relationships between the sub–parts of the two shapes. Multi–scale analysis [8], [6], [7] exploits a description at different levels of detail of a shape to highlight its characterizing elements. At each level, the shape can be partitioned in significant parts; as the resolution changes, from fine to coarse, adjacent parts tend to combine, to create more general structures, whose location, orientation and attributes are characteristics of the shape. Shapes which are partially different tend to exhibit similar characterizing elements if they are analyzed at coarse scales. This fact can be exploited to derive a grouping criterion based on the most perceptually salient features of the shapes. The coarser is the scale, the more the shapes are clustered according to their characterizing properties.

In this paper we present a method for the indexing of two dimensional, planar and closed shapes on the basis of their visual appearance. The proposed approach is based on a hierarchical description of the shapes at different levels of abstraction. Shapes are analyzed also at different scales of resolution. Through this analysis the details of the shape are gradually filtered out, while the characterizing elements of the shape are preserved. To preserve the inherent uncertainty of visual attributes, shape parts are described through fuzzy attributes. Through this multi–level multi–scale description, similar shapes are clustered according to the presence of similar characterizing elements. The index structure allows to select a tunable level of uncertainty to provide different degrees of selectiveness during the indexing process.

The paper is organized as follows: In Sect.2, it is introduced the problem of finding a description of a shape which is able to distinguish between the details of the shape and its characterizing elements. In Sect.3, it is explained how the proposed description can be used to carry out shape indexing. In Sect.4, considerations about the effectiveness of the approach are expounded with several examples.

2   Multi–scale shape analysis

Since the first work of Attneave [1], many contributions have appeared to point out the central role played in the partitioning process by those points where the shape bends more sharply. This idea has been the starting point for most of the successive efforts in shape partitioning, and it represents the starting point of this work too. In our method, it is assumed that the partitionment of a shape occurs at the points of minima of its curvature function. In general, the partitionment originated by the minima points decomposes the shape in a set of tokens. As there is a psychological evidence about the role played by these parts during the visual perception process [3], it seems to be quite reasonable to assume that a description of these parts should lead to a complete and meaningful discrimination among different shapes. However, partitioning a shape in sub-parts is just a part of the goal. Besides we must be able to detect those parts which represent *similarity prints*, apart from the details which appear in a particular instance.

If we assume to partition the shape in correspondence with the minima of the curvature function, each token of the shape can be viewed as a protruding or indenting part of the shape. Most of the times, if the shape represents the contour of a real object, the number of partitioning points of the shape is high. Every minimal detail in the contour of the object determines the presence of a protrusion or an indentation of the shape. It follows that with this great number of partition points it is very difficult to discriminate between points which model characterizing elements of the shape and those which are due to insignificant details.

The process by which the characterizing elements of a shape can be separated from the details derives by the analysis of shape and curvature at different scales. To provide a meaningful relationship among descriptions at different scales, we need to analyze the behavior of shapes under progressive smoothing. By smoothing the shape, its details can be filtered out, and what remains from this process is a coarser representation of the original shape, still keeping prominent features of shape appearance. This process can be applied several times, and each time, the new shape can be viewed as a generalization of the preceding ones, preserving its characterizing elements but loosing some details. This method is commonly referred to as *scale-space-filtering* [8].

2.1   Scale–space filtering

Mathematically, a planar, continuous, closed curve can be parameterized with respect to its arc-length t, and expressed as:

$$c(t) = \{x(t), y(t)\} \quad , \quad t \in [0, 1]$$

To analyze c at varying levels of detail, the functions $x(t)$ and $y(t)$ are convolved with a one dimensional Gaussian kernel $g(t, \sigma) = \frac{1}{\sigma\sqrt{2\pi}}e^{-\frac{t^2}{2\sigma^2}}$ [6]. The two components of the smoothed curve $C(t, \sigma)$ are therefore evaluated as:

$$X(t, \sigma) = \int_{-\infty}^{t} x(s)\, g(t - s, \sigma)ds \qquad Y(t, \sigma) = \int_{-\infty}^{t} y(s)\, g(t - s, \sigma)ds$$

The curvature $\Gamma(t, \sigma)$ of $C(t, \sigma)$ at the point $\{X(t, \sigma), Y(t, \sigma)\}$ can be expressed as ([7]):

$$\Gamma(t, \sigma) = \frac{X_t(t, \sigma)Y_{tt}(t, \sigma) - X_{tt}(t, \sigma)Y_t(t, \sigma)}{(X_t^2(t, \sigma) + Y_t^2(t, \sigma))^{3/2}}$$

where X_t, Y_t and X_{tt}, Y_{tt} are the first and second derivatives of X and Y with respect to t, respectively.

For a given value of σ we define $P_\sigma = \{p_n\}$ as the set of points p_n of the curve corresponding to the relative minima t_n of $\Gamma(t, \sigma)$, that is:

$$p_n = C(t_n, \sigma)$$

The set P_σ is made of points which partition the curve $C(t, \sigma)$ in tokens corresponding to the main protruding and indenting parts of the shape at the level of detail identified by σ. Of course, when σ varies, the number and locations of p_n vary; more precisely, the higher σ, the lower the number of p_n is. In order to discover the characterizing elements of a shape, we have to observe how the partition points change during the smoothing.

If we consider the evolution of the smoothed curve $C(t, \sigma)$, it can be argued that there are ranges for σ where the number of tokens keeps constant. In these intervals the minima translate along the curve, but no minima disappear. Values of σ where the number of minima changes mark structural changes in the aspect of the curve. A minimal but significant representation of the curve can thus be derived by describing the curve only in correspondence with these critical values of σ.

2.2 Shape Description

An effective description of a shape can be achieved by representing the visual features of each token at different scales. We will refer in the following to the scale k of a generic shape, as the smoothed shape with k minima of its curvature function.

For each token τ_n we consider its *equivalent triangle*, with vertices at the two token extrema p_n, p_{n+1} and the token center of mass b_n defined as:

$$b_{n_x} = \frac{\int_{C(t_n,\sigma)}^{C(t_{n+1},\sigma)} X\,ds}{\int_{C(t_n,\sigma)}^{C(t_{n+1},\sigma)} ds} \qquad b_{n_y} = \frac{\int_{C(t_n,\sigma)}^{C(t_{n+1},\sigma)} Y\,ds}{\int_{C(t_n,\sigma)}^{C(t_{n+1},\sigma)} ds}$$

The visual aspect of τ_n is represented by:

i) the symmetry $\mathcal{S}$ of the equivalent triangle with respect to its basis (p_n, p_{n+1}); $\mathcal{S}$ is evaluated considering the difference between the two angles $\widehat{b_n p_n p_{n+1}}$ and $\widehat{b_n p_{n+1} p_n}$;

ii) the orientation $\mathcal{O}$ of the vector $\mathbf{b_n m_n}$, where m_n is the median point of the segment (p_n, p_{n+1}); $\mathcal{O}$ is expressed through the angle θ_n which characterizes the vector in polar coordinates;

iii) the normalized token length $\mathcal{L}$; $\mathcal{L}$ is expressed through the ratio between the token and the shape length l_n/L.

Shapes of the same object can exhibit a high variability in terms of shape details or spatial arrangement of shape tokens. To improve the tolerance of shape description to this variability, fuzzy sets have been used to represent the values of the three properties. A set of attributes is associated with each property $\mathcal{S}$, $\mathcal{O}$ and $\mathcal{L}$, and a membership function μ_a is defined on each attribute a. The value of μ_a (a real value in $[0,1]$) computed for a token τ_n represents to what extent the visual aspect of τ_n conforms to the attribute a.

The value of the symmetry $\mathcal{S}$, which ranges in $[-\pi, \pi]$, is bucketed using the set of attributes (*left, center, right*). The value of the orientation $\mathcal{O}$, ranging in $[0, 2\pi]$, is bucketed using the set (*north, south, east, west*). The value of the ratio $\mathcal{L}$, which ranges in $[0, 1]$, is bucketed using the set (*short, med, long*).

A symbolic description is derived by thresholding values of the membership functions. This description retains the most relevant visual feature of a token, according to the value of the threshold α. For each token τ, $l_\alpha(\tau, p)$ is defined as the set of labels representing those attributes a of the property p such that $\mu_a > \alpha$.

The description of a generic shape C at scale k is characterized by two types of descriptors:

$D(C, k)$, the ordered set of 10–tuple storing the values of μ_a for all the attributes of each token τ_n with $n \in \{0, \dots, k-1\}$.

$L_\alpha^p(C, k)$, the set of symbolic labels associated with tokens τ_n for the property p, according to the threshold α:

$$L_\alpha^p(C, k) = l_\alpha(\tau_0, p) \times l_\alpha(\tau_1, p) \times \dots l_\alpha(\tau_{k-1}, p)$$

As an example, in Fig. 1 they are shown a shape C with 4 partition points and its fuzzy description $D(C, 4)$. If we assume $\alpha = 0.4$, the symbolic description for the orientation $\mathcal{O}$ can be computed as:

$$l_{0.4}(\tau_0, \mathcal{O}) = \{north\}$$
$$l_{0.4}(\tau_1, \mathcal{O}) = \{west\}$$
$$l_{0.4}(\tau_2, \mathcal{O}) = \{south, east\}$$
$$l_{0.4}(\tau_3, \mathcal{O}) = \{north\}$$

$$L_{0.4}^{\mathcal{O}}(C, 4) = \{(north, west, south, north),$$
$$(north, west, east, north)\}$$

A symbolic description retaining the most relevant features of all the three properties, is obtained by considering the Cartesian product of symbolic descriptions computed on the individual properties:

$$L_\alpha^{SOL}(C, k) = L_\alpha^S(C, k) \times L_\alpha^O(C, k) \times L_\alpha^L(C, k)$$

In our approach, a shape C at scale k is associated with a representation structure including the complete fuzzy shape description $D(C, k)$, a description $L_\alpha^{SOL}(C, k)$, and a description $L_\alpha^O(C, k)$. This scheme provides three levels of abstraction for the description of a shape: The fuzzy description corresponds to the lowest level of abstraction and is used for a fine analysis of shape properties. At the intermediate level, the shape is represented through symbolic labels computed on all the properties of the tokens. At the highest level only the labels computed on the orientation property are taken into account, thus capturing only the prominent perceptual features of the shape. In Fig. 2 the representation corresponding to the shape of Fig. 1 is shown. The representations at the two highest levels are symbolic, and depend on the value of the threshold α. With high values of α, the symbolic descriptions retain only those attribute which have a high value of the membership function. In this case, the description captures only the prominent perceptual attributes of each token. Differently, with low values of α, even non prominent visual features are represented at the highest level of abstraction.

Since at the coarsest scales, tokens mark characterizing elements of the shape, it is reasonable to assume that at these scales, similar shapes share similar tokens. In Fig.3 representation schemes associated with two shapes are shown. Each shape represents a horse at scale 4. Dotted arrows highlight symbolic labels which are equal apart from circular shifting. In this way, invariance is achieved with respect to the location of the first token along the object contour.

3 Index Structure

Shape descriptions of different objects have been embedded into an index structure which mirrors the multi–level multi-scale representation of the shapes.

At each scale k, symbolic descriptions of different objects are clustered, separately for $L_\alpha^{\mathcal{O}}(\cdot)$ and $L_\alpha^{\mathcal{SOL}}(\cdot)$. Clusters define nodes of a graph. A–nodes store the symbolic labels $L_\alpha^{\mathcal{O}}(\cdot)$, B–nodes the $L_\alpha^{\mathcal{SOL}}(\cdot)$ labels and C–nodes the fuzzy descriptions $D(\cdot)$.

Nodes are connected through arcs. Two types of arcs are provided:

i) Arcs between nodes of the same type at different scales k_1 and k_2, modeling the relationships between descriptions of a certain object at different scales. Only A–nodes are connected by this type of arcs.

ii) Arcs between nodes of different types at a certain scale k, modeling the relationships between descriptions at different levels of abstraction, from coarse to fine.

In Fig.4 they are sketched the representation structures for three distinct scales of two horse shapes. Each node corresponds to a description of the shape at a certain level of abstraction. Links between nodes correspond to relationships between descriptions at the same scale (vertical links) or at different scales (horizontal links, only at the highest abstraction level). In Fig.5 the two representation structures of Fig.4 are combined into a single representation in which descriptions shared by the two shapes are associated with a single node.

The threshold α determines the number of symbolic labels that are associated with each description, and tunes the tolerance of the index structure to the imprecision of part description. The lower is α, the higher is the number of labels associated with each description. Differently, with a high value of α, only a few labels are associated with the shape, thus reducing the complexity of the index structure but, at the same time, reducing the level of imprecision managed by the index.

3.1 Traversing the index

Given a query shape C_q, selection of database shapes sharing similar characterizing elements is accomplished by comparing the descriptions of C_q obtained at different scales, against the graph nodes.

Starting from the coarsest scale k_1, the elements of the set $L_\alpha^{\mathcal{O}}(C_q, k_1)$ are compared with the A–nodes of the graph. As a match is detected the elements of the set $L_\alpha^{\mathcal{SOL}}(C_q, k_1)$ are compared with B–nodes which are linked to the matched A–node. The procedure is similarly extended to the third level of abstraction: the fuzzy description $D(C_q, k_1)$ is compared with the C–nodes of the graph, and the matching scores are computed.

A and B–nodes contain ordered sets of symbolic labels. Two generic labels l_1 and l_2 match iff: i) l_1 and l_2 refer to the same scale; ii) it exists a number r of circular shifts of the symbols in l_1 such that the two labels are equal. By allowing circular shifting in the matching procedure, invariance is achieved with respect to the location of the first token along the object contour.

C–nodes contain numeric values corresponding to the fuzzy description $D(C, k)$ of a database shape. Descriptions are compared by evaluating the average correlation between the fuzzy description of the corresponding tokens. The matching score is normalized in $[0, 1]$ and provides a measure of the similarity between the two shapes at the scale k.

The same analysis is propagated to the following scale descriptions through the links between the A–nodes. The procedure terminates when the nodes corresponding to the finest scale are analyzed. Since a database shape can be matched at several scales, global matching scores are computed. Presently, they are obtained by averaging matching scores computed at each scale. Assuming that a shape C has been matched at scales k_1, k_2, ..., k_N with matching scores m_1, m_2, ..., m_N, respectively, then the global matching score M is computed as:

$$M = \frac{1}{N} \sum_{i=k_1}^{k_N} m_i \; .$$

4   Experimental results

Experiments have been carried out using a sample database of over 400 shapes taken from 20th century paintings. Shapes are derived by extracting the contour of relevant objects represented in the images. Each shape is manually extracted and sampled at 100 equally spaced points. Shapes represent the contours of objects of different sizes and in different positions. Many shapes are derived from occluded objects and miss a considerable part of their original contour, in some cases. Shapes are derived from images by extracting the contour of relevant objects represented in the images.

Descriptions are automatically extracted from each shape, and an index structure is built following the technique expounded in Sec. 3. Each shape is described at most at four scales, corresponding to $2, 3, 4, 5$ curvature minima.

Queries are performed by drawing sketches on a graphic interface. Once a query has been issued, the user tunes the value of two parameters (α and β in $[0, 1]$) which trigger the degree of selectiveness during the indexing process: α controls the tolerance of the index to imprecision of part description; β restricts the number of the best matching items that are displayed.

Retrieval results are presented for a few sample queries in Figs. 6-7.

Fig. 6 shows a sketch representing a fruit dish and the output of the indexing procedure. The output comprises all the shapes of fruit dishes and other shapes which all exhibit similar characterizing elements. All these shapes present a bone–shaped aspect if analyzed at a coarse scale.

In Fig. 7, the sketch of a more complex shape is shown, roughly representing the contour of a horse and the corresponding indexed shapes are presented. The system selects not only those shapes which closely resemble the sketch, but also shapes that represent a similar object with different postures. Neither the difference in the number of legs of the animals, nor the absence of some occluded part affect the performance of the system. In this example, since the multi–scale analysis detects the saliency of parts corresponding to the two front and rear legs, three shapes of a hat contour are also selected. This is due to the fact that the hat brim resembles the front and rear legs of an animal at a coarse level of resolution.

In order to assess the indexing accuracy of the proposed technique, performance figures obtained from our experiments are reported. For a given query, let T be the total number of relevant items available, R_r the number of relevant items retrieved, and T_r the total number of retrieved items. Then the *precision* $\mathcal{P}$ is defined as R_r/T_r and the *recall* $\mathcal{R}$ as R_r/T. Both parameters are function of α and β; they are interdependent, in the sense that one cannot be increased without decreasing the other. In Fig.8(a)(b) values of $\mathcal{R}$ and $\mathcal{P}$ are shown as functions of α for several values of β. It can be noticed that, by tuning the values of α and β, the system moves from a state in which almost all the similar shapes are selected ($\alpha = 0.25$, $\beta = 0.2$, $\mathcal{R} = 99\%$) to an opposite state where the precision of the system is improved with a minimal decay of the recall.

The efficiency of the proposed indexing technique has been measured by considering the number of comparisons effectively saved with respect to a sequential scanning of the whole database. To give a qualitative estimate of this pruning capability, in Fig.8(c) it is shown the percentage of C–nodes effectively analyzed during the indexing process. The figure shows that, in the average case, from 85% to 90% of comparisons are saved with respect to a sequential scanning.

5 Conclusions

In this paper, we presented a technique for shape indexing which exploits a multi–level multi–scale analysis of shapes to detect their characterizing elements. Since characterizing elements are responsible for the perceived aspect of the shape, and since they are shared by different instances of similar shapes, the proposed technique is able to provide an effective indexing of shapes on the basis of their visual appearance. The shape description is exploited to derive a layered graph structure that groups shapes sharing similar parts, thus providing selective filtering of shapes dissimilar from the query.

Experimental results have proven that the proposed technique allows to effectively index a database of shapes, based on the characterizing appearance of the shapes. Performance of the indexing procedure has been analyzed with respect to its computational complexity, its precision (average number of similar items which are not selected), and its efficiency with respect to a sequential scanning of the database.

References

1. F.Attneave "Some Informational Aspects of Visual Perception". *Psych. Review,* vol. 61, pp. 183-193, 1954.
2. I.Biederman "Recognition by Components". *Psych. Review,* vol. 94, pp. 115-147, 1987.
3. D.D.Hoffman, W.A.Richards "Parts of Recognition". *Cognition,* vol. 18, pp. 65-96, 1985.
4. M.Leyton "Inferring Causal History from Shapes". *Cognitive Science,* vol. 13, pp. 357-387, 1989.
5. C.Faloutsos, M.Flickner, W.Niblack, D.Petkovic, W.Equitz, R.Barber, "The QBIC Project: Efficient and Effective Querying by Image Content". Res.Report 9453, IBM Res.Div. Almaden Res.Center, Aug.1993.
6. A.K.Mackworth, F.Mokhtarian, "Scale-based Description of Planar Curves". *Proc. 5th Canadian Soc. Computational Studies of Intell.,* London, Ont., Canada, May 1984, pp. 114-119.
7. A.K.Mackworth, F.Mokhtarian, "A Theory of Multiscale, Curvature-based Shape Representation for Planar Curves". *IEEE PAMI.,* Vol. 14, n. 8, August 1992 pp. 789-805.
8. A.P.Witkin, "Scale-space Filtering". *Proc. of 7th Int. Joint Conf. Artificial Intell.,* Karlsruhe, Germany, 1983, pp. 1019-1022.
9. W. I. Grosky, R. Mehrotra "Index-Based Object Recognition in Pictorial Data Management". *Computer Vision, Graphics and Image Processing,* Vol. 52, 1990, pp.416-436.
10. R.Mehrotra, F.K.Kung, W.Grosky, "Industrial Part Recognition Using a Component-index". *Image and Vision Computing* No.3, pp. 225-231, 1990.
11. W. I. Grosky, P. Neo, R. Mehrotra "A Pictorial Index Mechanism for Model-based Matching". *Proc. 5th Int. Conf. on Data Engineering,*Los Angeles, CA, Feb 1989, pp.180-187
12. R. Mehrotra, J. E. Gary "Similar-Shape Retrieval in Shape Data Management". *IEEE Computer,* September 1995, pp. 57-62.
13. A. Del Bimbo, P. Pala "Visual Image Retrieval by Elastic Deformation of User Sketches", To appear on *IEEE Transactions on PAMI.*
14. C. Teh, R.T. Chin "On Image Analysis by Method of Moments", IEEE Transactions on PAMI, vol.10, pp. 496-513, 1988.
15. A. Khotanzad, Y.H. Hong "Invariant Image Recognition by Zernike Moments", IEEE Transactions on PAMI, vol.12, pp. 489-497, 1990.
16. S. Sclaroff, A. Pentland "Object Recognition and Categorization Using Modal Matching", Proc. 2nd CAD-based Vision Workshop, Champion, PA, Feb. 1994.
17. G. Congiu, A. Del Bimbo, E. Vicario "Iconic Retrival from Databeses of Cardiological Image Sequences", Proc. of the third Int. Conf. on Visual Database, Lausanne, Switzerland, March 1995.

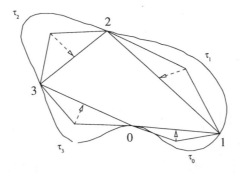

token	$\mathcal{S}$			$\mathcal{O}$				$\mathcal{L}$		
	left	*center*	*right*	*south*	*north*	*east*	*west*	*short*	*med*	*long*
0	0.01	0.99	0.00	0.00	0.93	0.07	0.00	0.27	0.73	0.00
1	0.04	0.96	0.00	0.34	0.00	0.00	0.66	0.00	0.71	0.29
2	0.00	0.96	0.04	0.52	0.00	0.48	0.00	0.00	0.91	0.09
3	0.02	0.98	0.00	0.00	0.65	0.35	0.00	0.11	0.89	0.00

Fig. 1. The shape of a horse at scale 4. For each shape token the values of the membership functions associated with all the attributes are reported.

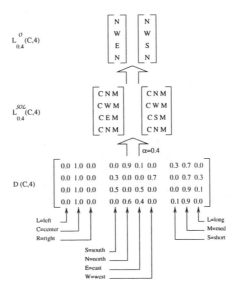

Fig. 2. Representation structure associated with the shape of Fig.1

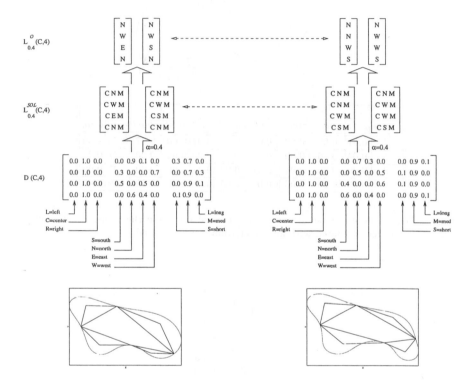

Fig. 3. Representation structures associated with the shapes of two horses. Correspondences between symbolic labels are highlighted with dotted arrows. Equivalence between the labels is achieved by a unitary circular shift of the tokens of the second shape. According to this, the first token $\tau_0(C_0)$ of the first shape corresponds to the second token $\tau_1(C_1)$ of the second shape; $\tau_1(C_0)$ to $\tau_2(C_1)$, $\tau_2(C_0)$ to $\tau_3(C_1)$ and $\tau_3(C_0)$ to $\tau_0(C_1)$.

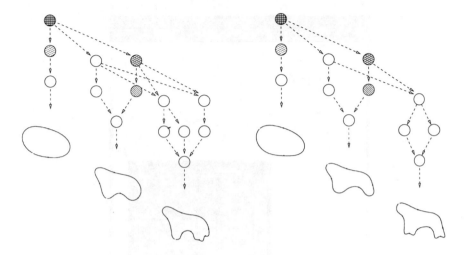

Fig. 4. Multi–level representation structures at three distinct scales for two different shapes of horses. Node textures highlight equal descriptions.

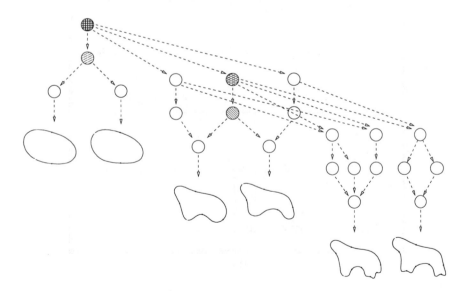

Fig. 5. Index structure for the representations of the two shapes in Fig.4. The structure keeps only one node description for nodes with the same descriptions.

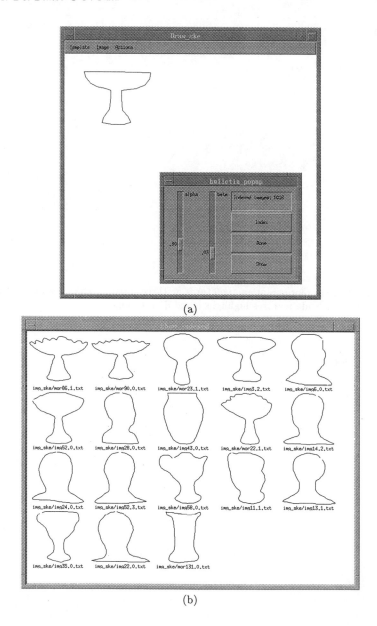

Fig. 6. The sketch of a fruit-dish (a) and the indexed shapes (b).

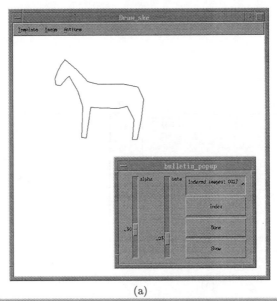

(a)

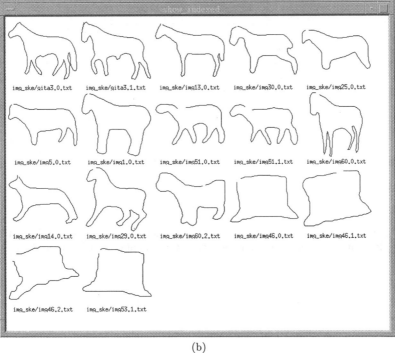

(b)

Fig. 7. A horse like sketch (a) and the indexed shapes (b).

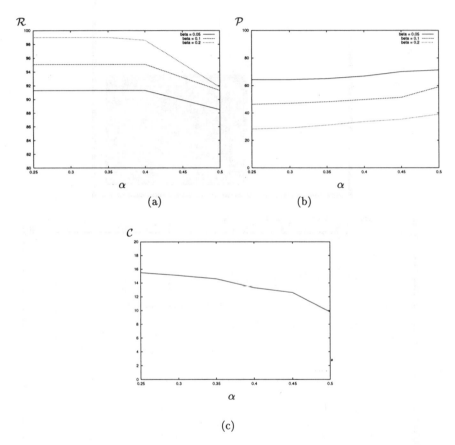

Fig. 8. (a) System recall and (b) precision as functions of α for three values of β. (c) Percentage of crossed C–nodes wrt their total number as a function of α.

Document Databases

Handling Multiple Instances of Symbols in Pictorial Queries by Image Similarity

Aya Soffer[1] and Hanan Samet[2]

[1] CESDIS, Goddard Space Flight Center and
Center for Automation Research, University of Maryland at College Park and
Computer Science and EE Department, University of Maryland Baltimore County
5401 Wilkens Avenue, Baltimore, MD 21228-5398
E-mail: aya@umiacs.umd.edu ***
[2] Computer Science Department and,
Center for Automation Research and Institute for Advanced Computer Science
University of Maryland at College Park, College Park, Maryland 20742
E-mail: hjs@umiacs.umd.edu †

Abstract. A method is presented for processing pictorial query specifications that consist of a query image and a similarity level that must hold between the query image and database images. The similarity level specifies the *contextual similarity* (how well does the content of one image match that of another) as well as the *spatial similarity* (the relative locations of the matching symbols in the two images). This method allows more than one instance of each object in the database image (while still requiring only one instance of each object in the query image). The algorithm tries to satisfy the contextual similarity first and then tries to satisfy the spatial constraints using an auxiliary graph data structure. The running time of this method is exponential in the number of objects in the query image.

1 Introduction

A basic requirement of an image database is the ability to query the database pictorially. The most common method of doing this is querying via an example image. The problem with this method is that in an image database we are usually not looking for an exact match. Instead, the goal is to find images that are similar to a given query image. The main issue is how to determine if two images are similar and whether the similarity criteria that are used by the database system match the user's notion of similarity. There are a few commercial systems that support retrieval of images by pictorial specification [5, 11]. Numerous prototype research IDMS's deal with storage and retrieval of images [1, 3, 4, 6, 7, 10].

*** The support of USRA/CESDIS and NASA Goddard Space Flight Center is gratefully acknowledged.
† The support of the National Science Foundation under Grant IRI-92-16970 is gratefully acknowledged.

In [9] we introduced a method for specifying queries to an image database pictorially that enables the user to indicate the level of required similarity between the query image and the database images. This method of query specification and the corresponding query processing techniques are applicable to images where the set of objects that may appear in them is known a priori, and where these objects are represented by graphical symbols. For example, in the map domain, graphical symbols are used to indicate the location of various sites such as hospitals, post offices, recreation areas, scenic areas etc. We call this class of images *symbolic images*. The query image is constructed by positioning objects so that the desired spatial constraints hold. Two image similarity factors are considered: (1) *contextual similarity*: how well does the content of one image match that of another. For example, should the database image contain all of the objects in the query image or may it just contain some of these objects. (2) *spatial similarity*: the relative locations of the matching symbols in the two images. By specifying the desired contextual and spatial similarity levels along with the query image, users can specify the extent of the required similarity. We have used this method as a user interface for a map image database system that we have developed [8] named MARCO (denoting MAp Retrieval by COntent).

The query processing algorithms in [9] assume only one instance of each symbol in the query image as well as in the database images. In this paper we present a method that allows the occurrence of more than one instance of each symbol in the database image (while still requiring only one instance of each symbol in the query image). This method tries to satisfy the contextual similarity first and then tries to satisfy the spatial constraints using an auxiliary graph data structure. The running time of this algorithm is exponential in the number of objects in the query image. All of the examples in this paper are from the map domain. However, images from many other interesting applications fall into the category of symbolic images. These include CAD/CAM, engineering drawings, floor plans, and more. Hence, the methods that we describe here are applicable to them as well.

2   Pictorial Query Specification

To specify queries pictorially, the user creates an image containing the required symbols positioned so that the desired spatial constraints hold. The user must also specify the image similarity level required to satisfy the contextual and spatial constraints. Throughout this paper we use the following definitions and notation. A *symbol* is a group of connected pixels that together have some common semantic meaning. A *class* is a group of symbols that all have the same semantic meaning. $cl(s)$ denotes the class of symbol s. We say that symbol $s1$ *matches* symbol $s2$ if $cl(s1) = cl(s2)$.

We define the following four levels of contextual similarity between a query image QI and a database image DI:

1. Every symbol in QI has a distinct matching symbol in DI, and every symbol in DI has a matching symbol in QI.

2. Every symbol in QI has a distinct matching symbol in DI (DI may contain additional symbols from any class).
3. Every symbol in DI has a matching symbol in QI.
4. At least one symbol in QI has a matching symbol in DI (DI may contain additional symbols from any class).

In addition, we define the following five levels of spatial similarity:

1. The matching symbols of QI and DI are in the exact same locations in both images.
2. The relative position of the matching symbols of QI and DI is the same, and the distance between them is bounded from below by some given value L and bounded from above by the distance between the symbols in QI. By default $L = 0$. If $L = 0$, then $0 \le dist(s_i, s_j) \le dist(s_k, s_l)$ (i.e., it is a range search). If $L = dist(s_k, s_l)$, then $dist(s_i, s_j) = dist(s_k, s_l)$ (i.e., it is an exact distance search).
3. The relative position of the matching symbols of QI and DI is the same, but the distance between them may vary.
4. The relative position of the matching symbols of QI and DI may vary, but the distance between them is bounded from below by some given value L and bounded from above by the distance between the symbols in QI. By default $L = 0$.
5. The location of the matching symbols, the distance between them, and the relative position of these symbols may vary (i.e., no spatial constraints).

The total similarity between QI and DI is defined by combining the two similarity factors. For example, $DI \equiv_{2,3} QI$ denotes that the contextual similarity and the spatial similarity of the two images is at levels 2 and 3, respectively. That is, for each symbol in QI there is a matching symbol from the same class in DI, the location of the symbols and the distance between them may vary, but the inter-symbol spatial relationship between them is the same. In general, if $DI \equiv_{csl,ssl} QI$ and if S' is the set of all the symbols of DI that match some symbol in QI, then the set of classes of the symbols of S' is a subset of the set of classes of the symbols of QI. Furthermore, for every pair of symbols s_1 and $s_2 \in S'$ the spatial constraints dictated by ssl and the positions of the matching symbols in QI hold.

More complex queries may be specified by combining query images with "AND" and "OR" operators. For example, to specify a query with spatial constraints between some symbols, but with no spatial constraints between other symbols, two separate query images with different values of ssl can be combined via the AND operator. For example, consider the query in Figure 1 which requests "all images with a hotel within 6 miles of a beach and with a cafe or a restaurant". No spatial constraints are specified for the restaurant and cafe symbols; however, the hotel must be within 6 miles of a beach. This method of splitting a query into several components can also be used to specify more than one acceptable spatial constraint. For example, Figure 2 requests "all images with a camping site within 5 miles of a fishing site OR with a hotel within 10 miles of a fishing site AND with an airfield northeast of and within 7 miles of

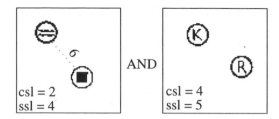

Fig. 1. A pictorial query to "find all images with a hotel within 6 miles of a beach and with a cafe or a restaurant"

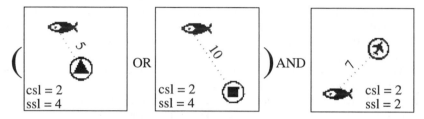

Fig. 2. A pictorial query to "find all images with a camping site within 5 miles of a fishing site OR with a hotel within 10 miles of a fishing site AND with an airfield northeast of and within 7 miles of the fishing site"

the fishing site". Note that the dotted lines with the distance that appear in the query images in Figures 1 and 2 are only used to denote the distance between symbols in the figure; they are not actually part of the query image. The query image only contains symbols. The distance (and relative directions) between the symbols is specified implicitly in the query image QI by the actual distance (and relative direction) between the symbols in QI.

3   Pictorial Query Processing

Pictorial queries are processed by a function called *GetSimilarImages* that takes as input the query image (QI), the contextual similarity level (csl), and the spatial similarity level (ssl). It returns the set of databases images B so that each image DI of B satisfies the pictorial query (i.e., $DI \equiv_{csl,ssl} QI$ for all $DI \in B$). *GetSimilarImages* constructs a set of candidate images from the database in which the contextual constraints hold and then invokes function *checkSsl* for each candidate image to determine if the spatial constraints dictated by ssl hold in it. An image in which the spatial constraints do not hold is removed from the candidate-image set. Pictorial queries involving more than one query component are executed by performing a separate pictorial query for each component and then computing the intersection of the results for components joined by an AND operator, and the union of the results for those joined by an OR operator.

Algorithm *checkSsl* determines whether the spatial constraints dictated by a query image QI and spatial similarity level ssl hold in an image DI. Figure 3

```
            checkSsl(logical image DI, QI, similarity level ssl)
if ssl = 5 ∨ |DI| = 1 then /* no need to check anything */
    return TRUE
/* compute distances and relative location between QI symbols*/
foreach qel₁ ∈ QI
    foreach qel₂ ∈ QI − {qel₁}
        if (ssl = 2) ∨ (ssl = 4) then
            dists[cl(qel₁), cl(qel₂)] ← getDist(loc(qel₁), loc(qel₂))
        if (ssl = 2) ∨ (ssl = 3) then
            relDirs[cl(qel₁), cl(qel₂)] ← getReldir(loc(qel₁), loc(qel₂))
/* now check that these hold in the input image */
foreach del₁ ∈ DI
    foreach del₂ ∈ DI − {del₁}
        if (ssl = 2) ∨ (ssl = 4) then
            if getDists(loc(del₁), loc(del₂)) > dists[cl(del₁), cl(del₂)] then
                return FALSE
        if (ssl = 2) ∨ (ssl = 3) then
            if getReldirs(loc(del₁), loc(del₂)) ≠ relDirs[cl(del₁), cl(del₂)] then
                return FALSE
return TRUE /* everything is OK */
```

Fig. 3. Algorithm *checkSsl* to determine whether the spatial constraints dictated by a query image QI and spatial similarity level ssl hold in a logical image DI.

summarizes this algorithm. The input to *checkSsl* is QI' and DI' which are sub-images of the original QI and DI that contain only those symbols that were matched to each other by *GetSimilarImages* when checking the contextual constraints. Thus, the set of classes of the symbols of DI' and QI' is identical although $|DI'|$ may be larger than $|QI'|$ since DI and hence DI' may have multiple instances of the same class. The algorithm first computes the distance and/or the relative directions between the symbols of QI'. It then computes them for DI' and checks whether the required spatial constraints between each symbol pair in DI' hold. See Figure 4 for example sub-images QI' and DI'.

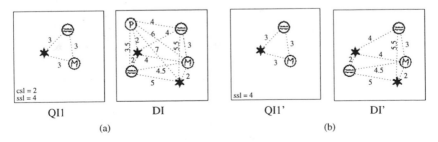

Fig. 4. (a) Query image $QI1$ and database image DI. (b) The corresponding sub-images $QI1'$ and DI' that contain only the matching symbols.

4   Multiple Symbol Instances in Database Images

Figure 5 illustrates the complexity that arises from allowing multiple instances of the same symbol in database images. Although there is one pair of symbols in DI' that satisfies the spatial constraints for each query-image pair (denoted by solid lines in the part of the figure corresponding to DI'), there is no triplet of symbols that does this. In other words, $checkSsl$ cannot verify a triplet of conditions but it can catch the three pairs. Therefore, a pair-wise algorithm such as $checkSsl$ cannot work here. Instead, a new and more complex version of $checkSsl$ would be needed that checks every possible triplet combination. In general, for a query with $|QI'|$ symbols, we need to check for the occurrence of every possible combination of them. This new version of $checkSsl$ would thus take $O(|QI'|^2 + \binom{|DI'|}{|QI'|})$ time, which is exponential ($|QI'|^2$ to compute the distance between every pair of symbols in QI', and $\binom{|DI'|}{|QI'|}$ to check if these distances hold for any combination of size $|QI'|$ in DI').

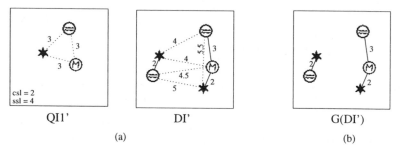

QI1'   DI'   G(DI')

(a)   (b)

Fig. 5. (a) Query sub-image $QI1'$, and database sub-image DI' that does not satisfy the spatial constraint specified by ssl. (b) The corresponding query graph $G(DI')$ does not have a clique of size $|QI1'| = 3$.

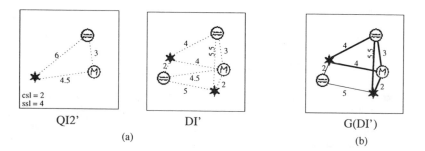

QI2'   DI'   G(DI')

(a)   (b)

Fig. 6. (a) Query sub-image $QI2'$, and database sub-image DI' that does satisfy the spatial constraint. (b) The corresponding query graph $G(DI')$. It has two cliques of size $|QI2'| = 3$, indicated by thick lines.

One solution for this problem is based on the following definition and theorem. Note that the discussion here assumes that $ssl = 4$, i.e. the spatial constraints are only based on distance, however the results hold for cases involving relative directions as well.

Definition. A *clique* in an undirected graph $G = (V, E)$ is a subset $V' \subseteq V$ of vertices, each pair of which is connected by an edge of E. In other words, a clique is a complete subset of G. A clique of size k is a complete subgraph of G where $|V'| = k$.

Theorem 1. *Let* $G(DI') = (V, E)$, *where* $V = $ *all symbols s in* DI'. *Let* $(v_i, v_j) \in E$ *if* $dist(v_i, v_j)$ *in* DI' *is less than or equal to* $dist(cl(v_i), cl(v_j))$ *in* QI'. DI' *satisfies the spatial constraints specified by* QI' *if and only if graph* $G(DI')$ *has a clique of size* $|QI'|$.

We first observe the use of this theorem by means of an example and then present a proof of it. Figure 5b shows graph $G(DI')$ that corresponds to the query $QI1'$ in Figure 5a. There is no clique of size $|QI1'| = 3$ in $G(DI')$, and thus DI' does not satisfy $QI1'$. However, for query sub-image $QI2'$, as seen in Figure 6, $G(DI')$ (in Figure 6b) has two cliques of size 3, and therefore DI' does satisfy $QI2'$. Recall that we are still assuming that there is only one instance of each symbol in the query image.

Proof. We first prove the "if" part (i.e., if $G(DI')$ has a clique of size $|QI'|$, then DI' satisfies the spatial constraints specified by QI'). If $G(DI') = (V, E)$ has a clique whose elements are $V' \subseteq V$ and if $|V'| = |QI'|$ then by definition of a clique each pair of elements of V' are connected by an edge of E. We denote this complete subgraph by $G'(DI')$. Each one of the vertices $v \in V'$ corresponds to exactly one of the symbols in QI'. The reason for this is that since we assume that QI (and thus QI') has only one instance of each symbol, and since the edges in $G(DI')$ correspond to constraints between symbols in QI', there are no edges in $G(DI')$ between multiple instances of the same symbol. Therefore, V' consists of $|QI'|$ unique symbols and there is a one-to-one correspondence between the vertices of $G'(DI')$ and the symbols of QI'. Furthermore, since $G'(DI')$ is a complete graph, all of the constraints dictated by QI' hold. Otherwise, the corresponding edge would not have been inserted into $G(DI')$. Thus, if $G(DI')$ has a clique of size $|QI'|$, then DI' satisfies the spatial constraints specified by QI'. We now prove the "only if" part (i.e., if DI' satisfies the spatial constraints specified by QI', then $G(DI')$ has a clique of size $|QI'|$). If DI' satisfies the spatial constraints specified by QI' then by the definition of $DI \equiv_{csl,ssl} QI$ in Section 2 and by the definition of DI' and QI' in Section 3 there exists a set of symbols $S' \in DI'$ where $|S'| = |QI'|$ in which for every pair of symbols s_1 and $s_2 \in S'$ the spatial constraints dictated by ssl for the matching symbols in QI' hold. According to the rule for constructing $G(DI')$, its set of vertices V contains one vertex for each symbol in DI'. In particular, it contains the set of vertices corresponding to the symbols in $S' \subseteq V$. Furthermore, an edge will be inserted between every two vertices corresponding to symbols in S'. Thus the subgraph of $G(DI')$ consisting of the vertices corresponding to the symbols of S' will be complete, and since $|S'| = |QI'|$, it is a clique of $G(DI')$ of size $|QI'|$.

Corollary 2. $DI \equiv_{csl,ssl} QI$ *if and only if* DI *satisfies* QI *in terms of csl and* DI' *satisfies* QI' *in terms of ssl.*

Proof. Immediate from the definitions of $\equiv$, DI', and QI' and from Theorem1.

The *clique problem* is known to be NP-Complete [2], and thus we cannot expect to check for the spatial constraints using this method in polynomial time. However, the number of instances of query-image symbols in a database image is most likely not very large and is not a function of the size of the database. Instead, it is a function of the average number of symbols in an image which is a constant. Therefore, checking the spatial constraints by searching for cliques of size QI' is quite reasonable. The total cost of the modified version of *checkSsl* (called *McheckSsl*) that builds the graph and looks for cliques is $O(|DI'|^2 + 2^{|DI'|})$ where $|DI'|$ is the number of symbols in the database image that have matching symbols in the query image ($|DI'|^2$ for building graph $G(DI')$, and $2^{|DI'|}$ for searching for cliques of size $|QI'|$ in $G(DI')$). Note that this solution still assumes only one instance of each class in the query image.

5 Concluding Remarks

The method presented in this paper still assumes only one instance of each symbol in the query image. Handling multiple instances of symbols in query images is more complex since in this case each symbol in the database image may potentially be matched to more than one symbol in the query image. While one particular choice of matching may not yield a hit for the query, another choice may result in a positive result for the query. In addition, once a particular matching is chosen we must keep track of this binding in order to ensure that the other conditions hold with this particular binding. We are currently working on a solution for this problem.

Using our query specification method, the same query may be formulated in more than one way (by using different combinations of *csl* and AND/OR operators). One formulation may be more efficient to process than others. Furthermore, some combinations of AND and *csl* values may be impossible to satisfy in that the same image cannot satisfy both clauses of the AND. Therefore, query optimization methods for processing pictorial queries are required. This is a subject for future research.

References

1. S. K. Chang, Q. Y. Shi, and C. Y. Yan. Iconic indexing by 2-D strings. *IEEE Transactions on Pattern Analysis and Machine Intelligence*, 9(3):413–428, May 1987.
2. M. R. Garey and D. S. Johnson. *Computers and Intractability, A Guide to the Theory of NP-Completeness*. W. H. Freeman and Co., San Francisco, 1979.
3. V. Gudivada and V. Raghavan. Design and evaluation of algorithms for image retrieval by spatial similarity. *ACM Transactions on Information Systems*, 13(2):115–144, April 1995.

4. A. Gupta, T. Weymouth, and R. Jain. Semantic queries with pictures: the VIM-SYS model. In G. Lohman, editor, *Proceedings of the Seventeenth International Conference on Very Large Databases*, pages 69–79, Barcelona, Spain, September 1991.
5. W. Niblack, R. Barber, W. Equitz, M. Flickner, E. Glasman, D. Petkovic, and P. Yanker. The QBIC project: Querying images by content using color, texture, and shape. In *Proceeding of the SPIE, Storage and Retrieval of Image and Video Databases*, volume 1908, pages 173–187, San Jose, CA, February 1993.
6. D. Papadias and T. K. Sellis. A pictorial query-by-example language. *Journal of Visual Languages and Computing*, 6(1):53–72, March 1995.
7. A. Pentland, R. W. Picard, and S. Sclaroff. Photobook: Content-based manipulation of image databases. In *Proceeding of the SPIE, Storage and Retrieval of Image and Video Databases II*, volume 2185, pages 34–47, San Jose, CA, February 1994.
8. H. Samet and A. Soffer. MARCO: MAp Retrieval by COntent. *IEEE Transactions on Pattern Analysis and Machine Intelligence*, 18(8):783–798, August 1996.
9. A. Soffer and H. Samet. Handling multiple instances of symbols in pictorial queries by image similarity. In *Proceedings of the First International Workshop on Image Databases and Multi Media Search*, pages 51–58, Amsterdam, The Netherlands, August 1996.
10. M. Swain. Interactive indexing into image databases. In *Proceeding of the SPIE, Storage and Retrieval for Image and Video Databases*, volume 1908, pages 95–103, San Jose, CA, February 1993.
11. M. Ubell. The montage extensible dataBlade architecture. In *Proceedings of the ACM SIGMOD International Conference on Management of Data*, page 482, Minneapolis, MN, June 1994.

Content Based Hypertext Creation in Text/Figure Databases

Marcel Worring and Arnold W.M. Smeulders

Intelligent Sensory Information Systems
Department of Computer Science
University of Amsterdam, The Netherlands
worring@wins.uva.nl

Abstract. We consider the construction of hypertext for documents containing a mixture of text and figures to provide convenient access to the content of both the text *and* the figures. The focus in this paper is on detecting alphanumeric labels in the figures to be used as anchors in the hypertext construction.

1 Introduction

More and more documents are becoming available in their digital form and are stored in document databases or made accessible through the World Wide Web. Most of the documents contain a mixture of text and figures. Full text retrieval and automatic extraction of text-to-text type hyperlinks [4] are becoming more and more commonplace. Such a level of functionality has not yet been realized for figures or the combination of text and figures. However, for many classes of documents, access is determined by the possibility to include the content of the figures as well. After all they have been included by the authors to underline the most important points they wish to make.

Notably in patent applications and manuals the accompanying text consists mostly of extended captions of the figures. Consider for example a user manual for a PC. In such a manual there will be a figure showing the monitor where labels are attached to different buttons. These buttons have a description in the accompanying text. Such a reference may be at a considerable distance with respect to the linear reading order of the document.

In accessing large files of digital documents it is therefore of great value to have available the non-linear hypertext structure of the document. If this is the case one can create separate text and figure channels where clicking a keyword in the text automatically turns the focus of attention in the figure channel to the corresponding figure (even if that is in another chapter, e.g. where the definition is) and to the proper position within this figure. Vice versa when clicking in the figure the associated text should be displayed.

The above is not easy to achieve as in almost any digital document the figure is available in its bitmap format only. In document image databases this is even more complicated as these are usually created by scanning paper documents and hence the whole document is stored as a bitmap. As a consequence most systems providing hyperlink access to (scanned) documents [4, 5, 6] limit their attention to links between fragments of text or links to figures as a whole. One of the few systems making relations between text and figure details is the Piction system [7] developed for analyzing newspaper photographs by means of the caption. Although their goal was not hypertext construction it can be viewed as such.

We are developing a system for hypertext construction within the domain of patent applications and manuals or other documents with figures created by a drawing package [9, 10]. Current topics of the system will be described in this paper. which is organized as follows. In section 2, an overview of the system is given and a classification of different labels in a figure is made. For the particular class of alphanumeric labels we present a new detection algorithm in section 3. Results are presented in section 4.

2   The hyperdocument system

2.1   Hypertext

The essence of *hypertext* is formed by the *links* from and to *(composite) components* and *anchors* within the components [2].

For text/figure documents the composite components are typically defined by the logical structure [1] which among others defines the linear reading order. The components are the individual textblocks, figures and lines. Finally, anchors are keywords in textblocks and labels (or other details) in the figures.

Hence, when the input to the system is a scanned document our goal is to

1. find the components by analyzing the image of the document
2. find anchors in both text and figures
3. create the relevant links to anchors and/or components

The first step in the analysis is the classification of the different document parts into the geometric classes text, figure, line etc. Many algorithms are known e.g. [8]. We have developed a similar bottom-up approach with a visual algorithm editor allowing fast adaptation to new application domains. For efficiency reasons this classification is performed at a reduced resolution (in our case reduction by a factor 4 in both x- and y-direction). The later analysis of figures is performed at full resolution as otherwise small details are lost. In all cases the parameters are specified in actual document parameters rather than pixels. Hence, increasing the resolution always yields more accurate results. If required the user can interactively correct the classification.

Every block in the image classified as text is sent to an external Optical Character Recognition program to reveal the ASCII text conveyed by the facsimile of the text. These pieces of text and the figures in the document form the basis for the hypertext construction. Note that at this point the distinction between a scanned document and a generic ASCII text combined with figures is only that the former might contain more errors due to improper recognition.

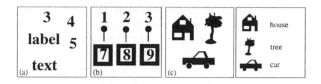

Fig. 1. *(a) plain alphanumeric labels, (b) two examples of generic alphanumeric labels, (c) icon labels, and (d) legend labels*

2.2 Anchors and links

We now turn our focus to the figures in the document where we aim to detect labels to be used as anchors. We distinguish four different types of labels which can be present (see figure 1) namely :

- *plain alphanumeric labels* : text strings without a generic visual part.
- *generic alphanumeric labels* : text strings with an associated generic visual part.
- *icon labels* : labels distinguished by their shape alone
- *legend labels* : icon labels with an associated textual definition.

The detection of the last three types in order to be used as anchors has been studied in [10]. In the next section we consider the detection of plain alphanumeric labels in figures.

Link creation to all but the icon labels is on the basis of the associated textual meaning. This ASCII string can be retrieved through Optical Character Recognition of the facsimile of the textual part of the label. This ASCII string can then be used in a keyword search in the associated text. For icon labels, links will always be to positions in the document, either figure or text, where the same icon is present.

3 Label detection and recognition

3.1 Introduction

We consider the detection of alphanumeric labels in figures. For scanned paper maps this is studied, among others, in [3]. They make a preselection of objects in the image on the basis of expected width and height of the characters. From there domain knowledge is used to improve recognition. In our case we have a more general situation where no extensive domain knowledge is present. As a consequence the detection of labels should be on the basis of the similarities within the set of characters rather than their distinction from the environment as non-character objects can have arbitrary unknown properties. Furthermore, as no predefined notion of scale is present the method should be scale independent.

The analysis is performed in a number of steps. First; *connected objects are detected.* These objects can be either individual characters, individual characters accidently connected in horizontal direction, or graphics. We only consider horizontal connections between characters as vertical spacing is usually much larger and hence accidental connections are unlikely. For each of the detected objects the relevant *features are computed*. On the basis of these features the *selection of candidate labels* is performed. Finally, OCR is used to *retrieve the ASCII content* of each label. This can also result in rejects of individual characters or complete labels. Hence, this provides a further verification.

3.2   Features

In this section we consider which features should be used in the detection. The assumption is that a consistent font is used for the labels in the figure. As the method should work for every character local (shape) information cannot be used as feature. Hence, only global features are considered. Candidate features are *height* of characters. The *width* and finally features based on the *stroke width*.

Height is usually very consistent within one document and varies only depending on whether ascenders (e.g. "b,l,k"), descenders (e.g. "j,p,q"), or none of the two are present (e.g. "a,c,e"). Capitals usually have the same height as objects with ascenders. Width is varying much more for different characters e.g. "W" versus "i", and furthermore two subsequent characters in a label might be connected. Both width and height are easily computed from the bounding box of the connected binary objects.

As a measure of stroke width we consider the average stroke width, which varies for different types of fonts (e.g. italic versus bold). As consistent font is assumed the average stroke width should be similar for all characters. It is computed from the discrete distance transform. First, the distance transform of the binary object is computed, local maxima of which are used to compute the medial axis. Then the average of the distance values on the axis can be used as an approximation of the average stroke width.

3.3   Label selection

When detecting the connected objects in the image we regard any object which has an area smaller than $(0.05\ cm)^2$ as noise. Objects with a width or height larger than 1.0 cm are disregarded (i.e. classified as graphics).

In the next step candidate characters are merged into candidate labels. This has two functions. First, after merging, the selection on width can be made on the basis of complete words rather than the individual characters circumventing the above described problems. Second, for a complete label, average feature values are more robust than values for single characters.

The following characteristics are used to decide whether two label fragments should be merged. 1. The horizontal spacing between the two fragments should be small and 2. The two fragments should have a substantial overlap in the vertical direction

As stated before measures for these characteristics should be scale invariant. As width varies with the number of characters in the fragment scale independence must be achieved by defining measures relative to the height of the fragments.

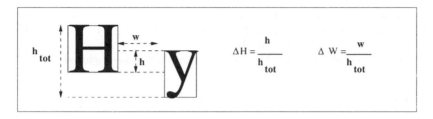

Fig. 2. *Graphical impression of the computation of the measures ΔH and ΔW.*

To be precise let $x^i_{min}, x^i_{max}, y^i_{min}, y^i_{max}$ define the bounding box for label fragment i, then the following equations measure the spacing and overlap of fragments i and j.

$$\Delta W = \frac{max(x^i_{min}, x^j_{min}) - min(x^i_{max}, x^j_{max})}{max(y^i_{max}, y^j_{max}) - min(y^i_{min}, y^j_{min})}$$

$$\Delta H = 1 - \frac{|y^i_{min} - y^j_{min}| + |y^i_{max} - y^j_{max}|}{max(y^i_{max}, y^j_{max}) - min(y^i_{min}, y^j_{min})}$$

The measures are exemplified in figure 2. Candidate label fragments are only merged if $\Delta W \leq W_t$ and $\Delta H \geq H_t$. The process continues until there are no more changes to the set of fragments. Note that negative values of ΔH indicate no overlap at all whereas negative values of ΔW do indicate overlap. From the characteristics of characters with and without ascenders/descenders we conclude that an appropriate setting for overlap is $H_t = 0.5$. We further set $W_t = 0.75$.

As labels in the figure are set in some fixed font, we expect to find many objects with similar height and stroke width. We therefore compute the modal height h_m and modal average stroke width s_m by making histograms of height and average stroke width for all objects. As these values will vary much more for graphical objects the modal height and stroke width will correspond to the characters. To be precise we expect these values to correspond to the characters without ascenders/descenders.

Now candidate labels for which the height $h_{obj} \notin [(1 - \alpha)h_m, (1 + \beta)h_m]$, for properly chosen α and β can be classified as graphics. Again from the characteristics of characters we set $\alpha = 0.5, \beta = 2.0$. When multiple fonts are used in the figure each maximum in the height histogram should be analyzed. In the resulting set one can still expect non-character objects. Therefore labels with average stroke width $s_{obj} \notin [(1 - \gamma)s_m, (1 + \omega)s_m]$ should also be discarded.

As this is document dependent γ and ω are not fixed. Finally, if the number of characters in a label is known to be at least n_{char}, labels are discarded when $w_{obj} < n_{char} * h_m$. Note, that again all steps are invariant to change of scale.

In summary the algorithm is given by:

1. : join characters into labels
2. : discard labels on basis of height
3. : discard labels on basis of stroke width
4. : discard labels on basis of width
5. : perform OCR and discard characters or labels if not recognized

4   Results

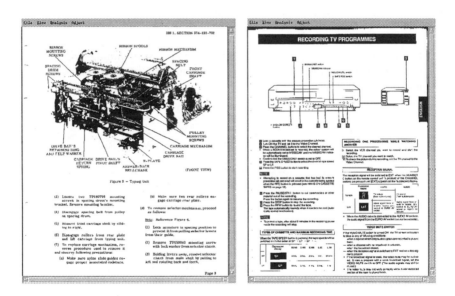

Fig. 3. *Representative example documents used in the text. Documents of class 1 (left) are from an old (1964) manual of a tele-typewriter where photographs, text, and graphics have been mixed. The documents of class 2 (right) are taken from a manual for a VCR and are completely drawing package generated.*

To illustrate the algorithm we have applied it to a set of 9 documents of which the documents in figure 3 are representatives. In total there are 2337 objects larger than the noise value and width and height smaller than 1.0cm, of which 1551 are genuine characters.

We have experimented with different values of γ and ω but it turned out that we could not find values yielding good results. Either genuine characters were removed or not a single non-character was classified as such. Hence, for the current experiments we do not use step 3 of the algorithm. For the selection on width we set $n_{char} = 3$. After this selection, remaining labels are sent to the commercial OCR-package OmniPage.

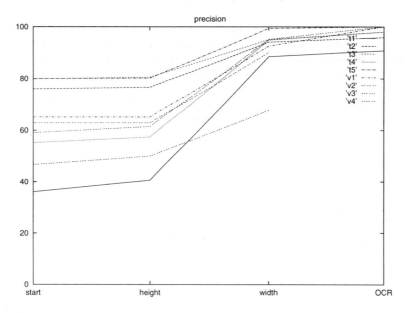

Fig. 4. *Precision as function of the different processing steps in the algorithm for images of class 1 (t1-t5) and class 2 (v1-v4).*

To judge the performance of the algorithm we consider the

- *recall*: proportion of genuine characters retrieved, and
- *precision* : proportion of genuine characters in the selected set

We measure those after each step in the algorithm where we note that it is important that no labels are missed. Hence, recall should stay high after each step. Precision should clearly not decrease.

The resulting precision is presented in figure 4. From the figure it is observed that precision is very high. Especially the selection on width gives a significant increase. For two documents precision after OCR is not shown as OmniPage was not capable of handling the remaining graphics, mainly lines in the figures. Hence, no textual labels could be retrieved.

After step 1-4 the recall of the algorithm was high (5*100%, 99%, 98%, 97%, and 94%). Most prominent error is the deletion of dashes in words. Except for the above mentioned two documents recall did not change after OCR. Furthermore, only 3 of the genuine characters were assigned the wrong ASCII label.

5   Conclusion

Content based access to a database containing textdocuments with associated figures should make the hypertext structure of the document explicit including links to details in figures. In this paper we have presented an algorithm for detecting alphanumeric labels in bitmap figures to be used as anchors in hypertext construction.

The results show that the algorithm has good performance based on a limited set of assumptions and hence can effectively support the process of hypertext creation. However, the results also show that precision should be improved further. This can be achieved by considering other measures of stroke width than the average stroke width we have used or by using other features like e.g. the aspect ratio to classify lines in the image and locally to detect dashes in words.

Further research will consider larger sets of documents and include a complete hypertext construction including derivation of logical document structure. Also other invariances (e.g. rotation) and multiple fonts will be considered.

References

1. I.R. Campbell-Grant. Introducing ODA. *Computer Standards & Interfaces*, 11:149–157, 1991.
2. F. Halasz and M. Schwartz. The Dexter hypertext reference model. *Communications of the ACM*, 37(2):30–39, 1994.
3. C.P. Lai and R. Kasturi. Detection of dimension sets in engineering drawings. *IEEE Transactions on Pattern Analysis and Machine Intelligence*, 16(8):848–855, 1994.
4. A. Myka and U. Güntzer. Using electronic facsimiles of documents for automatic reconstruction of underlying hypertext structures. In *Second International Conference on Document Analysis and Recognition, Tsukuba Science City, Japan*, pages 528–532, 1993.
5. G. Nagy, S. Seth, and M. Viswanathan. A prototype document image analysis system for technical journals. *IEEE computer*, 25(7):10–22, 1992.
6. S. Satoh, A. Takasu, and E. Katsura. A collaborative approach supporting method between document processing and hypertext construction. In *Second International Conference on Document Analysis and Recognition, Tsukuba Science City, Japan*, pages 533–536, 1993.
7. R.K. Srihari. Automatic indexing and content-based retrieval of captioned images. *IEEE Computer*, 28(9):49–56, 1995.
8. S. Tsujimoto and H. Asada. Major components of a complete text reading system. *Proceedings of the IEEE*, 80(7):1133–1149, 1992.
9. M. Worring, R. Buitenhuis, and A.W.M. Smeulders. An ODA/Dexter hyperdocument system with automated link definition. In S. Spaccapietra and R. Jain, editors, *Proceednigs of Visual Database Systems III, Lausanne*, pages 346–359, 1995.
10. M. Worring, R. van den Boomgaard, and A.W.M. Smeulders. Structured hyperdocument generation using OCR and icon detection. In *Third International Conference on Document Analysis and Recognition, Montreal*, pages 1180–1183, 1995.

This article was processed using the LaTeX macro package with LLNCS style

Video Analysis

A New Method for Key Frame Based Video Content Representation♣

Alan Hanjalic, Reginald L. Lagendijk, Jan Biemond

Department of Electrical Engineering, Information Theory Group
Delft University of Technology
P.O. Box 5031, 2600 GA Delft, The Netherlands
Phone: +31-15-2783084, Fax: +31-15-2781843
{alan,inald,biemond}@it.et.tudelft.nl

Abstract

Compact video representation is an important step when developing tools for search through large video data bases. It has been shown in many publications that the usage of representative video frames (key frames) for this purpose is indeed an appropriate way of preserving the entire temporal information flow of the sequence in a considerably smaller amount of data - if the key frame set is obtained properly. In this paper we describe a novel method for key frame based video representation. The main advantage of this approach is that the resulting set of key frames, as opposed to recent methods from literature, is not dependent on subjective thresholds or any other manually given parameters. It gives a key frame set based on "objective" model for the video information flow. Another advantage is that this key frame set contains not more than the maximal number of frames, which is set beforehand for the entire sequence.

1 Introduction

We are witnessing an immense growth in the development of digital libraries. Collected in such libraries are large volumes of digitized multimedia data, which are reachable via electronic networks by any user world-wide. Libraries containing a variety of well-organized digital data bring many advantages, such as preservation of quality of stored information and almost unlimited possibilities to manipulate and browse through data using comfortable user interfaces.

The development in the field of digital libraries depends on achievements in several areas. The US digital library initiative addresses several of these challenges [6]. Achievements in digital storage media technology cause a continuously increasing ratio between *storage capacity* and corresponding *costs*. With this increase of capacity the problem arises of locating desired parts of stored data in a quick and reliable way. The development of search and access methods is therefore as crucial as the storage technology itself for efficient usage of digital libraries. This has been recognized also by the International Organization for Standardisation, which started the new project "Multimedia Content Description Interface" (in short MPEG-7). This project should standardize the description of various types of multimedia

---

♣ This work was supported in part by the EU ACTS program under the contract AC018: *SMASH* (Storage for Multimedia Applications Systems in the Home)

information. The description should be related to the actual content and allow fast and efficient retrieval of any part of the stored information [12].

In the European project *SMASH* [http://www-it.et.tudelft.nl/pda/smash], new storage systems for multimedia are under investigation, as well as several search strategies. The goal of the project is to develop a large capacity home storage device, capable to store tens of Gbytes of various multimedia data on a combined tape-disk mass storage unit and being equipped with a tool for efficient and reliable tracing and retrieval of any desired part of the stored information. The main application focus of the SMASH system is on storage of digital *video* services: DVB (Digital Video Broadcasting) is the European standard for transmission of digital services [8], now being adopted also in other countries and organisations worldwide. Due to this focus, the development of search strategies within the project is oriented primarily to video sequences.

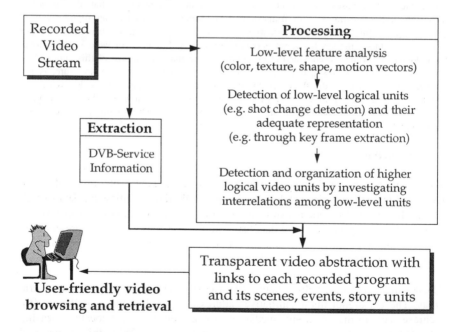

Figure 1: One possible temporal scheme of all activities related to a user-friendly organisation of the recorded video, followed by the browsing and retrieval procedure on a transparent video abstraction. Reduced, key frame based video representation eases the third processing step in the scheme to a great extent

In order to allow the user to efficiently browse for, select and retrieve a desired video part without having to deal directly with GBytes of stored (compressed) data, several activities have to be carried out as a preparation for such user interaction. Figure 1 illustrates this on the example of DVB-like information. The main goal of these procedures is to provide the user a compact and easy understandable overview of the complete stored video information. The user can browse through such abstraction, easily build up an impression of the entire stored video and make a selection leading to a retrieval of the corresponding video segment.

In this paper we concentrate on one of the most important steps in making a video browsing tool: *compact representation of the video temporal information flow*. This representation is done by first segmenting the entire sequence in elementary content units called *video shots* (unbroken series of frames, e.g. a zoom of a person talking [11]), and then reducing each shot to a number of characteristic frames. The proposed novel method for extracting key frames has been developed to suite specific requirements of a fully automated video analysis system, being a part of the SMASH browsing tool. These requirements are

- high degree of process automation (parameter independence)
- sequence independence
- representation objectivity
- controllability of the total key frame number

In this paper we assume that a reliable video parsing algorithm (e.g. [4]) is used to detect changes between consecutive video shots.

2 Key frame based video content representation

Video representation through characteristic frames (*key frames*) has been addressed very frequently in literature (e.g. [1, 3, 4, 5, 9, 10, 13, 14]) as an elegant and efficient way of preserving the whole temporal information flow of the sequence in a considerably smaller amount of data. The underlying assumption is that if these frames are extracted using an appropriate video sampling method, the visual content of each segment of the sequence can be easily recognized by looking at given samples. Such compact video representation appears thus to be suitable for the purpose of video browsing. Also when considering query processes where the search for video parts containing some specific objects, persons or features is performed, the concept based on key frames can be useful since features collected from key frames can be used. If detection of higher logical ("semantic") units of a video is intended, which is to be done by investigating interrelations among different video shots, key frames can be useful as shot-representatives for comparison purposes.

2.1 Existing approaches

A simple method to select key frames is to take the first frame of each shot [9]. More reliable content representation requires non-uniform sampling of the video shot. In [10], Pentland et al. have found the frames at the beginning and the end of a shot, in the middle of no-motion segments or in the middle of segments where the camera is tracking a foreground object, to be good key frames to represent the content of a shot. Some other approaches [1, 3, 14], based on measuring the differences between the last selected frame and the remaining frames and extracting a subsequent key frame if the measured difference exceeds the given threshold, are typically sequential processes leading generally to unpredictable results. In particular, the final number of key frames for the entire sequence cannot be estimated for any given threshold. We can end up with a huge number of key frames or simply with too few key frames - not enough for browsing or other intended procedures. This makes it difficult to predict the capacity needed for storing extracted key frames (in spite of possible "key frame pruning", as proposed in [14] for further reduction of already obtained key frame sets). Secondly, it is rather difficult, especially in [1] and [3] to relate any particular parameter value by threshold setting to the key frame collection resulting from that setting. Furthermore, the dependency of the approach on subjective and usually data dependent thresholds, limits its applicability in fully automated systems and leads to non-reproducible results.

3 New key frame extraction approach

Aiming at a key frame based video representation, which fulfils the requirements indicated in the introduction to this paper, we have developed a new two-step key frame extraction method.

In the first step, the assignment of a number of key frames per shot is carried out depending on total "content" of a shot and also of the entire sequence. The term "content" is explained in the following section. This key frame assignment is done such that the sum of all assigned key frames along the sequence is close to a given maximal number of allowable key frames N for the entire sequence. The number N can be adjusted depending on the type of the program to be stored.

The assignment step is followed by a threshold independent and objective procedure for optimal distribution of the assigned number of key frames along each video shot.

In the following sections we present results of our investigations concerning both of these steps. Important fact to be noticed is that the distribution of key frames along the shot in the second step is performed by a *numerical algorithm* delivering the best possible shot representation, given the number N and with respect to the used measure for the information flow dynamics along a shot [7].

3.1 Measures for the information flow dynamics along a video shot

There the possibility to simulate variations in the temporal information flow of the sequence by choosing an appropriate analytical function. This function measures relevant changes between each two consecutive frames of a sequence and indicates with its values the magnitude of such changes.

This leads to the problem of finding appropriate visual features and metrics to perform the described frame-to-frame comparison. For minimizing the influence of non-relevant temporal variations, "global" frame visual features should be used, such as color and intensity histograms. In our approach we adapted the method proposed in [4] and defined an analytical function for describing the relevant *frame-to-frame difference* (further referred to as *FFD*) between frames *k* and *k-1* as:

$$FFD(k) = d_{yuv}(k,k-1) = \sum_{i} \sum_{j=Y,U,V} |h_k^j(i) - h_{k-1}^j(i)| \qquad (1)$$

This formula proved to be relatively robust with respect to the elimination of non-relevant temporal fluctuations, such as small object or camera movements, focal length changes, etc.

If the *FFD(k)* values in the shot *i* are accumulated from the beginning of the shot up to the shot frame *k*, i.e.

$$C_i(k) = \sum_{n=2}^{k} FFD(n) \qquad (2)$$

than $C_i(k)$ indicates the *total magnitude of temporal flow fluctuations up to the final summation point.*

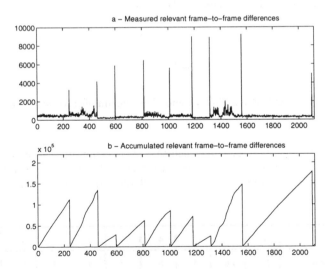

Figure 2a: Measured relevant frame-to-frame differences for first nine shots of the sequence "Nature".
Figure 2b: Curves of accumulated frame-to-frame differences, obtained for each shot using (2).

$C_i(k)$ has a close-to-linear behaviour in shot parts with uniform temporal information flow and changes in steepness wherever changes in the flow dynamics occur. The function $C_i(k)$ we take as the model for the *information flow dynamics* in the shot i. We will refer to it in the further text as the "content development" function of the shot i. Figure 2b illustrates the behaviour of $C_i(k)$ for the *FFD(k)* curve from Figure 2b.

If the summation process stretches along the entire shot, we obtain the *total magnitude of temporal flow fluctuations in the shot*, that we can also refer to as the total "content" of the shot:

$$C_i = \sum_{k=2}^{L} FFD(k) \qquad (3)$$

In this formula, k is the frame index and L is the number of frames in the shot.

3.2 Key frame allocation for each video shot

By spreading given maximal number of key frames N along the entire video sequence, each shot of the sequence gets assigned a fraction of given N key frames according to its relative share of "content" to the total "content" of the sequence. We therefore assign K_i key frames to shot i as:

$$K_i = \frac{C_i}{\sum_{j=1}^{S} C_j} N \qquad (4)$$

C_j is the "content" of the shot j and S is the number of shots in the entire sequence.

The resulting number of key frames delivers, after being normalised by the shot length, the *key frame density*. This density corresponds now to the relative amount of temporal variations of a shot, compared to all other shots in the sequence.

Shot Index	1	2	3	4	5	6	7	8	9
Key frames and densities using (4)	14	16	4	8	11	9	3	18	22
	1:18	1:13	1:34	1:27	1:17	1:19	1:45	1:13	1:24
Key frames and densities using (5)	12	12	3	8	10	9	3	17	21
	1:20	1:18	1:45	1:27	1:19	1:19	1:45	1:14	1:11

Table 1: *Number of assigned key frames and resulting key frame rates per shot*

Table 1 illustrates the key frame assignment for the sequence used to compute *FFD(k)* curve in Figure 2a. The given maximal number of key frames was $N=100$.

Equation (4) assumes that the entire sequence is available prior to the assignment process, so that the total "content" of the sequence (denominator in (4)) is known. If, however, the assignment procedure is to be done sequentially or on-the-fly, we propose the following approximation:

$$K_i = \frac{C_i}{\sum\limits_{j=1}^{s} C_j} N = C_i \frac{N}{T} \frac{T}{\sum\limits_{j=1}^{s} C_j} \approx C_i \frac{N \sum\limits_{j=1}^{i} T_j}{T \sum\limits_{j=1}^{i} C_j} \tag{5}$$

Here, T is the total sequence length, and T_j is the length of the shot j. The intention by such approximation is to obtain similar assignment results as by (4), however only using the information available at the moment where K_i is computed. Since the information about the total "content" of the entire sequence (denominator in (4)) is not known, we can only summarize until the shot i. This action alone could change assignment results considerably if applied in (4), and we try to compensate it by taking into consideration also the time parameters, e.g. shot and sequence lengths. We assume that the ratio between the total sequence length and the total sequence "content", can be well approximated by the ratio between the sequence length and "content", both taken only up to the current shot i. Assignment results in Table 1 show only minor differences, compared to results where (4) was used.

3.3 Key frame distribution along a shot

After assigning a certain number of key frames to each video shot, the next step is to find locations for these key frames within a shot so that they approximately capture the entire temporal information flow of a shot.

We use the "content development" curve from (2) as reference, since it represents the process of building up the entire shot "content" by accumulating relevant temporal variations along all shot frames. By its varying steepness, the curve indicates exactly all locations "where something interesting happens": steeper parts correspond to strong and flatter parts to more stationary temporal variations.

It is now our intention to perform the same "content building" operation, but using only a limited number of shot frames, e.g. assigned number of key frames. Basic idea can be seen in Figure 3, with 7 assigned key frames. The actual "content development" is approximated by the curve $C_i(k_j)$ composed of rectangles, each one defined by k_j and t_j and each corresponding to one key frame. Here k_j $(j=1,...,K_i)$ are the temporal positions of the key frames, while t_{j-1} and t_j are the *breakpoints* between the shot segments that are represented by key frame k_j. Note that t_0 and t_{K_i} are the (known) temporal begin and endpoints of i-th shot. The approximation process leads automatically to a key frame density which corresponds to the behaviour of the actual "content development" curve, e.g. higher density in steeper segments. In this way, the optimal representation of a (variable) temporal information flow along a shot can be achieved. It can be said, that each key frame represents all shot frames within its rectangle.

Technically, the key frame distribution along a shot results from minimizing the following criterion function:

$$g(k_1, \ldots, k_{K_i}, t_1, \ldots, t_{K_{i-1}}) = \sum_{j=1}^{K_i} \int_{t_{j-1}}^{t_j} \left| C_i(x) - C_i(k_j) \right| dx \qquad (6)$$

The numerical procedure for obtaining the optimal key frame distribution along a video shot by minimizing the criterion function (6) is explained in more details in [7].

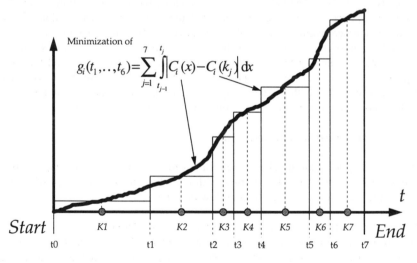

Figure 3: *Illustration of the key frame distribution within a video shot by assigned 7 key frames. An approximation of the accumulation can be obtained using 7 flexible rectangles.*

3.3.1 Key frame distribution experiments

Let us first check the performance of the distribution procedure on a fictive shot with the "content development" represented by the curve in Figure 4. The curve shows a variable temporal information flow along the shot. Three characteristic parts can be recognized, two with a stationary and the middle one with a non-stationary "content development". 13 key frames were assigned to this shot and the result of their distribution along the shot can also be seen in Figure 4.

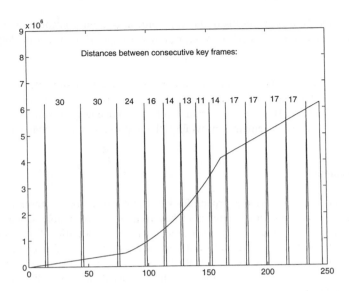

Figure 4: *Application of the approach to a fictive video shot. Obtained variable key frame densities picture the actual content development*

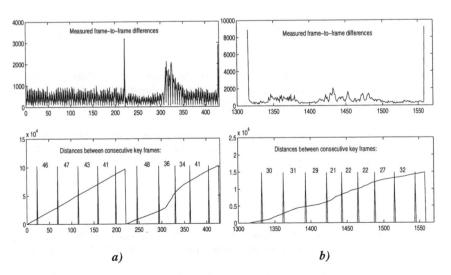

a)   *b)*

Figure 5a: *Two shots of the movie Four Weddings and a Funeral. Frame-to-frame differences, accumulated differences and assigned key frames can be seen.*
Figure 5b: *Same analysis for one shot of the Nature movie*

Figures 5a and 5b present results of the key frame allocation procedure on example of two real video sequences (*Four Weddings and a Funeral* -courtesy of Polygram, *Nature*).

In each case, the variability of the key frame density along a shot depends on the variability in the temporal information flow, e.g. behaviour of the "content development" curve. However, a certain level of homogeneity in spreading of key frames along the shot remains, providing the representation of the entire shot material.

4 Conclusions

In this paper a new two-step approach for key frame extraction is presented taking into account given maximal number of key frames for the whole sequence and spreading it corresponding to the measured temporal information flow along the sequence. The global key frame allocation method assigns a number of key frames to a shot depending on the total amount of changes in the information flow along the shot. These key frames are then optimally distributed over the shot in a threshold independent way.

In comparison to key frame extraction procedures proposed in the literature, this approach has following important properties:

- It allows the regulation of the maximal number of key frames per video sequence by setting the maximum of key frames N.

- Spreading of N given key frames along the sequence and their positioning within each shot is not based on any parameter (threshold) setting but on the analysis of the actual temporal information flow in the given sequence.

The quality of obtained key frame representation of the video sequence depends strongly on the robustness of frame-to-frame difference metric against non-relevant fluctuations in the analysed information flow.

References:

[1]   Zhang H., Low C.Y., Smoliar, S.W.: "Video Parsing and Browsing Using Compressed Data", Multimedia Tools and Applications, 1, pp 89-111, Kluwer Academic Publishers, 1995.
[2]   Yeung M.M., Yeo B., Wolf W., Liu B.: "Video Browsing using Clustering and Scene Transitions on Compressed Sequences", IS&T/SPIE Multimedia Computing and Networking, February 1995
[3]   Yeung M.M., Liu B.: "Efficient Matching and Clustering of Video Shots", Proceedings of ICIP, Vol.1, pp 338-341, Washington, D.C., USA, 1995.
[4]   Yeo B., Liu. B.: "Rapid Scene Analysis on Compressed Video", IEEE Transactions on Circuits and Systems for Video technology, Vol.5, No.6, December 1995

[5]   Furth B., Smoliar S.W., Zhang H.: "Video and Image Processing in Multimedia Systems", Kluwer Academic Publishers, 1995

[6]   COMPUTER - IEEE Computer Magazine, Vol. 29, Issue 5, May 1996

[7]   Lagendijk R.L., Hanjalic A., Ceccarelli M., Soletic M., Persoon E.: "Visual Search in a SMASH System", Proc. ICIP '96, Lausanne, CH, 1996

[8]   ETS 300 421, "Digital broadcasting systems for television, sound and data services; framing structure, channel coding and modulation for 11/12 Ghz satellite services", EBU/ETSI JTC, December 1994.

[9]   Arman F., Hsu A., Chiu M.-Y.:"Image Processing on Compressed Data for Large Video Databases", Proc. ACM Multimedia '93, Annaheim, CA, 1993

[10]   Pentland et al.: "Video and Image Semantics: Advanced Tools for Telecommunications", IEEE MultiMedia, Summer 1994

[11]   Picard R.W.: "Light-years from Lena: Video and Image Libraries of the Future", *Proc. of the IEEE Int. Conf. on Image Processing 1995*, vol. 1, pp. 310-313, Washington DC, USA, 1995.

[12]   ISO/IEC JTC1/SC29/WG11: "MPEG-7: Context and Objectives (v.3)", Bristol, April 1997

[13]   Gerek O.N., Altunbasak Y.:"Key Frame Selection from MPEG Video Data", Proc. of SPIE Vol. 3024, San Jose 1997

[14]   Xiong W., Ma R., Lee J.C.-M.:"A Novel technique for Automatic Key Frame Computing", Proc. of SPIE Vol. 3022, San Jose 1997

Multimedia Navigation

Towards Multimedia Thesaurus Support for Media-based Navigation

Paul H. Lewis, Hugh C. Davis, Mark R. Dobie and Wendy Hall

The Multimedia Research Group,
Department of Electronics and Computer Science
University of Southampton, England, SO171BJ,
tel: +44 1703 593715, E-mail phl@ecs.soton.ac.uk

Abstract. This paper describes an open hypermedia system which allows content based navigation and retrieval from both text and non-text media. The system provides a variety of link types including the generic link which, once authored from a particular selection, may be followed from any instance matching that selection. The paper also describes the concept of a multimedia thesaurus and illustrates how it may be used to enhance the navigational capabilities of the system, allowing links to be authored on one representation of an object and followed from a different representation.

1 Introduction

The use of hypermedia links to navigate through multimedia information collections has increased dramatically with the increasing popularity of the World Wide Web. Typically the links in the web are from one point to another and the source anchors of links tend to be text based.

During the last six years the Multimedia Research Group in Southampton University has developed Microcosm, an open architecture for hypermedia systems handling large multimedia information collections[4, 7, 6, 11]. The architecture is three layered: an applications layer in which general and special purpose media viewers, together with third party applications packages, provide the user interface to the multimedia collection, a link service layer in which any number of communicating processes provide the hypermedia functionality and a storage layer where the documents, link information and other databases are maintained.

One of the important features of the architecture is that link information is held in link databases, separately from the documents being linked, so that documents remain in their native format and may be prepared and viewed via third party applications packages. This also means that links may be established with media on read only devices such as CD-ROM.

A second important feature is the generic link. Generic links differ from the more common point to point links in that, once a link has been authored between a source selection and a destination point, it may be followed from every occurrence of the source selection in any document which has access to the linkbase. Thus a generic link from the word *Amsterdam* to a video of the city may be followed from any occurrence of the word *Amsterdam*. The generic link works at the link authoring stage by storing the content of the source selection (ie the word *Amsterdam*) as the source anchor of the link and at the link following stage, by matching the user selection with source anchors in the linkbase.

We have recently extended the Microcosm architecture to create MAVIS (Microcosm Architecture for Video, Image and Sound) which provides a framework for authoring and following generic links from non-text media[11]. Thus, a user may select part of an image by dragging a rectangle over the required region with the mouse, and may specify this selection as the source anchor for a generic link. A user making another sub-image selection in another image may follow the link if the selection is similar to the source anchor on which the link was authored. The generic links in non-text media work by extracting a variety of representations or signatures from the selection and using pattern matching between signatures at the link following stage.

It should be clear that the generic link works by matching representations of the selection *content*. Hence we can refer to navigation with generic links as content based navigation.

In the next section we briefly refer to related work and in section 3 we give more detail of generic link following with MAVIS. In section 4 we discuss how a digital thesaurus could enhance generic link following from text and then extend the approach by describing, with a prototype example, how a multimedia thesaurus could provide enhanced generic link following from text and non-text media. The paper concludes with some final comments and a note on future work.

2   Related Work

There has recently been a rapid development in the use of content for retrieving images from image databases with many papers describing a wide range of techniques [1, 10, 13]. Sometimes these are tuned to specific application domains but some systems provide basic content based image retrieval tools of wider applicability. A good example is the QBIC, Query By Image Content, system [5, 14], developed by IBM, which uses combinations of colour, shape and texture for image retrieval and the Manchester Content Addressable Image Database [12].

Typically the aim is to retrieve an image from the database if it contains *features* specified by the user, either by drawing a sketch or identifying similar features in a displayed image. However, little work has been published on navigating from images to other parts of a multimedia information collection when using image content as the key with which to determine the available routes to be navigated. Part of the reason for this is that most hypermedia systems rely on fixed or hard wired links between parts of the multimedia information collection even when navigating from text. A notable exception is the system under development at NEC [8, 9], which is a hypermedia system in which non-textual information may be retrieved using media-based queries.

3   Generic Links and Non-Text Media

In the Microcosm architecture, a link in the linkbase, which has been authored from text, consists of information about the source anchor and the destination anchor of the link. For a specific or point to point link the source anchor includes the selection content, the file in which it occurs and the location in the file at which it occurs. To be able to follow a specific link from a particular selection in a particular document, all three items in the source anchor must match those for the selection. When authoring a generic link from text only the selection itself is recorded in the linkbase for the source anchor. To follow a generic link from a particular selection, only the selection needs to match the selection in the link. Thus, a generic link may be followed from any instance of the source selection in any document. This gives a substantial reduction in link authoring effort, but until the introduction of MAVIS the generic link was only available from text.

In order to provide generic links from non-text media, the MAVIS architecture was developed. The architecture recognised that it was not simply a matter of recording the media based selection in the link source anchor and then matching selections when link following. Text selections are matched exactly, but with non-text selections, similarity estimation is required. The MAVIS architecture also recognises that in order to provide content based retrieval and navigation from non-text media it is necessary to be able to extract and match a wide range of representations from a range of different media types. This functionality is provided by modules controlled by a media table subsystem. Each module is responsible for handling all the processing associated with one particular representation for one particular medium and must contain algorithms to extract the representation, to index the representation for rapid retrieval and to estimate a similarity value, given two representations to be matched.

The main modules implemented so far include a colour histogram module based on the Tek HVC colour representation, a texture module which uses statistical geometric texture statistics [3], a shape module which uses rotation, scale and translation invariant moments, a further shape module which uses chord length distribution and a demonstrator sound module which uses the Fourier transform of the selection from a digital sound file as the representation. The media table subsystem maintains an association between the different media and the modules which can process selections from them. The user can control which modules are active via the subsystem and the weighting associated with different representations if retrieval or link following is to be based on more than one representation. The architecture is designed so that additional modules may be added to support other representations as required. More details of the MAVIS architecture and its use for content based retrieval and navigation have already been published [11].

4   Thesaurus Enhanced Generic Links

In the previous sections we saw that generic link following succeeds by matching representations of user selections with the source anchors of links. In the case of text, an exact match or word stem match is appropriate whereas for non-text it is necessary to use similarity matches. However, even in the case of text, the basic generic link has a severe limitation. For the generic link to be successful the user must choose the same word or words as those used when the link was authored. Synonyms and semantically linked concepts are not catered for in the current implementation. If a generic link is authored on the word car, it can not be followed from the word automobile. For non-text media there are equivalent problems. For example, for images, if a link is authored on the shape of an object from one particular view it will not be possible to follow it from an image in which the view is substantially different.

One way to approach a solution to this problem for text is to introduce a digital thesaurus. This should contain all the vocabulary (words or terms) appropriate to the application domain, arranged as a network with at least the following relations: broader term, narrower term, equivalent term and related term. The thesaurus could be invoked either at the link authoring or the link following stage or both. In the first case, if the thesaurus is invoked when a generic link is authored, links could be automatically generated and stored from all terms equivalent to the selected source anchor term. This would increase the linkbase size but have the advantage of increasing the speed of link following. Alternatively, the authoring stage could remain unchanged, ie a single link is generated from the author's selection, but at the link following stage the user's selection is expanded via the thesaurus to a set of equivalent terms and each is compared with the linkbase source anchors to find any available links. This will be less expensive in linkbase storage but will slow down the linkbase search.

More elegantly the thesaurus could contain an indicator of a preferred term for each set of equivalent terms. At the authoring stage, the source anchor term is switched to its preferred term via the thesaurus and at link following, the user's chosen term is also switched to its preferred term, via the thesaurus, before the linkbase search is commenced.

All transactions via the thesaurus described so far can be invisible to both author and user, providing an appropriate thesaurus is available containing all terms likely to be encountered. Indeed, within the Microcosm architecture, the thesaurus could be introduced as a filter between the viewers and the linkbase, without substantial disturbance to the current architecture. However, an additional level of functionality may be achieved if, at the link following stage, the user is given access to the thesaurus to broaden or narrow down the generic links from a particular selection. For example, a user reading a document on analytical chemistry may wish to try and follow links on *mass spectrometry*. If an option to view the thesaurus at this point is available the user may choose narrower terms such as *high resolution mass spectrometry* or broader terms such as *spectrometry* to act as the selection for link following. Indeed the user could also choose to switch on a particular level of automatic broader or narrower term fan out for selections when generic link following. In this case, whenever a term is chosen, all broader terms or all narrower terms or both could also be compared with the linkbase source anchors to find appropriate links to follow.

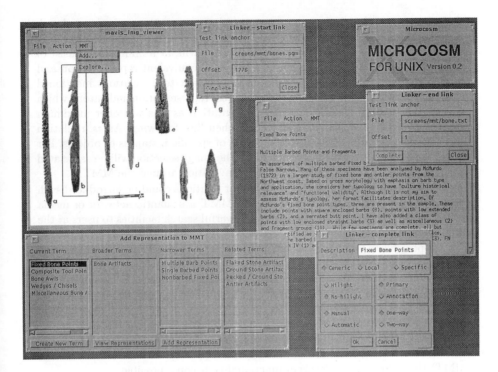

Fig. 1. A User Interface for the MMT with MAVIS

4.1 A Multimedia Thesaurus

The thesaurus described so far is similar to thesauruses which have been used in information retrieval systems for many years. However, the integration of a digital thesaurus and generic link following offers a significant enhancement in the potential of generic link following from text. More importantly, we propose a multimedia extension to the basic digital thesaurus concept which will provide enhanced generic link following from non-text media as well as from text.

The multimedia thesaurus(MMT) consists of a network of representations. Many of these will be text, corresponding to a traditional digital thesaurus, but some will be representations of terms extracted from other media. We have seen that in order to provide generic links from non-text, indexes of features such as shape or texture description vectors or sound representations are accumulated. In the multimedia thesaurus these will be associated with equivalent text representations. A new set of relations in the network will, at a minimum, consist of broader representation, narrower representation, equivalent representation and related representation as generalisations of the text term relations mentioned earlier. The MMT will also include preferred representation indicators which will typically be attached to a text representation as this will offer maximum storage efficiency and matching efficiency when link following. An *is_a* relation will also be used to indicate representations of specific instances of objects. For image based representations, thumbnails of the image selection will be associated with the node to facilitate more informed navigation around the MMT.

In a natural extension to the MMT, other relations could be introduced such as *is-part-of*, *is-older-than* etc making the MMT a semantic network of media based representations and allowing more powerful search facilities to users at the link following stage.

It is possible to view the MMT structurally in two parts. The first is a network of concepts and their relationships which is the MMT but with only the preferred terms. This contains all the important conceptual/semantic relationships in the MMT. The second part consists of all the equivalent representations which are linked to their preferred term nodes in the concept network. We have already prototyped a concept network as an aid to enhanced link following[2].

By associating media based representations with equivalent term nodes in the MMT at the generic link authoring stage (if they are not already in the MMT) the following new levels of functionality become possible.

- When a generic link is authored from a representation of an object which is in the MMT, it will be possible to follow the link from any of the media based representations for the object which are also present. Thus, a generic link could be authored from an image of a Greek amphora using a shape representation and followed from a text document via selection of the text term *Greek amphora*.
- In particular application areas, multiple views of objects may be available. For example in a multimedia museum application, multiple views of an exhibit may be provided and representations of these could be associated with each other via the MMT. A generic link from one view could then be followed from any of the other views of the same artefact.
- As in the case of text described earlier, it will be possible to use the MMT at the link following stage to broaden or narrow the specificity of the attempt at generic link following by navigating the broader and narrower representation relations in the MMT.

Although the use of an MMT offers significant enhancements for generic link following, the construction of the MMT is a non-trivial activity and will involve substantial time overheads. However, for some applications the text thesaurus may already exist or the the time investment may be deemed worthwhile.

4.2 The User Interface

When authoring a generic link in an MMT supported, open hypermedia environment, the user may wish to attach the source selection representation to the MMT at the authoring stage if it is not already present. In figure 1 a generic link is being authored from the shape of a particular archaeological artifact (a multiple barbed point) to some text about bone points (the end link). The shape for the start link has been selected by dragging a rectangle around it and specifying the shape representation module to be used in MAVIS via the media table (not shown).

Before completing the link by selecting *Ok* in the complete link window (bottom right) the author could link the representation into the MMT by selecting an MMT tools menu and choosing an *Add* option. A prototype example is shown in the figure.

The list of top level terms from the MMT is displayed and the appropriate preferred term is selected by scrolling and clicking. Selecting *Add Representation* would then complete the addition of the representation to the MMT. If no appropriate entry points are present, MMT building tools would be used to add appropriate new terms and their relations.

Once the representation is linked in to the thesaurus, the generic link may be followed not only from similar shape selections but also from the text representation *multiple barb points*. No user interaction with the thesaurus would be required here if automatic MMT based generic link following is initiated. A user, following a generic link in this way, may also decide to use the MMT explicitly to explore links from representations nearby. The user will be able to navigate to other representations within the MMT and then choose to follow links from selected representations.

5 Conclusions and Future Work

In this paper we have described the Microcosm open hypermedia system and MAVIS, an extension to Microcosm to allow content based navigation from non-text media as well as text. We have discussed the idea of a multimedia thesaurus(MMT) and shown how an MMT could be used to provide more powerful generic link authoring and following.

We are currently in the process of implementing the thesaurus, integrating it into the Microcosm/MAVIS architecture and developing intelligent agents to improve/automate the grouping of representations in the MMT and the matching of selections during link following. There is substantial scope for introducing further enhancements to content based navigation and retrieval facilities using the capabilities of the multimedia thesaurus.

Acknowledgement

This research is being undertaken with the support of the EPSRC, grant number GR/L03446.

References

1. Special issue on content based retrieval. *IEEE Computer 28*, 9 (1995).
2. BEITNER, N. B., GOBLE, C. A., AND HALL, W. Putting the media into hypermedia. In *SPIE Proceedings, Multimedia Computing and Networking* (1995), pp. 12–23.
3. CHEN, Y., NIXON, M., AND THOMAS, D. Texture classification using statistical geometrical features. *Pattern Recognition 28*, 4 (1995), 537–552.
4. DAVIS, H., HALL, W., HEATH, I., HILL, G., AND WILKINS, R. Towards an integrated information environment with open hypermedia systems. In *Fourth ACM Conference on Hypertext (ECHT '92)* (Milan, Italy, December 1992), D. Lucarella, J. Nanard, N. M., and P. Paolini, Eds., pp. 181–190.
5. FALOUTSOS, C., BARBER, R., FLICKNER, M., HAFNER, J., NIBLACK, W., PETKOVIC, D., AND EQUITZ, W. Efficient and effective querying by image content. *Journal of Intelligent Information Systems 3* (1994), 231–262.
6. HALL, W., DAVIS, H. C., AND HUTCHINGS, G. A. *Rethinking Hypermedia: the Microcosm Approach.* Kluwer Academic Press, Amsterdam, 1996.
7. HILL, G. J., WILKINS, R. J., AND HALL, W. Open and reconfigurable hypermedia systems: A filter-based model. *Hypermedia 5*, 2 (1993), 103–118.
8. HIRATA, K., HARA, Y., SHIBATA, N., AND HIRABAYASHI, F. Media-based navigation for hypermedia systems. In *Hypertext '93* (Seattle, Washington, USA, November 14-18 1993), ACM Press, pp. 159–173.
9. HIRATA, K., HARA, Y., TAKANO, H., AND KAWASAKI, S. Content-oriented integration in hypermedia systems. In *Proceedings of the Seventh ACM Conference on Hypertext* (Washington DC, March 1996), B. Ladd, Ed., pp. 11–21.
10. JAIN, R., MURTHY, S., CHEN, P., AND CHATTERJEE, S. Similarity measures for image databases. In *SPIE Proceedings, Storage and Retrieval for Image and Video Databases III* (1995), pp. 58–65.
11. LEWIS, P. H., DAVIS, H. C., GRIFFITHS, S. R., HALL, W., AND WILKINS, R. J. Media-based navigation with generic links. In *Proceedings of the Seventh ACM Conference on Hypertext* (March 1996), ACM, pp. 215–223.
12. OAKLEY, J., SHANN, R., DAVIS, D., AND HUGUEVILLE, L. A database management system for vision applications. In *5th British Machine Vision Conference* (York, U.K., 13-16 September 1994), BMVA Press, pp. 629–639.
13. SMOLIAR, S., AND ZHANG, H. Content-based video indexing and retrieval. *IEEE Multimedia 1*, 2 (1994), 62–72.
14. TREAT, H., ORT, E., VO, M., JANG, J.-S., HALL, L., TUNG, F., AND PETKOVIC, D. Searching images using Ultimedia manager. In *SPIE Proceedings, Storage and Retrieval for Image and Video Databases III* (1995), pp. 204–213.

Enhancing Video Navigation with Existing Alternate Representations

Ken Yap, Bill Simpson-Young, Uma Srinivasan

Research Data Network CRC/CSIRO Australia
Locked Bag 17, North Ryde 2113, Australia
Email: {Ken.Yap,Bill.Simpson-Young,Uma.Srinivasan}@dit.csiro.au
Tel: +61 2 3253100 Fax: +61 2 3253101

Abstract. We describe FRANK, an application that we have developed for remote browsing of film archives. FRANK uses alternate representations of video in the form of text, image, or structured data that have a time-based mapping. We describe the motivation for the project, the work processes of the users, and the operation of the resulting prototype. Finally we suggest some techniques for deriving timecodes in the absence of time-stamped alternate representations.

1 Introduction

Alternate representations of video are material in the form of text, image or structured data that have a time-based mapping to specific video material. Alternate representations are often generated during the work process for a video production and, in the case of documentary videos (the material we are working with), include transcripts and shotlists.[1] We describe how this material is integrated into FRANK (Film/TV Researchers Archival Navigation Kit) to enhance the quality of the navigation.

Our application, FRANK[1], is a tool that allows filmmakers and researchers to browse a video archive remotely (intercity via a broadband ATM network). These users need to do more than just view a video using standard VCR type controls. They need to be able to selectively search a video with the help of the alternate representations. In their current work practices they have transcripts and shotlists at hand. Therefore FRANK had to be more than a standard Video On Demand system. Our challenge was to design an architecture and implement a prototype that satisfied the users' requirements.

2 Work processes in film research

In the first part of the project, we did a user requirement study[2]. This involved interviewing a group of typical users, comprising film producers, film researchers, and librarians. Our focus was the research part of the film production process, where the users are evaluating potential material for inclusion in the production.

---

[1] Shotlists are textual descriptions of video sequences.

In the initial stage of a search, a researcher uses catalogs, printed material, personal contacts and accumulated expertise to narrow the field of search. In the next phase, they scan candidate videos, looking for potential material, making shot notes as they go. They may also have at their disposal screenplays, transcripts and shot lists, which were created either in the screen writing process, the production process (e.g. transcripts of interviews) or in the post-production process (e.g. transcripts for subtitling). In these days of office automation, these resources are available in machine readable form.[3] Some contain timecodes which can be used for synchronisation with the video. Our architecture takes advantage of this existing material by assimilating it into our database and providing a navigation engine to work with the video server.

3   FRANK functionality and architecture

The FRANK software system allows a film or TV researcher to browse remote video (using *start*, *stop*, random access, etc) and to browse remote alternate representations such as transcripts and shotlists (using *next page*, full-text searching, etc). The researcher can use the alternate representation to locate material of interest (e.g. by performing a search for a desired word in a transcript) and, with the press of a button, request that the video be played from the corresponding position. They can specify that they want tight coupling of the video with the alternate representation so that as they browse and jump through, say, a transcript, the video will always keep synchronised (or vice versa).

The architecture of the FRANK system is a client-server architecture and has a separation of the video server from the server providing navigation and searching of the alternate representations (see Figure 1). The FRANK client performs the synchronisation and display of the material provided by the two servers.

4   Navigation

The key to effective use of alternate representations is to provide tight coupling of the navigation through the video and its representation such that the users feel that they are navigating through a common information space[4]. In FRANK, this is achieved not only by providing the coupled navigation through text/images and video, but also by making the video navigation buttons (e.g. *next* and *prev*) context-dependent such that the effect of a button depends on the alternate representation currently in effect. For example, when viewing a shotlist, pressing the *next* button would advance the video to the next shot specified in the shotlist, whereas when viewing a set of stills indicating positions of interest (e.g. the results of a search), the *next* button would advance to the next such position. In providing this support, FRANK is allowing navigation through the information space rather than navigation through the video as a sequence of frames as in the VCR or standard video control model.

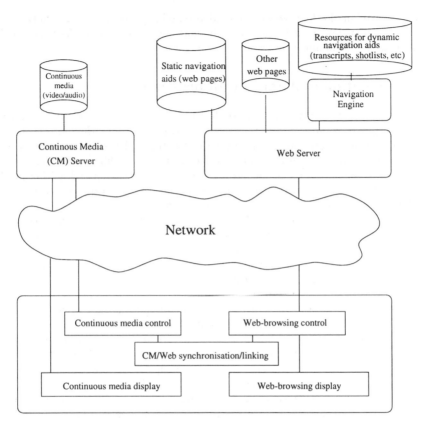

Fig. 1. FRANK architecture

The appearance of the resulting FRANK prototype is shown in Figure 2. The left half is the navigational text while the right half is the video viewer.

For the practical use of alternate representations for video navigation in a network environment, it is advantageous to separate them from the video on the network as is done with the FRANK architecture. In doing this, the alternate representations can be used as navigation aids for videos available from existing video servers on a network (assuming the video servers support a protocol for random access) without the video server having any knowledge of the existence of external navigation aids. This allows alternate representations to be provided as a value-added service aiding navigation of existing video services.

As well as being useful for material such as transcripts and shotlists, the FRANK architecture is suitable for any representation of video that has a time dimension and can be determined by pre-processing of the video. Thus the FRANK architecture is appropriate for content-based retrieval and navigation

such as searching for footage within a video matching specified image characteristics (e.g. texture). In such cases, the alternate representation is the timecoded
image metadata obtained by pre-processing the video.

5   Generation of Alternate Representations

The initial material on which FRANK has been used has timecode information
already present in the alternate representations. For example, the material from
Film Australia's Australian Biography series has timecodes approximately every
paragraph. We have found that this is sufficient for use by film researchers, who
want to find the part of a video where a topic is being discussed and neither need
nor want the video to be cued exactly to a specified word. Transcripts are often
available where the material is likely to be exported (and hence translated) or
where the material is expected to be of important historical value. In Australia,
a filmmaker can also get a greater tax advantage when they donate material
to a national archive and the estimated value is greater if a transcript exists.
Whether or not timecodes are included in a transcript will depend on the policy
of the body sponsoring the transcript creation.

In situations where there are no timecodes on transcripts, some pre-processing
needs to be done in order to synchronise available information with the corresponding video segment. In such cases the method used necessarily is context dependent depending on factors such as the structure of the material (e.g. whether
it's a narrative documentary, a sequence of newsclips, etc.) and the nature of the
available alternate representations (e.g. a transcript of the audio component, a
full shotlist of the video component, a short shotlist in a catalogue entry, etc.).

We intend to use FRANK on material with a variety of different characteristics. The material that we are using, and some characteristics of each, includes:

1. Material from Film Australia's Australian Biography series. Each half-hour
   program is primarily a recorded interview with interspersed archival stills
   and footage. The audio of the interview has been created from a longer
   taped interview but is intended to appear as a continuous narrative. The
   audio usually continues over the stills and some archival footage leading
   to a close relationship between the transcript and the audio component but
   usually not the video component. A separate shotlist exists that describes the
   visual component with descriptions of archival footage used. The transcripts
   have timecodes corresponding to approximately every paragraph of spoken
   text and the shotlists have a timecode entry for each shot.
2. Material from the Australian Broadcasting Corporation's "4 Corners" documentary series. The transcript includes a full textual version of the audio
   component and also a textual description of shots used in the program. The
   transcripts do not have timecode information.

This section describes the broad categories of options that we intend to investigate for the generation of alternate representations and/or timecode information.

5.1 Alternate Representation Synthesis

This category of techniques is used for the generation of an alternate representation where there is no use made of existing textual alternate representations. The category includes techniques such as:

1. Automatic transcript generation using speech analysis techniques.
2. Video segmentation using video analysis techniques to find first or a representative frame from each shot and/or scene.
3. Context-based sampling techniques to capture the timecodes of corresponding segments, for example; every 2000th frame for an action movie; first frame of every shot for a news clip[5]; or camera shift for documentary/interviews[6].

5.2 Content-based Timecode Generation

This category of techniques includes using techniques such as those above to enhance the usefulness of existing textual representations by matching the textual representation with the audio or video content in order to insert timecode information into the textual representation. The techniques include those for:

1. Synchronisation of audio with transcript. The synchronisation process can utilise various cues. For example, an interview usually consists of two persons taking turns to speak. They will have distinctive audio signatures and the transitions between their parts can be used to time stamp the transcript.
2. Synchronisation of video with shotlist.

5.3 Interpolation on Parallel Media

This category of techniques includes using techniques in both of the categories above and additionally using interpolation in one representation based on relative positions in another representation. For example, the transcript length in words can be used to estimate the approximate duration of the shot, and the transcript and video can be synchronised by interpolation.

5.4 Interactive Timecode Insertion

This category of techniques include all those discussed above and in addition include user involvement and user-feedback on the heuristics being used.

For example, the base FRANK system will support manual insertion of timecodes into a transcript while a video is being viewed (by the user clicking the Insert Timecode button when the footage corresponding to the text insertion cursor position is played). A great deal of time can be saved if, after a timecode is entered and the text cursor repositioned by the user, a guess is made for the next timecode needed (using interpolation techniques) and the video cued to the corresponding position.

It might also be possible for the user, often an experienced researcher, to estimate the transcript length and corresponding shot duration.

5.5   Use of These Techniques

We are accumulating a stock of heuristics and trying to infer a more general architecture for a browsing tool that will allow users to apply these techniques, singly or in combination, to find the material they need.

6   Status of Prototype

Initial demonstrations of the FRANK system to film and television researchers and librarians has met with an overwhelmingly positive response. Although developed to experiment with applications of wide-area broadband networks, we have had a great deal of interest in the system being used across local area networks for internal use within archives. We are now commencing a technology trial of FRANK in several archives.

7   Summary

We have shown how alternate representations are critical in our architecture to provide the quality of video archive navigation demanded by our users.

We analysed the work habits of our user group and discovered that alternate representations are commonly used as aids in current work processes.

We have developed an architecture and a prototype based on that design for remote video browsing. In our design, the navigation aids are stored separately from the video. This allows small service providers to provide a high-quality service with the help of a shared resource, that is, the large media servers providing the video streams. This in turn reduces the entry costs for a media service provider.

We have identified some approaches we will be investigating for generating timecodes in the absence of time-based alternate representations.

8   Acknowledgements

We acknowledge the support provided by the Cooperative Research Centre for Research Data Network established under the Australian Government's Cooperative Research Centres Program. We also thank Film Australia and the Australian Broadcasting Corporation for supplying material and film researching/archiving expertise to the project.

References

1. K. Yap and B. Simpson-Young, The BIOS Trials on the Telstra Experimental Broadband Network, in Australian Telecommunication Networks and Applications Conference 1995, Sydney, December 1995.

2. B. Simpson-Young and K. Yap, Work Processes of Film and Television Researchers, CSIRO Division of Information Technology Technical Report 95/11, March 1995. See http://www.syd.dit.csiro.au/projects/dimmis/bios/tr95_11.ps

3. James Griffioen, Raj Yavatkar, and Robert Adams. An Object-oriented Model for Semantic Intepretation of Multimedia Data. In ACM Multimedia'95 Proceedings, CA 1995.

4. Howard D. Wactlar, Takeo Kanade, Michael A. Smith, and Scott M. Stevens. Intelligent Access to Digital Video: Informedia project. IEEE Computer **29** (5) May 1996.

5. Zhang, H J, and Smoliar S.W. Developing Power Tools for Video Indexing and Retrieval. In Proceedings IS&T/SPIE symposium on Electronic Imaging Science and Technology: Storage and Retrieval for Image and Video Databases II 140–149. San Jose, CA, 1994.

6. Akioi Nagasaka and Yuzuru Tanaka. Automatic Video Indexing and Full-Video Search for Object Appearances. Visual Database Systems II **A-7** 113–119. Elsevier Science Publishers B.V. (North Holland). IFIP 1992.

An Experimental Result in Image Indexing Using GEP-2D Strings

Qing-Long Zhang,* Shi-Kuo Chang*, and Stephen S.-T. Yau[†]

Abstract

An experimental result in image indexing using GEP-2D strings is reported. Each 2D image is modelled as a generalized extended pseudo-symbolic picture, which has the GEP-2D string representation. In [10] it is proven that there is an efficient algorithm to generate the GEP-2D string representation of a 2D image. In this paper we describe the implementation of the GEP-2D string indexing algorithm using C language on a SUN Sparc workstation and the timing result, which empirically verified the theoretical time complexity upperbound of $O(N^3)$ for this algorithm, where N is the number of all objects involved in a picture.

1 Introduction

Image database systems have been extensively studied over the past ten years. One of the most important problems in the design of image database systems is how images are stored in the image databases. Content-based image indexing techniques need to be developed for facilitating image information retrieval from an image database. With the recent interest in multimedia systems, content-based image/multimedia document retrieval has attracted the attention of researchers across several disciplines.

Tanimoto [5] suggested the use of picture icons as picture indexes, thus introducing the concept of iconic indexing. Subsequently, Chang et al. [2] developed the concept of iconic indexing by introducing the 2D string representation of the image. Since then, the 2D string approach has been studied further in the literature. A detailed exposition on the 2D string approach has recently been given by Chang and Jungert [1], and experimental systems

---

*Knowledge Systems Institute, 3420 Main Street, Skokie, IL 60076, USA; E-mail: {qzhang, changsk}@ksi.edu. The second author is also with the Department of Computer Science, University of Pittsburgh, Pittsburgh, PA 15260, USA; E-mail: chang@cs.pitt.edu.

[†]Department of Mathematics, Statistics, and Computer Science, University of Illinois at Chicago, 322 Science and Engineering Offices, 851 South Morgan Street, Chicago, Illinois 60607, USA; E-mail: yau@uic.edu.

based on the 2D string approach are presented in Chapter 6 of this book [1]. Sistla et al. [4] developed a rule system $\mathcal{R}$ for reasoning about spatial relationships in picture retrieval systems. One obvious distinction between the work of Sistla et al. [4] and the work such as [1] [2] is that, the spatial operators in [4] are defined by absolute spatial relationships among objects, while the spatial operators in the other approaches are defined by relative spatial relationships among objects.

Yau and Zhang [6] addressed the completeness problem, proposed in [4], of reasoning about planar spatial relationships in picture retrieval systems. In that paper, they presented two efficiently decidable classes of planar pictures: *pseudo-symbolic pictures* and *extended pseudo-symbolic pictures*, which have pseudo-2D string representation and extended pseudo-2D string representation respectively. Zhang and Yau [8] then proposed a new iconic indexing, called the combined 2D string representation, for extended pseudo-symbolic pictures by unifying both the extended pseudo-2D string representation and the usual 2D string representation. Later, Zhang et al. [9] extended the earlier work on the extended pseudo-symbolic pictures to model the whole images. In this approach, each 2D image is modelled as a generalized extended pseudo-symbolic picture, which has the GEP-2D string representation. This approach can also be applied to 3D scenes. A detailed extension to modelling the whole images can be found in Zhang et al. [10]. For the detailed theoretical framework, the reader may refer to Zhang [7].

In this paper we consider the implementation of the GEP-2D string approach. We have implemented GEP-2D string indexing algorithms using C on SUN Sparc workstation. Section 2 presents the background. The GEP-2D string indexing algorithms are described in Section 3. Implementation and experimental result are reported and discussed in Section 4. Finally, conclusion and future research are given in Section 5.

2   Background Work

We use $<_r$ and $<_a$, respectively, to represent relative and absolute spatial relationships involving *left-of* and *below* (and *in-front-of* for 3D scenes only). We first recall the definitions of symbolic picture and 2D string [2].

2.1   Symbolic Pictures

Definition 2.1 *Given a set V of symbols, a symbolic picture f over V is an $m \times n$ matrix, in which each slot of the matrix is assigned a (possibly empty) subset of V.*

Definition 2.2 *A (reduced) 2D string (u, v) over V is defined as a pair of strings*

$$(x_1 y_1 x_2 y_2 \ldots y_{t-1} x_t, x_{p(1)} z_1 x_{p(2)} z_2 \ldots z_{t-1} x_{p(t)}),$$

where $x_i \in V$ and y_i, z_i are either $<_r$ or null symbols and $p: \{1, 2, \ldots, t\} \longrightarrow \{1, 2, \ldots, t\}$ is a permutation function.

The 2D string approach is based on the idea that the spatial knowledge contained in a real picture can be suitably represented by a symbolic picture. A 2D string representing a symbolic picture is derived from the picture by orthogonally projecting its symbols by columns and by rows. This approach allows for an efficient and natural way to construct iconic indexes for two-dimensional pictures.

The non-redundant 2D string representation of a symbolic picture is given by Costagliola et al. [3].

2.2 Extended Pseudo-Symbolic Pictures

Now we introduce the definitions of pseudo-symbolic picture and extended pseudo-symbolic picture [7] [6]. We consider the following basic absolute spatial relationship symbols: *left-of*, *below*, (*in-front-of* for 3-dimensional scenes only), *inside*, *outside*, and *overlaps*.

The concept of a local scene plays a key role in pseudo-symbolic pictures and extended pseudo-symbolic pictures.

Definition 2.3 *Given a set V of symbols, a local scene over V consists of a subset $U \subseteq V$ and a set $\boldsymbol{F}$ of spatial relationships among symbols in U satisfying that $\boldsymbol{F}$ contains only inside, outside, and overlaps relationships, but no left-of or below relationships, and exactly one of "x outside y" and "x overlaps y" is in $\boldsymbol{F}$ for any two distinct symbols x and y in U.*

Definition 2.4 *Given a set V of symbols, a pseudo-symbolic picture (abbr. P-symbolic picture) f over V is an $m \times n$ matrix, in which each slot is assigned a (possibly empty) local scene over V.*

To avoid ambiguity of 2D string representation, we associate multiple occurrences of the same object with different nonnegative integers.

Let f be a pseudo-symbolic picture. We represent each nonblank slot by a super-symbol e_i ($i \geq 0$). Then f becomes a simple symbolic picture f_s over the set of super-symbols under "$<_a$". We call f_s *the reduced symbolic picture of f*. As with 2D strings, the pseudo-2D string of f is obtained by projecting the super-symbols of f_s by columns and by rows.

The concept of extended pseudo-symbolic pictures is an extension of the concept of pseudo-symbolic pictures.

Definition 2.5 *A regular partition on an $m \times n$ matrix is a collection of sets of slots T $= \{T_i \mid i \in I\}$ such that*

(1) for each set of slots T_i, there exist integers $1 \leq i \leq j \leq m$ and $1 \leq k \leq l \leq n$ such that

$$T_i = \{(x,y) \mid i \leq x \leq j, k \leq y \leq l\},$$

where each pair (x,y) denotes the (x,y)-slot in the given $m \times n$ matrix. We call i, j, k, and l, respectively, below-bound, above-bound, left-bound, and right-bound;

(2) for any two distinct subscripts i, j in I, $T_i \cap T_j = \emptyset$;

(3) $\cup_{i \in I} T_i = \{(i,j) \mid 1 \leq i \leq m, 1 \leq j \leq n\}$;

(4) for $1 \leq i \leq m$ and $1 \leq j \leq n$, there exist T_{k1} with below-bound i, T_{k2} with above-bound i, T_{k3} with left-bound j, and T_{k4} with right-bound j.

Definition 2.6 *Given a set V of symbols, an extended pseudo-symbolic picture (abbr. EP-symbolic picture) f over V is a regular partition on an $m \times n$ matrix $T = \{T_i \mid i \in I\}$, in which each T_i is assigned a (possibly empty) local scene over V such that T satisfies the following property, called the minimality condition of rows and columns: for any $1 \leq i \leq m$ and $1 \leq j \leq n$, there exist T_{k1} with below-bound i, T_{k2} with above-bound i, T_{k3} with left-bound j, and T_{k4} with right-bound j such that each of them is assigned a non-empty local scene.*

Let f be an EP-symbolic picture and $T = \{T_i \mid i \in I\}$ be its regular partition on an $m \times n$ matrix. We represent each T_i assigned with a non-empty local scene by a super-symbol e_j $(j \geq 0)$. Then f will become a symbolic picture f_s over the set of super-symbols under "$<_a$" if, for each $T_k \in T$ associated with a super-symbol e (possibly blank if T_k is assigned an empty local scene), every slot $(p,q) \in T_k$ is assigned the super-symbol e (possibly blank). We call f_s the reduced symbolic picture of f. Now the extented pseudo-2D string representation of f is just the non-redundant 2D string of f_s.

2.3   GEP-Symbolic Pictures

In this section we introduce generalized extended pseudo-symbolic pictures to model all 2D images [9] [10] [7]. To achieve this goal, we extend the definition of extended pseudo-symbolic picture to that of generalized extended pseudo-symbolic picture by generalizing the concept of a local scene and possibly discarding some spatial relationships.

Definition 2.7 *Given a set V of symbols, a generalized local scene over V consists of a subset $U \subseteq V$ and a consistent set F of spatial relationships among symbols in U satisfying that exactly one of "x outside y" and "x overlaps y" is in F for any two distinct symbols x and y in U.*

Definition 2.8 *Given a set V of symbols, a generalized pseudo-symbolic picture (abbr. GP-symbolic picture) f over V is an $m \times n$ matrix, in which each slot is assigned a (possibly empty) generalized local scene over V.*

Let f be a GP-symbolic picture. Similar to the case of P-symbolic pictures, we can get a reduced symbolic picture f_s of f. Then the generalized pseudo-2D string (abbr. GP-2D string) of f is obtained by projecting the super-symbols of f_s by columns and by rows.

Now we introduce an extension of GP-symbolic pictures, called generalized extended pseudo-symbolic pictures, which can model all 2D scenes.

Definition 2.9 *Given a set V of symbols, a generalized extended pseudo-symbolic picture (abbr. GEP-symbolic picture) f over V is a regular partition on an $m \times n$ matrix $T = \{T_\alpha \mid \alpha \in I\}$, in which each T_α is assigned a (possibly empty) generalized local scene over V such that T satisfies the following property, called the minimality condition of rows and columns: for any $1 \leq i \leq m$ and $1 \leq j \leq n$, there exist T_{α_1} with below-bound i, T_{α_2} with above-bound i, T_{α_3} with left-bound j, and T_{α_4} with right-bound j such that each of them is assigned a nonempty generalized local scene.*

Let f be a GEP-symbolic picture and $T = \{T_i \mid i \in I\}$ be its regular partition on an $m \times n$ matrix. Similar to the case of EP-symbolic pictures, we can get a reduced symbolic picture f_s of f. Then the generalized extented pseudo-2D string (abbr. GEP-2D string) representation of f is just the non-redundant 2D string of f_s.

3 GEP-2D String Indexing Algorithms

In this section, we present GEP-2D string indexing algorithms for images in image databases.

3.1 Algorithms for Generating P-2D and EP-2D Strings

Yau and Zhang [6] considered the decidability problem for (extended) pseudo-symbolic pictures. That is, is there a decidable procedure to determine whether a given planar picture is (extended) pseudo-symbolic? For a planar picture f, we assume all objects and spatial relationships in f are given. Yau and Zhang [6] proved the following two theorems.

Theorem 3.1 *There exists an efficient algorithm with time complexity of $O(n^2)$, where n is the number of all objects involved in a picture, to determine whether a given planar picture is pseudo-symbolic, and if it is, the algorithm also returns its pseudo-2D string representation.*

Theorem 3.2 *There exists an efficient algorithm with time complexity of $O(n^3)$, where n is the number of all objects involved in a picture, to determine whether a given planar picture* *is extended pseudo-symbolic, and if it is, the algorithm also returns its extended pseudo-2D string representation.*

Now, we present the algorithms given in [6] [7].

Algorithm I. *Decide whether a given planar picture f is pseudo-symbolic.*

Input: the set of objects O_f and the set of relationships R_f representing f.

Output: YES if f is pseudo-symbolic; NO, otherwise.

          And if YES, the pseudo-2D string representation of f is also produced.

Step 1. Encode local scenes by super-symbols

          Set $O = O_f$;

          While $O \neq \emptyset$ do

                  begin

                  Choose one symbol $x \in O$, and calculate the set E_x, then

                  check whether $\{x\} \cup E_x$ forms a local scene of f.

                  If yes, use a super-symbol e_i to represent it and continue;

                  otherwise, output "NO" and exit the procedure.

                  Reset $O = O - \{x\} \cup E_x$;

                  end;   /* while */

Step 2. Define *left-of* and *below* relationships among super-symbols

          For every pair of super-symbols e_i and e_j, check whether

          the bad condition between e_i and e_j occurs.

          If yes, then output "NO" and exit the procedure;

          otherwise, define either *left-of* or *below* relationships between them.

Step 3. Find local substrings of super-symbols

          /* Form local substrings of super-symbols w.r.t. *left-of* relationships. */

          Set $S = \{e_0, e_1, \ldots, e_{l-1}\}$;   /* the set of super-symbols */

          While $S \neq \emptyset$ do

                  begin

                  Choose one super-symbol $e \in S$, and calculate the set L_e, then check

                  whether $\{e\} \cup L_e$ forms a local substring w.r.t. *left-of* relationships.

                  If yes, represent it by L_i (i is some integer) and continue;

                  otherwise, output "NO" and exit the procedure.

                  Reset $S = S - \{e\} \cup L_e$;

                  end;   /* while */

          /* Form local substrings of super-symbols w.r.t. *below* relationships. The following

              code is the same as the above one except all *left-of*'s are replaced by *below*'s. */

          Set $S = \{e_0, e_1, \ldots, e_{l-1}\}$;   /* the set of super-symbols */

          While $S \neq \emptyset$ do

                  begin

Choose one super-symbol $e \in S$, and calculate the set B_e, then check
whether $\{e\} \cup B_e$ forms a local substring w.r.t. *below* relationships.
If yes, represent it by B_j (j is some integer) and continue;
otherwise, output "NO" and exit the procedure.
Reset $S = S - \{e\} \cup B_e$;
end; /* while */

Step 4. Produce the pseudo-2D string representation (u, v) of f
Sort $\{L_1, L_2, \ldots, L_p\}$ w.r.t. the natural *left-of* relationship, and use u
to store the sorted order;
Sort $\{B_1, B_2, \ldots, B_q\}$ w.r.t. the natural *below* relationship, and use v
to store the sorted order;
Replace all L_i's and B_j's in u and v by their represented local substrings of
super-symbols, respectively, and then output "YES" and (u, v).
/* End of the algorithm. */

Note that the above presented Algorithm I needs only the first three steps to verify
whether a given planar picture is pseudo-symbolic. And if it is, then the algorithm executes
Step (4) to output its pseudo-2D string at the extra cost of time complexity of at most $O(n^2)$.

Algorithm II. *Decide whether a given planar picture f is extended pseudo-symbolic.*

Input: the set of objects O_f and the set of relationships R_f representing f.

Output: YES if f is extended pseudo-symbolic; NO, otherwise.
And if YES, the extended pseudo-2D string representation of f is also produced.

Step 1. Encode local scenes by super-symbols
Same as Step 1 in the algorithm for deciding pseudo-symbolic pictures.

Step 2. Define *left-of* and *below* relationships among super-symbols
Same as Step 2 in the algorithm for deciding pseudo-symbolic pictures.

Step 3. Produce the extended pseudo-2D string representation (u, v) of f
/* Find the first component u of the pair (u, v). */
Set $u = \emptyset$ and $S = \{e_0, e_1, \ldots, e_{l-1}\}$; /* Initially S is the set of super-symbols */
While $S \neq \emptyset$ do
begin
Calculate the set u_1 of all left-most super-symbols in S and set $S_1 = S - u_1$;
/* ∘ means the concatenation operation of two strings. */
If $S_1 = \emptyset$ then $u = u \circ u_1$ and reset $S = \emptyset$;
else begin
$u = u \circ u_1 \circ <$;
Calculate the set u_{11} of all x's ending at the current column and set
$u_{12} = u_1 - u_{11}$;

Reset $S = S_1 \cup u_{12}$;
    end;
  end;   /* end of while */
/* Find the second component v of the pair (u, v). The following code is the same
    as the above one used to find u except replacing all *left-of*'s using *below*'s. */
Set $v = \emptyset$ and $S = \{e_0, e_1, \ldots, e_{l-1}\}$;   /* Initially S is the set of super-symbols */
While $S \neq \emptyset$ do
  begin
    Calculate the set v_1 of all below-most super-symbols in S and set $S_1 = S - v_1$;
    If $S_1 = \emptyset$ then $v = v \circ v_1$ and reset $S = \emptyset$;
    else   begin
        $v = v \circ v_1 \circ <$;
        Calculate the set v_{11} of all x's ending at the current row and set
        $v_{12} = v_1 - v_{11}$;
        Reset $S = S_1 \cup v_{12}$;
        end;
  end;   /* end of while */
  Output "YES" and (u, v).
/* End of the algorithm. */

Note that our above Algorithm II needs only the first two steps to verify whether a given planar picture is extended pseudo-symbolic. Hence, it takes only time complexity of $O(n^2)$ to verify the decidability problem for extended pseudo-symbolic pictures. And if it is, then the algorithm executes Step (3) to output its extended pseudo-2D string at the extra cost of time complexity of $O(n^3)$.

3.2 Algorithms for Generating GP-2D and GEP-2D Strings

Similar to the case of (extended) pseudo-symbolic pictures in Section 3.1, Zhang et al. [10] proved the following two theorems.

Theorem 3.3 *There exists an efficient algorithm with time complexity of $O(n^3)$, where n is the number of all objects involved in a picture, to determine whether a given planar picture is generalized pseudo-symbolic, and if it is, the algorithm also returns its generalized pseudo-2D string representation.*

Theorem 3.4 *There exists an efficient algorithm with time complexity of $O(n^3)$, where n is the number of all objects involved in a picture, to generate the GEP-2D string representation for a given planar picture.*

We now present the algorithms given in [10].

Algorithm III. *Decide whether a given planar picture f is generalized pseudo-symbolic.*

Input: the set of objects O_f and the set of relationships R_f representing f.

Output: YES if f is generalized pseudo-symbolic; NO, otherwise.

And if YES, the generalized pseudo-2D string representation of f is also produced.

Step 1. Encode generalized local scenes by super-symbols

Let $O_f = \{O_0, O_1, \ldots, O_{n-1}\}$, and $C = \{U_0, U_1, \ldots, U_{l-1}\}$ be a disjoint partition of O_f. Initially, set $U_i = \{O_i\}$ for each $0 \leq i \leq n - 1$, and $\mid C \mid = l = n$.

While (U_i and U_j in C are spatial-incomparable for some $0 \leq i < j \leq l - 1$) do

begin

Choose one pair of U_i and U_j in C ($0 \leq i < j \leq l - 1$) such that U_i and U_j are spatial-incomparable, and i and j are minimal. Then reset $C = (C - \{U_i, U_j\}) \cup \{U_i \cup U_j\}$;

end; /* while */

Step 2. Define *left-of* and *below* relationships among super-symbols

For every pair of super-symbols e_i and e_j, define either *left-of* or *below* relationships between them.

Step 3. Find local substrings of super-symbols

/* Form local substrings of super-symbols w.r.t. *left-of* relationships. */

Set $S = \{e_0, e_1, \ldots, e_{l-1}\}$; /* the set of super-symbols */

While $S \neq \emptyset$ do

begin

Choose one super-symbol $e \in S$, and calculate the set L_e, then check whether $\{e\} \cup L_e$ forms a local substring w.r.t. *left-of* relationships. If yes, represent it by L_i (i is some integer) and continue; otherwise, output "NO" and exit the procedure.

Reset $S = S - (\{e\} \cup L_e)$;

end; /* while */

/* Form local substrings of super-symbols w.r.t. *below* relationships. The following code is the same as the above one except all *left-of*'s are replaced by *below*'s. */

Set $S = \{e_0, e_1, \ldots, e_{l-1}\}$; /* the set of super-symbols */

While $S \neq \emptyset$ do

begin

Choose one super-symbol $e \in S$, and calculate the set B_e, then check whether $\{e\} \cup B_e$ forms a local substring w.r.t. *below* relationships. If yes, represent it by B_j (j is some integer) and continue; otherwise, output "NO" and exit the procedure.

Reset $S = S - (\{e\} \cup B_e)$;

end; /* while */

Step 4.   Produce the generalized pseudo-2D string representation (u, v) of f
Sort $\{L_1, L_2, \ldots, L_p\}$ w.r.t. the natural *left-of* relationship, and use u
to store the sorted order;
Sort $\{B_1, B_2, \ldots, B_q\}$ w.r.t. the natural *below* relationship, and use v
to store the sorted order;
Replace all L_i's and B_j's in u and v by using their represented local substrings
of super-symbols, respectively, and then output "YES" and (u, v).
/* End of the algorithm. */

Note that the above presented Algorithm III needs only the first three steps to verify
whether a given planar picture is generalized pseudo-symbolic. And if it is, then the algorithm executes Step (4) to output its generalized pseudo-2D string at the extra cost of time
complexity of at most $O(n^2)$.

Algorithm IV. *Generate the GEP-2D string representation for a given planar picture f.*

Input: the set of objects O_f and the set of relationships R_f representing f.
Output: Produce the generalized extended pseudo-2D string representation of f.
Step 1.   Encode generalized local scenes by super-symbols
Same as Step 1 in the algorithm for deciding generalized pseudo-symbolic pictures.
Step 2.   Define *left-of* and *below* relationships among super-symbols
Same as Step 2 in the algorithm for deciding generalized pseudo-symbolic pictures.
Step 3.   Produce the generalized extended pseudo-2D string representation (u, v) of f
/* Find the first component u of the pair (u, v). */
Set $u = \emptyset$ and $S = \{e_0, e_1, \ldots, e_{l-1}\}$;   /* Initially S is the set of super-symbols */
While $S \neq \emptyset$ do
begin
Calculate the set u_1 of all left-most super-symbols in S and set $S_1 = S - u_1$;
/* ∘ means the concatenation operation of two strings. */
If $S_1 = \emptyset$ then $u = u \circ u_1$ and reset $S = \emptyset$;
else   begin
$u = u \circ u_1 \circ\ <$;
Calculate the set u_{11} of all x's ending at the current column and set
$u_{12} = u_1 - u_{11}$;
Reset $S = S_1 \cup u_{12}$;
end;
end;   /* end of while */
/* Find the second component v of the pair (u, v). The following code is the same
as the above one used to find u except replacing all *left-of*'s using *below*'s. */
Set $v = \emptyset$ and $S = \{e_0, e_1, \ldots, e_{l-1}\}$;   /* Initially S is the set of super-symbols */

While $S \neq \emptyset$ do

    begin

        Calculate the set v_1 of all below-most super-symbols in S and set $S_1 = S - v_1$;

        If $S_1 = \emptyset$ then $v = v \circ v_1$ and reset $S = \emptyset$;

    else   begin

            $v = v \circ v_1 \circ\ <$;

            Calculate the set v_{11} of all x's ending at the current row and set

            $v_{12} = v_1 - v_{11}$;

            Reset $S = S_1 \cup v_{12}$;

            end;

        end;   /* end of while */

    Output the pair (u, v).

/* End of the algorithm. */

4 Implementation and Experimental Result

In this section, we begin to discuss our implementation of the four GEP-2D string indexing algorithms given in Section 3.

We have implemented the four GEP-2D string indexing algorithms, Algorithms I–IV given in Section 3, using C on SUN Sparc workstation. Then, our general GEP-2D string indexing algorithm works as follows: Given a planar picture f as an input (i.e., given the set of objects and the set of spatial relationships representing f), it first invokes Algorithm I to determine whether the picture f is pseudo-symbolic. If the output of Algorithm I is YES, the P-2D string representation of f is produced and the general GEP-2D string indexing algorithm stops. Otherwise (i.e., the output of Algorithm I is NO), the general GEP-2D string indexing algorithm will then invoke Algorithm II to decide whether the picture f is extended pseudo-symbolic. Again, If the output of Algorithm II is YES, the EP-2D string representation of f is produced and the general GEP-2D string indexing algorithm stops. Otherwise (i.e., the output of Algorithm II is NO), the general GEP-2D string indexing algorithm will invoke Algorithm III to decide whether the picture f is generalized pseudo-symbolic. Now, If the output of Algorithm III is YES, the GP-2D string representation of f is produced and the general GEP-2D string indexing algorithm stops. Otherwise (i.e., the output of Algorithm III is NO), the general GEP-2D string indexing algorithm will finally invoke Algorithm IV to produce the GEP-2D string representation of f. Thus, our general GEP-2D string indexing algorithm successively invokes Algorithms I–IV in order to generate the expected P-2D, EP-2D, GP-2D, or GEP-2D string representation.

For ease of implementation, we use vectors (i.e., one-dimensional arrays) and matrices

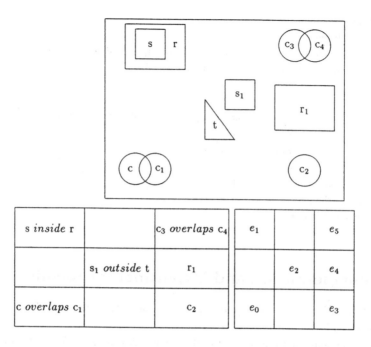

s *inside* r		c$_3$ *overlaps* c$_4$	e$_1$		e$_5$
	s$_1$ *outside* t	r$_1$		e$_2$	e$_4$
c *overlaps* c$_1$		c$_2$	e$_0$		e$_3$

Figure 1: An image, its pseudo-symbolic and reduced symbolic representations.

(i.e., two-dimensional arrays), respectively, to store the information on objects and spatial relationships in the picture. This would naturally cause the indexing algorithms to take the worst case of time complexity. By Theorems 3.1–3.4 in Section 3, all the four GEP-2D string indexing algorithms have at most the time complexity $O(N^3)$, where N is the number of all objects involved in a picture. Therefore, our general GEP-2D string indexing algorithm will have at most the time complexity $O(N^3)$.

In order to test our general GEP-2D string indexing algorithm, we select the following four source pictures, one for each of P-symbolic, EP-symbolic, GP-symbolic, and GEP-symbolic pictures. These four source pictures all have the same number of objects, 10.

Figure 1 shows an image, the pseudo-symbolic picture g representing it, and the reduced symbolic picture g_s of g. The set of symbols is $V = \{c, r, s, t\}$, where c, r, s, and t correspond to the objects *circle*, *rectangle*, *square*, and *right triangle*, respectively. Five occurrences of the circle (c) are represented by c_0 (simply c), c_1, c_2, c_3, and c_4, respectively. Two occurrences of the rectangle (r) are represented by r_0 (simply r) and r_1, respectively. Two occurrences of the square (s) are represented by s_0 (simply s) and s_1, respectively. Then, the pseudo-2D string representation of g is $(u, v) = (e_0e_1 <_a e_2 <_a e_3e_4e_5, e_0e_3 <_a e_2e_4 <_a e_1e_5)$, where

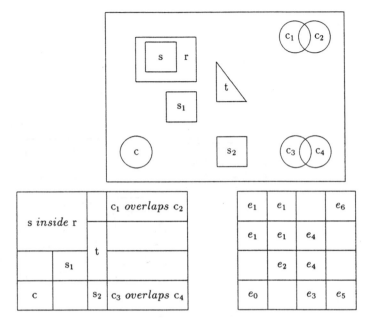

Figure 2: An image, its extended pseudo-symbolic and reduced symbolic representations.

e_0, e_1, e_2, e_3, e_4, and e_5, respectively, point to the local scenes $\{c\ overlaps\ c_1\}$, $\{s\ inside\ r\}$, $\{s_1\ outside\ t\}$, "c_2", "r_1", and $\{c_3\ overlaps\ c_4\}$.

Figure 2 shows an image, the extended pseudo-symbolic picture h representing it, and the reduced symbolic picture h_s of h. The symbols c, r, s, and t and the set of symbols V are the same as those in Figure 1. Then, the extended pseudo-2D string representation of h is $(u,v) = (e_0e_1\ <_a\ e_1e_2\ <_a\ e_3e_4\ <_a\ e_5e_6, e_0e_3e_5\ <_a\ e_2e_4\ <_a\ e_1e_4\ <_a\ e_1e_6)$, where $e_0, e_1, e_2, e_3, e_4, e_5$, and e_6, respectively, point to the local scenes "c", $\{s\ inside\ r\}$, "s_1", "s_2", "t", $\{c_3\ overlaps\ c_4\}$, and $\{c_1\ overlaps\ c_2\}$.

Figure 3 shows an image, the GP-symbolic picture g_1 representing it, and the reduced symbolic picture g_{1s} of g_1. The symbols c, r, s, and t and the set of symbols V are the same as those in Figure 1. Four occurrences of the circle (c) are represented by c_0 (simply c), c_1, c_2, and c_3, respectively. Two occurrences of the rectangle (r) are represented by r_0 (simply r) and r_1, respectively. Three occurrences of the square (s) are represented by s_0 (simply s), s_1, and s_2, respectively. Then, the GP-2D string representation of g_1 is $(u,v) = (e_0e_1\ <_a\ e_2\ <_a\ e_3e_4e_5, e_0e_3\ <_a\ e_2e_4\ <_a\ e_1e_5)$, where e_0, e_1, e_2, e_3, e_4, and e_5, respectively,

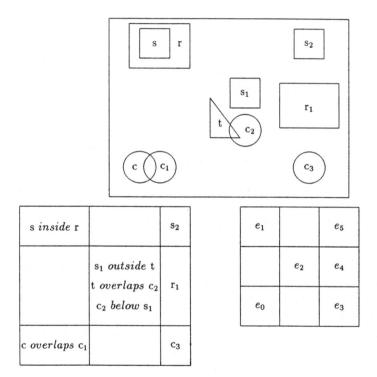

Figure 3: An image, its GP-symbolic and reduced symbolic representations.

point to the generalized local scenes $\{c \ overlaps \ c_1\}$, $\{s \ inside \ r\}$, $\{s_1 \ outside \ t, t \ overlaps \ c_2, c_2 \ below \ s_1\}$, "$c_3$", "$r_1$", and "$s_2$".

Figure 4 shows an image, the GEP-symbolic picture h_1 representing it, and the reduced symbolic picture h_{1s} of h_1. The symbols c, r, s, and t and the set of symbols V are the same as those in Figure 1. Then, the GEP-2D string representation of h_1 is $(u, v) = (e_0e_1 <_a e_1e_2 <_a e_3 <_a e_4e_5, e_0e_4 <_a e_2e_3 <_a e_1e_3 <_a e_1e_5)$, where e_0, e_1, e_2, e_3, e_4, and e_5, respectively, point to the local scenes "c", $\{s \ inside \ r\}$, "s_1", "t", $\{t_1 \ overlaps \ c_1, t_1 \ left\text{-}of \ s_2, c_1 \ below \ s_2\}$, and $\{c_2 \ overlaps \ c_3\}$.

We call the above four source pictures g, h, g_1, and h_1, respectively, as the type-1, type-2, type-3, and type-4 source pictures. Now, based on these four source pictures, we can build five classes of planar pictures $P_i(N)$, where $i = 1, 2, 3, 4$, and r (r means randomness), and N is the multiple of 10. We also call $P_i(N)$ a type-i picture. Let $N = 10n$ ($n > 0$). The type-i picture $P_i(N)$ ($i = 1, 2, 3$, or 4) is a picture with n copies of type-i source picture in it, and these n subscenes (copies) are arranged one by one in reverse-diagonal order such that, for any two of them, one must be completely on the left-below position of the other. The type-r picture $P_r(N)$ has the same form as a type-i picture $P_i(N)$ ($i = 1, 2, 3$, and 4) except that each of n subscenes (copies) in $P_r(N)$ is randomly chosen from the four source pictures g, h, g_1, and h_1. Clearly, $P_1(N), P_2(N), P_3(N)$, and $P_4(N)$ are, respectively, P-symbolic, EP-symbolic, GP-symbolic, and GEP-symbolic pictures. However, $P_r(N)$ could be either one of P-symbolic, EP-symbolic, GP-symbolic, and GEP-symbolic pictures, because of randomness of each subscene (copy) in $P_r(N)$. Note that, the major reason we choose the reverse-diagonal structure to build the pictures $P_i(N)$ ($i = 1, 2, 3, 4$, and r) is that we can easily generate the set of all objects and spatial relationships in $P_i(N)$.

We have measured the processor time that is being used when the general GEP-2D string indexing algorithm applies to the pictures $P_i(N)$ ($i = 1, 2, 3, 4$, and r). Table 1 shows the timing result, where the i-th column contains the timing result for the case of the pictures $P_{i-1}(N)$ ($i = 2, 3, 4, 5$) and the 6-th column contains the timing result for the case of the pictures $P_r(N)$. Note that each timing entry in the 6-th column is the average processor time of timing results for 40 samples of the pictures $P_r(N)$.

We can easily verify that each column of timing results generally satisfies the time complexity $O(N^3)$, where N is the number of objects in the picture. That is, if the time complexity $Time(N) = cN^3$ (c is a constant and $c > 0$), then $Time(N_1)/Time(N_2) = (N_1/N_2)^3$. This demonstrates the upperbound of the theoretical time complexity $O(N^3)$ of the general GEP-2D string indexing algorithm.

Table 1 shows that the timing result for the case of EP-symbolic pictures is more than that for the case of GP-symbolic pictures. This seems to contradict the intuitive thought that the general GEP-2D string indexing algorithm should take more time to generate the GP-2D

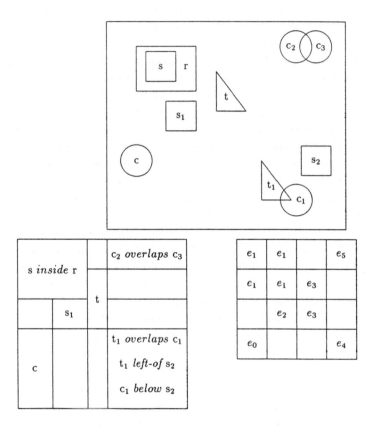

Figure 4: An image, its GEP-symbolic and reduced symbolic representations.

Table 1: A timing result for indexing algorithms

Number of	Time (seconds)				
Objects N	P-2D	EP-2D	GP-2D	GEP-2D	Random Case
50	0.717	1.633	1.367	2.167	2.283
70	1.900	4.533	3.600	5.766	6.009
100	5.450	12.733	10.216	16.399	16.770
200	42.498	99.713	78.697	126.412	130.547
300	151.477	353.686	269.973	441.032	459.188
400	356.802	840.683	645.324	1041.608	1089.346
500	697.622	1651.184	1262.916	2081.433	2101.846

string representation than to generate the EP-2D string representation, because the general GEP-2D string indexing algorithm does invoke Algorithm III in the GP-symbolic case, and not in the EP-symbolic case. As mentioned in Section 3.1, in fact, Algorithm II takes only time complexity of $O(N^2)$ to verify the decidability problem for extended pseudo-symbolic pictures, and if the input picture is extended pseudo-symbolic, Algorithm II then requires the extra cost of time complexity of $O(N^3)$ to produce the EP-2D string representation. Also note that Algorithm II should take more time to produce EP-2D string representation than Algorithm III to produce GP-2D string representation, because EP-2D strings are inherently more complex than GP-2D strings. Thus, our GEP-2D string indexing algorithm actually spends less time to generate GP-2D string representation for the pictures $P_3(N)$ than to generate EP-2D string representation for the pictures $P_2(N)$. Figure 5 is a plot for Table 1.

When generating a sample of the type-r pictues $P_r(N)$ ($N = 10n$ and $n > 0$), we use the random number generator to guarantee that each subscene (copy) in the sample picture is randomly chosen from the four type-i ($i = 1, 2, 3, 4$) source pictures. Note that a type-r sample picture is GEP-symbolic whenever at least one subscene (copy) in the sample is GEP-symbolic. Because of the equal possibility, the probability that a subscene (copy) in the picture $P_r(N)$ is not GEP-symbolic is 3/4. Then the probability that $P_r(N)$ ($N = 10n$ and $n > 0$) is not GEP-symbolic is $(3/4)^n$. So, the probability that a sample picture of $P_r(N)$ is GEP-symbolic is $1 - (3/4)^n$. Similarly, the probability that a sample picture of $P_r(N)$ is P-symbolic is $(1/4)^n$. When $n = 10$, $(1/4)^n = (1/4)^{10} = 9.53 * 10^{-7}$ and $1 - (3/4)^n = 1 - (3/4)^{10} = 0.9437$. This means that a sample picture of $P_r(100)$ is almost GEP-symbolic and almost could not be pseudo-symbolic. Thus, the timing result for the random case should have the similar timing result for the GEP-symbolic picture case.

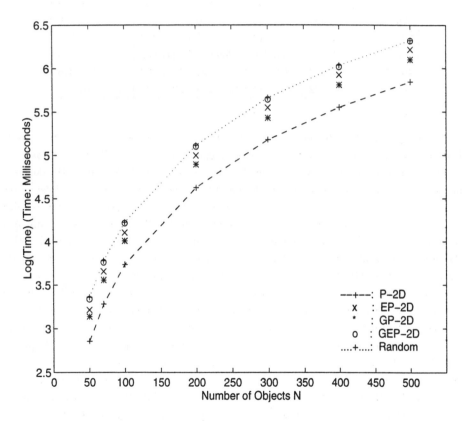

Figure 5: A timing result for indexing algorithms

Note that, our GEP-2D string indexing algorithm runs reasonably fast. For example, it only takes a few seconds to generate the GEP-2D string representation of a picture with 70 objects, while this picture may contain several thousands of spatial relationships. Since the algorithm needs to be applied only once for each picture, and a typical multimedia document contains less than 100 objects, this GEP-2D string indexing algorithm is practically applicable.

5 Conclusion and Future Research

In this paper we have considered the implementation of the GEP-2D string approach. We have implemented the GEP-2D string indexing algorithm for images in image databases, using C on SUN Sparc workstation. The timing result is reported and discussed. The experimental result empirically verified the theoretical time complexity upperbound of $O(N^3)$ for this algorithm, where N is the number of all objects involved in a picture.

Picture retrieval algorithms based on the GEP-2D string representation are being under further investigation and development. Applications of our GEP-2D string approach, such as Internet-based multi-media information search engine and virtual reality information retrieval, are also under investigation.

References

[1] S.-K. Chang and E. Jungert, *Symbolic Projection for Image Information Retrieval and Spatial Reasoning*, Academic Press, 1996.

[2] S.-K. Chang, Q. Y. Shi and C. W. Yan, "Iconic Indexing by 2-D Strings", *IEEE Trans. Pattern Anal. Machine Intell.*, 9, 3, 413–428, May 1987.

[3] G. Costagliola, F. Ferrucci, G. Tortora and M. Tucci, "Non-Redundant 2D Strings", *IEEE Transactions on Knowledge and Data Engineering*, 7, 2, 347–350, April 1995.

[4] A. P. Sistla, C. Yu and R. Haddad, "Reasoning about Spatial Relationships in Picture Retrieval Systems", *Proceedings of the 20th International Conference on Very Large Databases*, Santiago, Chile, 570–581, 1994.

[5] S. L. Tanimoto, "An Iconic Symbolic Data Structuring Scheme", *Pattern Recogn. and Artificial Intell.*, Academic Press, New York, 452–471, 1976.

[6] Stephen S.-T. Yau and Q.-L. Zhang, "On Completeness of Reasoning about Planar Spatial Relationships in Picture Retrieval Systems", Dept. of Mathematics, Statistics, and Computer Science, Univ. of Illinois, Chicago, *Preprint*, 1995.

[7] Q.-L. Zhang, *A Unified Framework for Iconic Indexing of Spatial Relationships in Image Databases*, Ph.D. Thesis, Department of Mathematics, Statistics, and Computer Science, The University of Illinois at Chicago, Illinois, USA, 1996.

[8] Q.-L. Zhang and Stephen S.-T. Yau, "A New Iconic Indexing for 2D and 3D Scenes", Department of Mathematics, Statistics, and Computer Science, Univ. of Illinois, Chicago, *Preprint*, 1995.

[9] Q.-L. Zhang, S.-K. Chang, and Stephen S.-T. Yau, "A Unified Approach to Indexing Images in Image Databases", *Proceedings of the First International Workshop on Image Databases and Multi Media Search*, Amsterdam, THE NETHERLANDS, pp. 99–106, August 22–23, 1996.

[10] Q.-L. Zhang, S.-K. Chang, and Stephen S.-T. Yau, "A Unified Approach to Iconic Indexing, Retrieval and Maintenance of Spatial Relationships in Image Databases", *Journal of Visual Communication and Image Representation* (Special Issue), December 1996.

Shape Encoding

Distance to Deformable Prototypes:
Encoding Shape Categories for Efficient Search

Stan Sclaroff

Computer Science Department, Boston University*
111 Cummington Street, Boston, MA 02215, USA

Abstract. An efficient shape-based indexing framework for content-based image retrieval is described. Rather than directly comparing a candidate shape with all entries in a database, shapes are ordered in terms of nonrigid deformations that relate them to a small subset of representative prototypes. The framework employs *modal matching*, a deformable shape decomposition that allows for automatic shape correspondence computation. In the modal representation, shape is decomposed into an ordered basis of orthogonal principal deformations. This allows selective invariance to in-plane rotation, translation, and scaling, and quasi-invariance to affine deformations. Retrieval accuracy and stability have been evaluated in experiments with 2D image databases. Experiments indicate that the method offers significantly better performance over moment-based invariants.

1 Introduction

Shape categories can be represented as deformations from a subset of standard or prototypical shapes; it is thought that this is one plausible mechanism for human perception [28]. This mechanism is appealing for its descriptive parsimony, and has served as inspiration for many of the prototype-based representations for machine vision. One advantadge of such schemes is that information about objects derived during categorization can be used to reduce the complexity of the identification process [12].

Our aim is to represent shape categories for interactive, image database search. Rather than directly comparing a candidate shape with all shapes in the database, we propose a method that first indexes shapes in terms of their relationship to a few shape prototypes. To do this, we will employ *modal matching* [31, 32, 33], a deformable shape decomposition that allows users to specify a few example shapes and has the computer efficiently sort the set of objects based on the similarity of their shape. In the modal representation, deformation is decomposed into an ordered basis of orthogonal principal components. This allows selective invariance to in-plane rotation, translation, and scaling, and quasi-invariance to affine deformations.

This chapter provides an overview of this new prototype-based approach, and then describes results of experiments that tested the approach's effectiveness for interactive shape-based image database search. The experiments indicate that this method offers significantly better performance over moment-based invariant methods. Experiments

---
* The work began while the author was at the MIT Media Laboratory and is now supported in part by Office of Naval Research Young Investigator Award N00014-96-1-0661, and the National Science Foundation Early Career Development Award IRI-9624168.

evaluating the stability of retrieval accuracy as a function of the number of prototypes are also described.

2   Overview of Approach

Our approach is related to *morphing*, a computer graphics technique that has become quite popular in advertisements. Morphing is accomplished by an artist identifying a large number of corresponding control points in two images, and then incrementally deforming the geometry of the first image so that its control points eventually lie atop the control points of the second image. Using this technique, in-between or novel views can be generated as warps between example views. This suggests an important way to obtain a low-dimensional, parametric description of shape: interpolate between known, prototype views. For instance, given views of the extremes of a motion (*e.g.*, systole and diastole, or left-leg forward and right-leg forward) we can describe the intermediate views as a smooth combination of the extremal views.

All that is required to determine this view-based parameterization of a new shape are: the prototype views, point correspondences between the new shape and the prototype views, and a method of measuring the amount of (nonrigid) deformation that has occurred between the new shape and each prototype view. The prototypes define a polytope in the space of the (unknown) underlying physical system's parameters. By measuring the amount of deformation between the new shape and extremal views, we locate the new shape in the coordinate system defined by the polytope. This coordinate in *prototype space* can be used for database indexing and fast search.

This general approach is related in spirit to the linear combinations of views paradigm, where any object view can be synthesized as a combination of linearly-warped example views of Ullman and Basri [34] and Poggio, *et al.* [27]. While the *view space* theorems associated with these methods do not apply to recognition of unfamiliar objects, recently Edelman has shown that a sufficient ensemble of prototypes can form a basis for a *shape space*, which is a provably faithful representation of unfamiliar shapes in a particular category [12].

The work proposed here differs from these proposals in two important ways. First, we are interested not only in recognizing shapes, but also in describing the types of deformations that relate them. We want to derive a low-dimensional parametric representation of the shape that can be used to recognize and compare shapes. Second, we cannot be restricted to a linear framework. Nonrigid motions are inherently nonlinear, although they *are* often "physically smooth." Therefore, to employ a combination-of-views approach we must be able to determine point correspondences and measure similarities between views in a way that takes into account at least qualitative physics of nonrigid shape deformation. In computer graphics it is the job of the artist to enforce the constraint of physical smoothness; in machine vision, we need to be able to do the same automatically.

To achieve this, we will employ modal matching, a method for (1) determining point correspondences using a energy-based model, (2) warping or morphing one shape into another using energy-based interpolants, and (3) measuring the amount of deformation between an object's shape and prototype views.

(a)   (c)   (e)

(b)   (d)   (f)

Fig. 1. The data needed to build deformable prototype shape models for two rabbit shape prototypes: original images (a,b), support maps (c,d), and edge maps (e,f).

Figure 1 shows the information required to build modal shape prototypes for two rabbit shape prototypes employed in our image database experiments. In our system a shape is defined by: a cloud of feature locations (*i.e.,* edges, corners, high-curvature points) and a region of support that tells us where the shape is. Given this input, deformable prototype models are built directly from feature data, using a finite element formulation that is based on Gaussian interpolants [33]. For efficiency, we can select a subset of the feature data as nodes for a lower-resolution finite element model and then use the resulting eigenmodes in finding the higher-resolution feature correspondences as described in [33]. This subset can be a set of particularly salient features (*i.e.,* corners, T-junctions, and edge mid-points) or a randomly selected subset of (roughly) uniformly-spaced features.

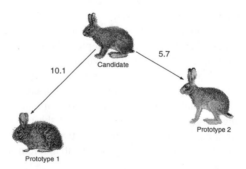

Fig. 2. Strain distance of candidate shape to two prototypes.

When a new shape is encountered, it is parameterized in terms of the energy needed to nonrigidly deform the prototype shape models into alignment with the new shape. Similarity is thus computed in terms of the amount of strain energy needed to deform each prototype to match it to the candidate shape, as illustrated in Fig. 2. The amounts of deformation are measured in terms of strain energy and stored as a n-tuple, where n is the number of prototype shapes employed. In this case, the resulting tuple is $(10.1, 5.7)$. The result is a low-dimensional parametric representation that can be used for efficient

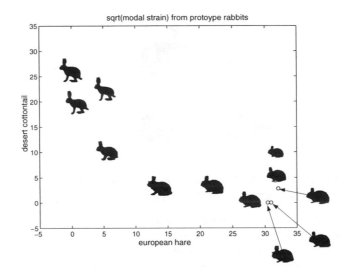

Fig. 3. Scatter plot of square-root modal strain energy for rabbit prototypes used in the image database experiment. The graph's x-axis depicts the square-root of strain energy needed to align the European Hare prototype with each rabbit shape, while the y-axis shows the energy needed to align the Desert Cottontail prototype with each rabbit shape.

shape-based image database search. Rather than directly comparing a candidate shape with all shape entries in a database, we instead compute similarity in a *distance to prototypes space*. Using this method, we compactly represent a category of shapes in terms of a few prototype views.

Fig. 3 shows a scatter plot of the two-dimensional "rabbit space" spanned by two rabbit shape prototypes. The graph's x-axis depicts the square-root of strain energy needed to align the European Hare prototype with each rabbit shape, while the y-axis shows the energy needed to align the Desert Cottontail prototype with each rabbit shape. Each of the 12 rabbit shapes has a coordinate in this strain-energy-from-prototype sub-space. As can be seen, the rabbits are clustered in terms of their 2-D shape appearance: long-legged, standing rabbits cluster at the top-left of the graph, while short-legged, seated rabbits cluster at the bottom right. There are two rabbits that map between clusters, showing the smooth ordering from long-legged, to medium-legged, to short-legged rabbits in this view-space.

3   Background and Notation

In the last few years researchers have made some progress toward automatic shape indexing for image databases. The general approach has been to calculate some approximately invariant statistic like shape moments, and use these to stratify the image database [5, 18, 19, 22, 24, 30] or curvature scale space information [23].

One problem with this general approach is that it discards significant perceptual and semantic information. While indexing methods provide a means to quickly narrow a search to a more manageable subset, they often do not provide a method for closer, direct comparison of *how* shapes are related. Rather than discarding useful similarity information by employing only invariants, we believe that one should use a decomposition that preserves as much semantically meaningful and perceptually important information as is possible, while still providing an efficient encoding of the original signal [25].

Another important problem with these approaches is that most are only robust for rigid shapes. Although many things move rigidly, in many cases this rigid-body model is inadequate. For instance, most biological objects are flexible and articulated. To describe these deformations, therefore, it is reasonable to model the physics by which real objects deform. This rationale led to the physical modeling paradigm of active contours or *snakes*[20] and deformable templates [8, 35]. A snake has a predefined structure that incorporates knowledge about the shape and its resistance to deformation. By allowing the user to specify forces that are a function of sensor measurements, the intrinsic dynamic behavior of a physical model can be used to solve fitting, interpolation, or correspondence problems.

While snakes enforced constraints on smoothness and the amount of deformation, they could not in their original form be used to constrain the *types* of deformation valid for a particular problem domain or object class. This led to the development of algorithms which include *a priori* constraints on the types of allowable deformations for motion tracking [2, 3, 6, 11].

Cootes *et al.*[7] use trainable snakes for capturing the invariant properties of a class of shapes, by finding the principal variations of a snake via the Karhunen-Loeve transform. Unfortunately, this method relies on the consistent sampling and labeling of point features across the entire training set and cannot handle large rotations. If different feature points are present in different views, or if there are very different sampling densities, then the resulting models will differ even if the object's pose and shape are identical.

We would like to avoid initialization and correspondence problems as much as is possible, by letting the data determine the parameterization in a natural manner. This philosophy is emodied in *modal matching*, where the data itself is used to define the deformable object, by building mass matrices that use the positions of image feature points as the finite element nodes [32, 33]. Due to space limitations, only a brief overview of the modal matching formulation can be provided in this chapter. Readers are directed to [31, 33] for extensive mathematical and algorithmic details.

3.1 Finite Element Method

The modal matching formulation employs finite element modeling techniques to provide an analytic characterization of shape and elastic properties over the whole surface. Problems caused by irregular sampling of feature points are thereby alleviated. Using Galerkin's method, we set up a system of polynomial shape functions that relate the displacement of a single point to the relative displacements of all the other nodes of an object. By using these functions, we can calculate the deformations which spread uniformly over the body as a function of its constitutive parameters.

Solution to the problem of deforming an elastic body to match the set of feature points then requires solving the *dynamic equilibrium equation*:

$$\mathbf{M}\ddot{\mathbf{U}} + \mathbf{D}\dot{\mathbf{U}} + \mathbf{K}\mathbf{U} = \mathbf{R}, \tag{1}$$

where $\mathbf{U}$ denotes a vector of displacement components at each element node, $\mathbf{R}$ is the load vector whose entries are the spring forces between each node point and the body surface, and where $\mathbf{M}$, $\mathbf{D}$, and $\mathbf{K}$ are the element mass, damping, and stiffness matrices, respectively [1, 26].

The FEM governing equations can be decoupled by posing the equations in a basis defined by the $\mathbf{M}$-orthogonalized eigenvectors of $\mathbf{K}$. These eigenvectors and values are the solution to the generalized eigenvalue problem:

$$\mathbf{K}\phi_i = \omega_i^2 \mathbf{M}\phi_i. \tag{2}$$

The vector ϕ_i is called the ith *mode shape vector* and ω_i is the corresponding frequency of vibration. Each mode shape vector describes how each node is displaced by the ith vibration mode. The mode shape vectors are $\mathbf{M}$-orthonormal; this means that $\Phi^T \mathbf{K}\Phi = \Omega^2$ and $\Phi^T \mathbf{M}\Phi = \mathbf{I}$. The ϕ_i form columns in the transform Φ and ω_i^2 are elements of the diagonal matrix Ω^2. We will assume Rayleigh damping (*i.e.*, $\mathbf{D} = a_0\mathbf{M} + a_1\mathbf{K}$), thus the damping matrix will also be diagonalized by this transform [1].

This generalized coordinate transform Φ is then used to transform between nodal point displacements $\mathbf{U}$ and decoupled modal displacements $\tilde{\mathbf{U}}$, $\mathbf{U} = \Phi\tilde{\mathbf{U}}$. We can now rewrite Eq. 1 in terms of these generalized or modal displacements, obtaining a decoupled system of equations:

$$\ddot{\tilde{\mathbf{U}}} + \tilde{\mathbf{D}}\dot{\tilde{\mathbf{U}}} + \Omega^2\tilde{\mathbf{U}} = \Phi^T \mathbf{R}, \tag{3}$$

allowing for closed-form solution to the equilibrium problem [26]. Given this equilibrium solution in the two images, point correspondences can be obtained directly.

By discarding high frequency modes the amount of computation required can be minimized without significantly altering correspondence accuracy. Moreover, such a set of modal amplitudes provides a robust, canonical description of shape in terms of deformations applied to the original elastic body. This allows them to be used directly for object recognition [26].

3.2   Modal Matching

Perhaps the major limitation of previous methods is the requirement that every object be described as the deformations of a *single* prototype object. For instance, in some schemes all shapes are represented as deformations from an elliptical or circular prototype [5, 13, 26]. Such approaches implicitly impose an *a priori* parameterization upon the sensor data, and therefore implicitly determine the correspondences between data and prototype. Furthermore, an elliptical prototype may be inadequate for many shapes, especially shapes that are not star-connected, or those that have long protrusions or deep concavities. We would like to avoid these problems as much as possible, by letting the data determine the parameterization in a natural manner. To accomplish this we use the data itself to define the deformable object, by building stiffness and mass matrices that use the positions of image feature points as the finite element nodes.

The resulting new modeling formulation is called *modal matching*, and is described in detail in [31, 33]. For each image we start with feature point locations, which are used as nodes in building a finite element model of the shape. We then compute the *modes of free vibration* Φ of this model using Eq. 2. The modes of an object form an orthogonal *object-centered* coordinate system for describing feature locations. That is, each feature point location can be uniquely described in terms of *how it projects onto each eigenvector, i.e.*, how it participates in each deformation mode. The transform between Cartesian feature locations (x, y) and modal feature locations (u, v) is accomplished by using the eigenvectors Φ as a coordinate basis:

$$\Phi = [\phi_1 \mid \ldots \mid \phi_{2m}] = \begin{bmatrix} \mathbf{u}_1 \\ \mathbf{v}_1 \\ \vdots \\ \mathbf{u}_m \\ \mathbf{v}_m \end{bmatrix} \tag{4}$$

where m is the number of nodes used to build the finite element model. The column vector ϕ_i is the ith *mode shape*, and describes the modal displacement (u, v) at each feature point due to the ith mode, while the row vector $\mathbf{u}_i$ and $\mathbf{v}_i$ are the ith *generalized feature vectors*, which together describe the feature's location in the modal coordinate system.

Normally only the n lowest-order modes are used in forming this coordinate system, so that (1) we can compare objects with differing numbers of feature points, and (2) ensure that the feature point descriptions are insensitive to noise. Depending upon the demands of the application, we can also selectively ignore rigid-body modes, or low-order projective-like modes, or modes that are primarily local. Consequently, we can match, describe, and compare nonrigid objects in a very flexible and general manner.

Point correspondences can now be determined by comparing the two groups of generalized feature vectors. The important idea here is that the low-order vibration modes computed for two similar objects will be very similar — even in the presence of affine deformation, nonrigid deformation, local shape perturbation, noise, or small occlusions. The points that have the most similar and unambiguous coordinates are then matched, with the remaining correspondences determined by using the physical model as a smoothness constraint [31, 33]. Currently, the algorithm has the limitation that it cannot reliably match largely occluded or partial objects.

Given point correspondences between two shapes, we can then determine the deformations required to align them. An important benefit of modal matching is that the eigenmodes computed for the correspondence algorithm can also be used to describe the rigid and non-rigid deformation needed to align one object with another. Once this *modal description* has been computed, we can compare shapes simply by looking at their mode amplitudes or — since the underlying model is energy-based — we can compute and compare the amount of deformation energy needed to align an object, and use this as a similarity measure. If the strain energy required to align two feature sets is relatively small, then the objects are very similar.

4   Encoding Modal Shape Categories

We can use distance to prototypes to define a low-dimensional space for efficient shape comparison. In such a scenario, a few prototypes are selected to span the variation of shape within each category. Every shape in the database is then aligned with each of the prototypes using modal matching, and the resulting modal strain energy is stored as an n-tuple Υ_i, where n is the number of prototypes, and the subscript i signifies the ith shape in the database. Each shape in the database now has a coordinate in this "strain-energy-from-prototypes" space; shapes can be compared simply in terms of their Euclidean distance in this space.

To measure distance from a prototype to a particular shape in the database, we employ a modified strain measure [32]:

$$\delta(A, B) = \left(\frac{1}{2a} \sum_{i \in \mathcal{S}} \tilde{u}_i^2 \omega_i^2 \right)^{\frac{1}{2}}, \tag{5}$$

where the ω_i are the modal stiffnesses, $\tilde{u}_i$ are the modal parameters that described the deformation needed to align shape A with shape B, and a is the shape A's area. The square root in Eq. 5 assures segmental additivity; i.e., $\delta(A, B) + \delta(B, C) = \delta(A, C)$, if B is on the line between A and C. The area normalization term assures that the metric satistifies the symmetry axiom; i.e., $\delta(A, B) \neq \delta(B, A)$. When a support map is available, this area can be computed directly. Otherwise, the area can be approximated by computing the minimum bounding circle, or the moments, for the data.

It may be desirable to make object comparisons rotation and/or position independent. To do this, we ignore displacements in the rigid body modes, thereby disregarding differences in position and orientation. In addition, we can make our comparisons robust to noise and local shape variations by discarding higher-order modes. This modal selection technique is also useful for its compactness, since we can describe deviation from a prototype in terms of relatively few modes.

One key advantage in using such a prototype-based approach is that of *data reduction*: given the multitude of possible viewpoints and configurations for an object, we need to reduce this multitude down to a more efficient representation that requires only a few *characteristic views*. Shapes are compared in terms of their relative distances to prototypes, rather than directly compared with one another.

4.1   Spanning Categories with Prototypes

In our current image database system, a human operator selects a few example shapes that approximately span each category. Our system performance is therefore dependent on the user's ability to select an adequately diverse and sufficient set of prototypes. It may be desirable to have a system that could automatically select prototypes in an unsupervised fashion. An unsupervised learning or clustering (e.g., k-means, hiearchical clustering, iterative optimization, Bayes classifiers) could be adapted for automatically selecting the prototype shapes based on modal matching and modal strain. Using such methods introduces a tradeoff, because for many pattern classification and learning schemes it is critical that training data sets be large and diverse enough to characterize the variations within a particular shape class [9]. This shifts the pressure from a human selecting adequate prototypes to a human providing sufficient diverse and large training data set (and providing the number of categories present). Finding these clusters without prototypes would (in general) require matching all shapes to all other shapes before optimal clusters could be obtained. In either case, qualities missing from either the training data or the prototypes may be ignored or misinterpreted.

Another issue is orthogonality. It is unlikely that the selected shape prototypes will describe orthogonal axes in some idealized category space. To ensure orthogonality we have employed a method based on finding the principal components. Given a set of prototypes, we compute the strain-to-prototypes feature vector Υ_i for each of a randomly selected subset of shapes in the database along with their covariance matrix. The eigenvectors of the covariance matrix are used to transform all Υ_i into new coordinates in an orthogonalized parameter space:

$$\Upsilon_i' = \Lambda^{-\frac{1}{2}}\Psi\Upsilon_i, \tag{6}$$

where the eigenvalues are stored in the diagonal matrix Λ, and the corresponding eigenvectors form the columns of the transform matrix Ψ.

Computing distances in this new space is equivalent to computing the Mahalonobis distance in the original strain-to-prototypes space. As before, variation orthogonal to the space spanned by the training set will not be represented. This may at first seem like a limitation; however, this property can be exploited to constrain the allowable deformations to only those that are statistically most likely. Furthermore, principal components with eigenvalues less than a threshold can be discarded to gain a lower-dimensional parameter space as well as better robustness to noise [15].

The transform to the orthogonalized parameter space is done as a precomputation (prior to repeated database search). The method has been tested in experiments with a database of handtool images, as will be detailed in Section 5.

4.2   Comparison Without Direct Correspondence Computation

Modal matching for feature correspondence is required in order to recover the nonrigid deformation parameters (and associated strain energy) that align objects with prototypes. In some cases, it is possible that two shapes are so different as to have no strongly corresponding modes within some threshold. A modified Hausdorff distance method enables modal comparison without computing feature correspondences [32]. Due to its better computational complexity, efficiency can be gained if the Hausdorff distance computation precedes direct point correspondence and shape alignment. If two shapes have no modes for which this Hausdorff distance falls within the reasonable tolerance for similarity, then the shapes will be flagged as "no similar modes." Lack of modal similarity is a strong clue that the shapes are probably from different categories, and therefore, attempting correspondence and alignment would be unreasonable.

(a)   (b)   (c)   (d)   (e)

Fig. 4. The five prototype shapes used in the image database experiments: (a) Squirrel Fish, (b) Spot Fin Butterflyfish, (c) Coney, (d) Horse Eye Jack, and (e) Southern Sennet.

5   Experiments in Interactive Search

In the first set of experiments, our method is used to structure an image database of fish. The images in this experimental database were digitized from a children's field guide [16]. Currently, there are 74 images of tropical fish in the database. Each image depicts a fish from the canonical viewpoint (side view), though orientation, position, and scale vary. Each fish is unoccluded and appears on a uniform background. Images for this and other experiments are available for anonymous FTP from `cs-pub.bu.edu` in the compressed tar file `sclaroff/pictures.tar.Z`.

We used the prototype-based shape description method formulated in Sec. 4, where each shape's strain-energy distance to the prototypes was precomputed and stored for interactive search later. First, for each image, a support map and edge image was computed, a finite-support shape model was built, and then the eigenmodes were determined. For the shapes in this experiment, approximately 60-70 finite element nodes were chosen so as to be roughly-regularly spaced across the support region.

Each shape in the database is then modal matched to a set of prototype images. There were five fish prototypes as shown in Fig. 4. These prototype images were selected by a human operator so as to span the range of shapes in the database. For fish prototypes, we chose prototypes that span the range from skinny fish (Fig. 4(e)), to fat fish (4(b)), and from smooth fish (4(c)) to prickly or pointy-tailed fish (4(a,d)).

Not all shapes in the database have similar modes (similarity is measured to within a threshold). This information was quickly deterined by using the Hausdorff distance measure described in Section 4.2. Using the more efficient Hausdorff distance, we can quickly determine when modes are nowhere near being similar, and no attempt at alignment and strain energy computation is made. Such shapes are simply flagged as being "not at all similar" to a particular shape prototype.

The resulting modal strain energy was then used as a similarity metric in Photobook, an image database management system developed at the MIT Media Lab [25]. Using Photobook, the user selected the image at the upper left, and the system retrieved the remaining images sorted by strain energy (shape similarity) from left to right, top to bottom. The similarity measure is shown below each image.

Fig. 5 shows two examples of database searches conducted using distance in prototype-space in Photobook. In each search, the user selected the image shown in the upper left corner. The system retrieved the remaining images sorting them by strain energy left to right, top to bottom. The similarity measure is shown below each image. When a Banded Butterflyfish was selected (Fig. 5(a)), the system retrieved other Butterfly Fish, and other fat-bodied fish. When a Crevalle Jack was selected (Fig. 5(b)), shapes rated most similar are other open water fish with similar body and tail shapes.

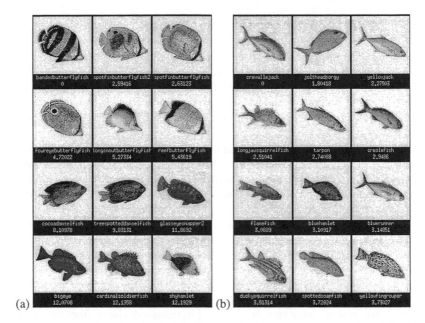

(a)

(b)

Fig. 5. Two examples of the ordering that resulted in searches for similar fish: (a) a Banded Butterfly Fish, and (b) a Crevalle Jack. The matches are shown in order, left to right, top to bottom, starting with the most similar.

In both searches, the fish judged "most similar" by the system appeared on the same page in the field guide. This type of similarity judgment performance is an encouraging result, since fish appearing under the same heading are nearly always in the same taxonomic category, *e.g.*, Groupers, Jacks, Snappers, Porgies, Squirrelfishes, Butterflyfishes, Hamlets, or Damselfishes. In the cases where fish listed under the same heading are not in the same taxonomic category it is because they were grouped together due to some shape similarity, *e.g.*, "Slim-bodied fishes" is the heading under which the Trumetfish, Bluespotted Cornetfish, Balao, Needlefish, Ballyhoo, and Houndfish appear.

Database queries like those just described were performed for each of the 72 fish images in the database. Overall, another fish under the same heading in the field guide was judged as most similar 71% of the time. To gain enhanced performance in capturing animal taxonomies, we suspect that modal matching would need to be part of a combined system that includes local shape features and color information.

For comparison, the same 72 queries were performed using moment invariants based on second- and third-order moments [10]. To gain better performance, the covariance matrix for the seven-dimensional feature vectors was computed and shapes where ordered in terms of their Mahalonobis distances to the selected shape. In this case another fish under the same heading in the field guide was judged as most similar 57% of the time.

5.1   Evaluating Retrieval Accuracy using AVRR

Thus far retrieval performance has been measured in terms of the percentage of times that a shape in the same category is retrieved as "most similar" over a number of trials. However, Photobook [25], and other query by example (QBE) image database systems (e.g., QBIC [14], Virage [17], Jacob [4]) provide a list of possible matches ordered in terms of their similarity distance from the example image. This is in contrast to retrieval systems based on "exact match."

In "exact match" systems the standard measures of precision and recall can be employed [29]. However, systems that offer a list of items sorted by similarity do not fall under the rubric of exact matching. We need a performance measure that embodies the positions in which target items appear in the retrieval. To evaluate retrieval performance in such situations, a *normalized recall* metric can be employed [13].

The normalized recall metric can be summarized as follows. Assume that the number of categories, shapes per category, and category membership for each shape are known in advance. Ideally, if there were a total of n items of the same category in the database, then these n items would appear in the first n positions for a similarity-based retrieval. It is emphasized that ordering of the items within the first these n positions is not as crucial; what matters most is that all n items from the category appear first in the retrieval. Retrieval accuracy must be measured in terms a deviation from the ideal average rank of relevant (IAVRR) items. The IAVRR is defined as the ideal average rank, when all relevant items are ranked at the top. For a database that contains n shapes in each category IAVRR $= \frac{n}{2}$.

In general, the database will contain categories of different sizes. We define a general equation for the ideal average rank as

$$\text{IAVRR} = \frac{1}{m} \sum_{i=1}^{c} \frac{n_i{}^2}{2}, \qquad (7)$$

where m is the total number of shapes in the database, c is the number of categories, and n_i is the number of shapes in the ith category.

Normalized recall is measured by comparing the IAVRR with the average rank of all relevant items (AVRR) for each retrieval. The AVRR is computed based on the actual ordered ranking of n_i shapes in a particular category for each database retrieval. Thus the ratio of AVRR to IAVRR can be used to give a measure of average retrieval accuracy over a number of experimental trials. Perfect performance would yield a ratio AVRR/IAVRR $= 1$.

Using this measure, the retrieval accuracy was evaluated for the previously described experiments with the fish image database in Photobook. The IAVRR for this database was 3.4. In other words, the average category contained approximately seven fish. Retrievals were computed for each 72 fish in the database. For modal matching, the AVRR = 8.9 and the ratio of AVRR/IAVRR = 2.6. In contrast, the AVRR was 17.7 and AVRR/IAVRR = 5.2 when moment invariants were used.

Fig. 6. Seven example images from the hand tools experimental image database. Because some tools were made of plastic, they could be bent in various ways. Tools appeared in a number of orientations and/or scales, with varying lighting.

5.2   Tool Image Database

In a second set of image database experiments we used a database of 63 grayscale images of hand tools. There were 21 images from each of three tool categories: wrenches, hammers, and crescent wrenches. The tools were placed on a uniform background so that a simple fuzzy c-Means clustering technique could be used for image segmentation [21]. Figure 6 shows example images taken from this database. Because some tools were made of plastic, they could be bent in various ways. Further, tools appeared in a number of orientations and/or scales, with varying lighting.

For each image, approximately 70-80 finite element nodes were chosen so as to be roughly-regularly spaced across the support region. Mode amplitudes for the first 32 modes were recovered and used to warp each prototype onto the other tools. Comparisons were made translation and rotation invariant by ignoring displacements in the rigid body modes. Comparisons were made scale invariant by recovering the scale factor before nonrigidly warping the shape to each prototype [33].

Matching experiments were then conducted using the coordinates produced via the orthogonalization procedure in Section 4. Database queries were performed for each of the 63 tool images in the database. Overall, another tool from the same category was judged as most similar 94% of the time, compared with 86% for the moments-based method.

Normalized recall experiments were also conducted. The IAVRR for this database is 10.5. For orthogonalized strain-from-prototypes, the AVRR was 18.2 and the resulting ratio AVRR/IAVRR = 1.7. The moments-based method produced AVRR = 23.1 and AVRR/IAVRR = 2.2. As another point of comparison, performance for shape-based search in QBIC was reported to have a AVRR/IAVRR ratio of 1.8 for a database of 777 airplane silhouettes coarsely categorized by viewpoint and overall shape [13].

5.3   Number of Prototypes and Retrieval Accuracy

Using the tool image database, experiments were conducted to evaluate retrieval accuracy as a function of the number of prototypes used. Multiple trials were conducted using between one and ten prototypes. These n prototypes were selected at random (uniformly distributed), in 1000 trials for each n. Average matching performance was evaluated using the coordinates produced via the orthogonalization procedure in Section 4. In each trial, database queries were performed for each of the 63 tool images in the database.

Figures 7 and 8 show the resulting performance curves. The graph in Fig. 7 shows how the number of prototypes affects the average performance for database queries

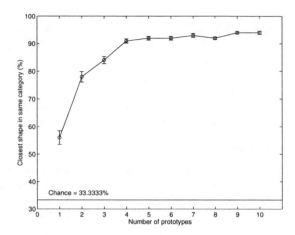

Fig. 7. Number of prototypes vs. average retrieval accuracy for the handtool database.

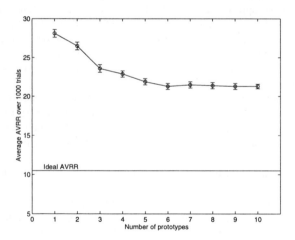

Fig. 8. Number of prototypes vs. average rank (AVRR) for the handtool database.

performed for each of the 63 tool images in the database. With only one prototype, another tool from the same category was judged as most similar 56% of the time. As the number of prototypes reached four, performance began to level off at approximately 90%.

The graph in Fig. 8 shows how the number of prototypes affects the average AVRR for retrieval of the 21 handtools in the same tool category. With only one prototype, the AVRR averaged 28.1. The average performance leveled out at 5 prototypes where AVRR = 21.9. The ideal AVRR would be 10.5. The ratio AVRR/IAVRR is greater than two.

6 Conclusion

We described a new image database search method that uses strain energy from deformable prototypes to encode shape categories. Retrieval accuracy of this approach has been demonstrated in a series of experiments with image databases of animals scanned from children's field guides and of deformable hand tools digitized via a video camera. In these experiments, the method performed consistently better than search on moment invariants. Experiments were also conducted to evaluate retrieval accuracy as a function of the number of prototypes used. Relatively few prototypes were needed to produce stable performance when a new orthogonalization scheme was employed.

References

1. K. Bathe. *Finite Element Procedures in Engineering Analysis.* Prentice-Hall, 1982.
2. A. Blake, R. Curwen, and A. Zisserman. A framework for spatiotemporal control in the tracking of visual contours. *International Journal of Computer Vision*, 11(2):127–146, 1993.
3. F. Bookstein. Principal warps: Thin-plate splines and the decomposition of deformations. *IEEE Trans. on Pattern Analysis and Machine Intelligence*, 11(6):567–585, June 1989.
4. M. La Cascia and E. Ardizzone. Jacob: Just a content-based query system for video databases. In *Proc. ICASSP*, Atlanta, 1996.
5. Z. Chen and S. Y. Ho. Computer vision for robust 3D aircraft recognition with fast library search. *Pattern Recognition*, 24(5):375–390, 1991.
6. I. Cohen, N. Ayache, and P. Sulger. Tracking points on deformable objects. In *Proc. European Conference on Computer Vision*, Santa Margherita Ligure, Italy, May 1992.
7. T. Cootes, D. Cooper, C. Taylor, and J. Graham. Trainable method of parametric shape description. *Image and Vision Computing*, 10(5):289–294, June 1992.
8. A. DelBimbo and P. Pala. Visual image retrieval by elastic matching of user sketches. *IEEE Trans. on Pattern Analysis and Machine Intelligence*, 19(2):121–132, February 1997.
9. R. O. Duda and P. E. Hart. *Pattern Recognition and Scene Analysis.* John Wiley, New York, 1973.
10. S. Dudani, K. Breeding, and R. McGhee. Aircraft identification by moment invariants. *IEEE Trans. Computers*, 26(1):39–47, 1977.
11. J. Duncan, R. Owen, L. Staib, and P. Anandan. Measurement of non-rigid motion using contour shape descriptors. In *Proc. CVPR*, pages 318–324, 1991.
12. S. Edelman. Representation, similarity, and chorus of prototypes. *Minds and Machines*, 5:45–68, 1995.
13. C. Faloutsos, R. Barber, M. Flickner, J. Hafner, W. Niblack, D. Petkovic, and W. Equitz. Efficient and effective querying by image content. *Journal of Intelligent Information Systems*, 3:231–262, 1994.
14. M. Flickner, H. Sawhney, W. Niblack, J. Ashley, Q. Huang, D. Dom, M. Gorkani, J. Hafner, D. Lee, D. Petkovic, D. Steele, and P. Yanker. Query by image and video content: The qbic system. *IEEE Computer*, pages 23–30, September 1995.
15. K. Fukunaga and W. Koontz. Application of the karhunen-loeve expansion to feature selection and ordering. *IEEE Trans. Communications*, 19(4), 1970.
16. I. Greenberg. *Guide to Corals and Fishes of Florida, th Bahamas and the Caribbean.* Seahawk Press, Miami, Florida, 1977.
17. A. Gupta. Visual information retrieval technology: A virage perspective. Technical Report Revision 3a, Virage Inc., 177 Bovet Road, Suite 540, San Mateo, CA 94403, 1996.

18. M. A. Ireton and C. S. Xydeas. Classification of shape for content retrieval of images in a multimedia database. In *Proc. Sixth International Conference on Digital Processing of Signals in Communications*, pages 111–116, Loughborough, UK, September 1990.

19. H. V. Jagadish. A retrieval technique for similar shapes. In *Proc. International Conference on Management of Data, ACM SIGMOD 91*, pages 208–217, Denver, CO, May 1991.

20. M. Kass, A. Witkin, and D. Terzopoulos. Snakes: Active contour models. *International Journal of Computer Vision*, 1:321–331, 1987.

21. Young Won Lim and Sang Uk Lee. On the color image segmentation algorithm based on the thresholding and the fuzzy c-means techniques. *Pattern Recognition*, 23(9):935–952, 1990.

22. R. Mehrotra and W. I. Grosky. Shape matching utilizing indexed hypotheses generation and testing. *IEEE Transactions of Robotics and Automation*, 5(1):70–77, 1989.

23. F. Mokhatarian, S. Abbasi, and J. Kittler. Robst and efficient shape indexing through curvature scale space. In *Proc. of BMVC*, 1996.

24. W. Niblack, R. Barber, W. Equitz, M. Flickner, E. Glasman, D. Petkovic, and P. Yanker. The QBIC project: Querying images by content using color, texture, and shape. In *Proc. SPIE Conf. on Storage and Retrieval of Image and Video Databases*, volume 1908, February 1993.

25. A. Pentland, R. Picard, and S. Sclaroff. Photobook: Tools for content-based manipulation of image databases. *International Journal of Computer Vision*, 18(3):233–254, June 1996.

26. A. Pentland and S. Sclaroff. Closed-form solutions for physically-based shape modeling and recognition. *IEEE Trans. on Pattern Analysis and Machine Intelligence*, 13(7):715–729, July 1991.

27. T. Poggio and F. Girosi. A theory of networks for approximation and learning. Technical Report A.I. Memo No. 1140, Artificial Intelligence Lab, MIT, Cambridge, MA, July 1989.

28. E. Rosch. Cognitive representations of semantic categories. *Journal of Experimental Psychology: General*, 104:193–233, 1975.

29. G. Salton and M. J. McGill. *Introduction to Modern Information Retrieval*. McGraw-Hill, 1989.

30. B. Scassellati, S. Alexopoulos, and M. Flickner. Retrieving images by 2D shape: comparison of computation methods with human perceptual judgements. In *Proc. SPIE Conf. on Storage and Retrieval of Image and Video Databases II*, San Jose, CA, February 1994.

31. S. Sclaroff. *Modal Matching: A Method for Describing, Comparing, and Manipulating Digital Signals*. PhD thesis, MIT Media Lab, January 1995.

32. S. Sclaroff. Deformable prototypes for encoding shape categories in image databases. *Pattern Recognition*, 30(4), 1997.

33. S. Sclaroff and A. Pentland. Modal Matching for Correspondence and Recognition. *IEEE Trans. on Pattern Analysis and Machine Intelligence*, 17(6):545–561, 1995.

34. S. Ullman and R. Basri. Recognition by linear combinations of models. *IEEE Trans. on Pattern Analysis and Machine Intelligence*, 13(10):992–1006, 1991.

35. A. Yuille, D. Cohen, and P. Hallinan. Feature extraction from faces using deformable templates. In *Proc. CVPR*, pages 104–109, San Diego, 1989.

A Modified Fourier Descriptor for Shape Matching in MARS

Yong Rui, Alfred C. She, and Thomas S. Huang [*]

Image Formation and Processing Lab, Beckman Institute
University of Illinois at Urbana-Champaign
Urbana, IL 61801, USA
E-mail: yrui@ifp.uiuc.edu, a-she@uiuc.edu, huang@ifp.uiuc.edu

Abstract. We propose a Modified Fourier Descriptor and a new distance measure for describing and comparing closed planar curves. Our method accounts for *spatial discretization* of shapes, an issue seldom mentioned, much less addressed in the literature.

The motivating application is shape matching in the Multimedia Analysis and Retrieval System (MARS), our content-based image retrieval system. The application requires a compact and reliable representation of object boundaries in the image database, and a similarity measure that can be computed in real time. We test our shape matching method on a set of Roman characters. Results indicate that our method is a feasible solution for real time shape comparison.

1 Introduction

Content-based retrieval (CBR) has gained considerable attention recently [1, 2, 3, 4, 5]. The most commonly researched image features used in retrieval are color, texture, and shape. Color and texture features are explored in [1, 2, 3, 4, 5]. Although shape features have also been studied[1, 5], it is still difficult to obtain a good solution.

To address the challenging issues involved in CBR, the Multimedia Analysis and Retrieval System (MARS) project was started at the University of Illinois [2, 6, 7, 8, 9, 10]. MARS supports user queries based on global color, texture, and shape, as well as queries on the spatial layout of color and texture. The on-line demo for MARS is http://jadzia.ifp.uiuc.edu:8000. MARS uses several shape matching methods, including Modified Fourier Descriptors (MFD), the proposed method presented in this paper. (For information on shape matching methods in MARS other than MFD, see [10], which describes fast algorithms we developed for Chamfer matching and Hausdorff matching. The reference also describes a relevance feedback mechanism that helps the user find the matching method that best fits his/her individual perception of shape feature.)

---

[*] This work was supported by the NSF/DARPA/NASA Digital Library Initiative under Cooperative Agreement No. 94-11318.

In general, a CBR system is useful only if it can retrieve acceptable matches in real time. This requires the choice of a suitable set of image features, a method for correctly extracting them, and a feature distance measure that can be computed in real time.

Our focus is on shape matching. We propose that a useful shape representation should satisfy the following four conditions:

1. *Robustness to Transformation* – the representation must be invariant to translation, rotation, and scaling of shapes, as well as the starting point used in defining the boundary sequence.

2. *Robustness to Noise* – shape boundaries often contain local irregularities due to image noise. More importantly, *spatial discretization* introduces distortion along the entire boundary. The representation must be robust to these types of noise.

3. *Feature Extraction Efficiency* – feature vectors should be computed efficiently.

4. *Feature Matching Efficiency* – since matching is done on-line, the distance measure must require a *very* small computational cost.

Some simple shape features are the perimeter, area, number of holes, eccentricity, symmetry, etc. Although these features are easy to compute, they usually result in too many false positives to be useful in a CBR system, thus they are excluded from our discussion.

Advanced methods that can represent more complex shapes fall into two categories. Region-based methods are the first category. A typical representative is the Moment-Invariants Method (MIM) [11]. The disadvantage of the MIM is its high computational cost (features are computed using the *entire* region, including interior pixels), and low discriminatory power. The descriptor tends to return too many false positives.

Boundary-based methods are the second category, and include the Turning Angle Method (TAM) [12] and Fourier Descriptors (FD) [13, 14]. These methods provide a much more complete description of shape than MIM; however, they are sensitive to the starting point of the shape boundary. They can discount the effect of the starting point only by solving a non-linear optimization problem, which is not feasible in a real-time CBR system. Also, to the extent of our knowledge, little research has been done on how to deal with the problem of *spatial discretization* when using these methods. We discuss this in detail in section 4.

We propose the Modified Fourier Descriptor (MFD), which satisfies our four conditions above. The FD method is the most closely related work, so we give a brief review of it in section 2. We discuss the proposed MFD in section 3. Comparisons between MFD and existing methods are given in section 4. Experimental results and conclusions are in sections 4 and 5, respectively.

List of symbols:

- N_V: number of vertices of a polygon;
- N_B: number of boundary points of a shape;
- N_C: number of FD coefficients used in shape reconstruction;
- V_i: the ith vertex of a polygon;
- N_{dense}: number of *dense* samples used in resampling in the MFD method;
- N_{unif}: number of *uniformly* spaced samples used in MFD method;
- α, β, γ: planar curves (shape boundaries).

2 Fourier Descriptors

There are two commonly known FD's, described in [13] and [14], which we denote as "FD1" and "FD2", respectively. FD1 has low efficiency in reconstructing the shape, so we discuss FD2 only.

Let γ be a clockwise-oriented simple closed planar curve with representation $z(l) = [x(l), y(l)]$, where l is the arc length along γ. A point moving along the boundary generates the complex function $u(l) = x(l) + jy(l)$. FD2 is defined as:

$$a_n = \frac{1}{L\left(\frac{2\pi n}{L}\right)} \sum_{k=1}^{N_V} (b_{k-1} - b_k) e^{-j\left(\frac{2\pi n l_k}{L}\right)} \tag{1}$$

where L is the total length of γ; $l_k = \sum_{i=1}^{k} |V_i - V_{i-1}|$ (for $k > 0$ and $l_0 = 0$); and $b_k = \frac{V_{k+1} - V_k}{|V_{k+1} - V_k|}$.

The distance metric is defined as the Euclidean distance in FD coefficient space. Let $\{a_n\}$ and $\{b_n\}$ denote the FD's of two curves α and β, respectively, and assume only N_C harmonics are used; the distance metric

$$d(\alpha, \beta) = \sqrt{\sum_{n=-N_C}^{N_C} |a_n - b_n|^2} \tag{2}$$

Now assume β is identical to α except for a translation, scale, and rotation, and that the curve is defined using a different starting point. Ideally, the distance between the two shapes should be zero. Translation is easily dealt with by omitting a_0 and b_0 when taking the sum in (2).

However, to account for the effects of scale (s), rotation (ϕ), and starting point (p), we must minimize the distance metric

$$d^*(\alpha, \beta) = \min_{s, \phi, p} \sum_{n=-M, n \neq 0}^{M} \left| a_n - s e^{j(np+\phi)} b_n \right|^2 \tag{3}$$

over the parameters (s, ϕ, p). This is a computationally expensive optimization problem and makes FD2 impractical for shape matching in a real-time CBR system, especially when the image database is large. Similarly, TAM has the same disadvantage.

3   Proposed Method – A Modified Fourier Descriptor

A point moving along the shape boundary generates a complex sequence (4-neighbor chain code):

$$z(n) = x(n) + jy(n), \quad n = 0, ..., N_B - 1 \tag{4}$$

where $x(n)$ and $y(n)$ are the x and y coordinates of the nth boundary points. The MFD is defined as the Discrete Fourier Transform (DFT) of $z(n)$:

$$Z(k) = \sum_{n=0}^{N_B-1} z(n)e^{-j\frac{2\pi nk}{N_B}} = M(k)e^{j\theta(k)} \tag{5}$$

where $k = 0, ..., N_B - 1$.

Next, we examine the properties of MFD and propose a distance measure which is both reliable and easy to compute.

Let $z'(n)$ be a boundary sequence obtained from $z(n)$: $z'(n)$ is $z(n)$ translated by z_t, rotated by ϕ, and scaled by α, with the starting point shifted by l. We know that $Z(k)$, for $k \neq 0$, is invariant to translation. Next, we examine rotation, scale, and starting point.

Explicitly, $z'(n)$ is related to $z(n)$ by

$$z'(n) = \alpha z(n - l)e^{j\phi} \tag{6}$$

The corresponding MFD of $z'(n)$ is

$$\begin{aligned}
Z'(k) &= \sum_{n=0}^{N_B-1} z'(n)e^{-j\frac{2\pi nk}{N_B}} \\
&= \sum_{n=0}^{N_B-1} \alpha z(n - l)e^{j\phi}e^{-j\frac{2\pi nk}{N_B}} \\
&= \alpha e^{j\phi} \sum_{n=0}^{N_B-1} z(n - l)e^{-j\frac{2\pi nk}{N_B}}
\end{aligned} \tag{7}$$

Setting $m = n - l$, we get

$$\begin{aligned}
Z'(k) &= \alpha e^{j\phi} \sum_{m=-l}^{N_B-l-1} z(m)e^{-j\frac{2\pi mk}{N_B}} e^{-j\frac{2\pi lk}{N_B}} \\
&= \alpha e^{-j(\phi+\frac{2\pi lk}{N})} Z(k) \\
&= M'(k)e^{j\theta'(k)}
\end{aligned} \tag{8}$$

where

$$M'(k) = \alpha M(k) \tag{9}$$

$$\theta'(k) = \phi + \theta(k) - \frac{2\pi lk}{N_B} \tag{10}$$

$$\phi = \theta_0 - \theta'_0; \tag{11}$$

where θ_0 and θ_0' are the orientations of the major axes of the two shapes, defined as

$$\theta_0 = \frac{1}{2} \tan^{-1} \left(\frac{2cm_{11}}{cm_{20} - cm_{02}} \right) \tag{12}$$

where cm_{ij} is the $(i,j)^{\text{th}}$ central moment of the shape.

The magnitude and phase angle of FD coefficients of $z'(n)$ are related to those of $z(n)$ in the way specified in (9) and (10). Based on these relations, we construct two sequences

$$ratio(k) = \frac{M'(k)}{M(k)}; \tag{13}$$

$$shift(k) = \frac{\theta(k) - \theta'(k) + \phi}{k}; \tag{14}$$

$$k = -N_C, ..., N_C, k \neq 0. \tag{15}$$

It is easy to see that if $z'(n)$ is indeed a transformed version of $z(n)$, then the two sequences above (eqs. (13)(14)) would both be constant in k. Specifically, $ratio(k) = \alpha$ and $shift(k) = 0$ for all k. On the other hand, if $z'(n)$ is completely different from $z(n)$, then $ratio$ and $shift$ will both have high variance with respect to the frequency index k. Based on this observation, the standard deviation is a good measure of the difference between two shapes. The distance measure for magnitude (D_m) and phase angle (D_p) are defined as

$$D_m = \sigma[ratio]$$
$$D_p = \sigma[shift] \tag{16}$$

where σ denotes standard deviation.

The overall distance measure is defined as the weighted sum of D_m and D_p:

$$Dist_{MFD} = w_m D_m + w_p D_p \tag{17}$$

where w_m and w_p are weighting constants. Empirically, we find that $w_m = 0.9$ and $w_p = 0.1$ gives good results for most of the images we tested.

Note that the proposed distance measure is invariant to translation, rotation, scale, and starting point, making it suitable for on-line matching in a CBR system.

4 Comparisons with the Existing Methods

We compare the MFD with FD1 and FD2 in terms of both computational complexity and practical robustness.

4.1 Computational Complexity

We mentioned in section 1 that a good shape representation method in the CBR system should be efficient in both feature extraction and feature matching, with much more emphasis on the latter. This is obvious since a CBR system typically does matching on-line, and may support multiple user queries simultaneously.

Tables 1 and 2 show the computation operation counts for MFD, FD1, and FD2 in feature extraction and feature matching, respectively. A subtract is counted as an add; a divide is counted as a multiply; absolute value is counted as 2 adds; math library functions (e.g., exponential, sine, square root) are counted as 16 multiplies.

We can see that although MFD requires a little bit more computation during feature extraction, it is much faster during feature matching. This is because the MFD distance measure is *intrinsically* invariant to translation, rotation, scale, and starting point. This is a very important advantage for the MFD since feature extraction is done off-line while matching is done on-line.

Table 1. Operation counts for feature extraction

	FD1	FD2	MFD
Adds	$O(N_V^2)$	$O(N_V^2)$	$O(N_B \log_2 N_B)$
Mults	$O(N_V)$	$O(N_V)$	$O(N_B \log_2 N_B)$

Table 2. Operation counts for feature matching

	FD1	FD2	MFD
Adds	$O(N_C^3)$	$Huge^*$	$O(N_C)$
Mults	$O(N_C^3)$	$Huge^*$	$O(N_C)$

$Huge^*$: beyond comparison since it requires finding all zeros of a trigonometric polynomial of degree N_c.

4.2   Robustness: Practice and Theory

Regardless of the different computational costs, FD1, FD2 and MFD are all valid shape representations, at least theoretically. But to be of practical use, a representation must be tested using the following procedure:

1. Use a camera to take two images of the same physical object, but at different scales, rotations, and translations.
2. Segment the two input images to obtain two shape boundaries, with arbitrary starting point.
3. Compare the features obtained from the each image.
4. If the match is good, conclude that the method is valid.

Note that the segmentation occurs *after* the transformation. This is the actual situation when comparing shapes from two different images. If we use this testing procedure, none of the existing methods give good results, including our proposed MFD method. This is because the boundaries used in these methods are sensitive to *discretization noise*. The discretization noise in many cases changes the boundary enough such that the Fourier coefficients become significantly different. Both FD1 and FD2 suffer from this problem.

The boundary extraction method of FD1 (described in [15]) is sensitive to noise. If we rotate the input image, both the number of vertices and the lengths between vertices will change. No boundary extraction method was mentioned in FD2. However, since FD1 was cited as a main reference in FD2, it most likely used the same boundary extraction method, thus, suffering from the same problem.

Since MFD uses the 4-neighbor chain code, it also suffers from discretization noise. A simple example illustrates this point (see Figure 1). We discretize the triangle using two different orientations. Note that the upper figure has *staircase effect* in edge c while the lower figure has *staircase effect* in edges a and b. The Fourier transform magnitudes, as well as $ratio(k)$ (defined in section 3) are shown in Figure 2. Note that the plot of $ratio(k)$ shows a large variance, even though the DFT coefficients were obtained from the *same* object.

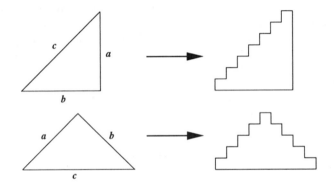

Fig. 1. Effect of spatial discretization on the chain code.

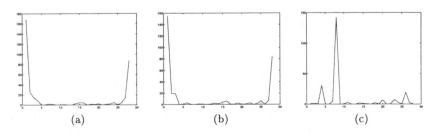

Fig. 2. (a) DFT magnitude of the upper triangle in Fig. 1; (b) DFT magnitude of the lower triangle in Fig. 1; (c) $ratio(k)$ vs. k.

We want to solve this *spatial discretization* problem while keeping the invariance properties of the MFD; we propose the following procedure:

1. Compute the DFT of the shape boundary $z(n)$, $Z(k)$, using (5);
2. Use the low frequency $[-N_C, +N_C]$ coefficients to reconstruct dense but possibly non-uniform samples $z_{dense}(n)$ of the original boundary:

$$z_{dense}(n) = \sum_{k=-N_C}^{N_C} Z(k)e^{-j\frac{2\pi nk}{N_B}}, \tag{18}$$

$$n = 0, ..., N_{dense} - 1$$

3. Use interpolation to trace the dense samples $z_{dense}(n)$ and construct uniform samples $z_{unif}(n)$, n = 0, ..., N_{unif}. The uniform samples $z_{unif}(n)$ are *uniformly* spaced on the boundary in terms of arc length;
4. Compute the DFT of $z_{unif}(n)$ to obtain coefficients $Z_{unif}(k)$, $k = -N_C, ..., N_C$.

In Figure 3, we have the two triangles re-sampled using the procedure described above. Note that the re-sampled points match more closely to the points that would have been sampled from the original (continuous) triangle.

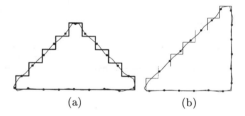

(a)   (b)

Fig. 3. (a) Uniform samples of the upper triangle in Fig. 1; (b) uniform samples of the lower triangle in Fig. 1.

5   Experimental Results

We chose to use a set of Roman characters (as opposed to object outlines from the MARS database) to evaluate the proposed method since Roman characters are more commonly available. This will allow other researchers to compare their methods to MFD more easily.

Our test images were created by printing the letters {m, n, u, h, l, t, f} on a laser printer and digitizing the printouts using a scanner. Letters were printed using 256 pt. Helvetica font. To test the robustness of the MFD method, we intentionally misaligned the letters slightly on the scanner, which introduced some boundary noise (Figure 4a).

We tested three aspects of our method: 1. its sensitivity to the choice of parameters N_C, N_{dense}, and N_{unif}, 2. its ability to discriminate between shapes, and 3. its robustness to image transformations.

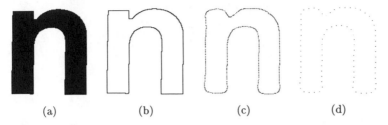

(a)   (b)   (c)   (d)

Fig. 4. (a) Original image; (b) Extracted boundary; (c) Low frequency reconstruction; (d) Uniform re-sampling.

Figure 4b shows the boundary extracted from the original image of the letter; Figure 4c shows the dense samples reconstructed using 40 MFD coefficients ($N_C = 20$); Figure 4d is the set of uniform samples obtained from Figure 4c.

We can see from Figure 4d that using the first 20 frequencies captures most of information contained in the boundary while reducing segmentation noise.

5.1 Sensitivity to choice of parameters

The letters "n" and "f" are used in the following experiments. "n vs. n" denotes the distance between "n" and a rotated version of "n", where the rotation angle is 27 degrees. "n vs. f" denotes the distance between an upright "n" and an upright "f".

1. *Sensitivity to N_C*

Table 3 shows Distance vs. N_C, where we can see that the MFD is very robust to N_C. We have a wide range to choose N_C from – it can range from 5 to 40 without significantly affecting the matching results for the images we used.

Table 3. Distance vs. N_C

N_C	10	15	20	25	30	35
n vs. n	0.095	0.090	0.059	0.051	0.051	0.051
n vs. f	1.984	1.806	1.930	1.713	1.907	1.705

2. *Sensitivity to N_{dense}*

N_{dense} is defined as

$$N_{dense} = \frac{boundary\ length}{N_{step}} \tag{19}$$

where N_{step} is the sampling interval. The finer the interval, the larger the number of dense samples. From Table 4 we see that the distance is almost constant for a wide range of N_{step}.

Table 4. Distance vs. N_{step}

N_{step}	2	4	6	8	10	12	14
n vs. n	0.059	0.059	0.059	0.059	0.059	0.059	0.060
n vs. f	1.912	1.912	1.913	1.912	1.931	1.932	1.932

3. Sensitivity to N_{unif}

N_{unif} is defined as

$$N_{unif} = (2N_C + 1)multi \qquad (20)$$

where *multi* makes N_{unif} a multiple of the number of total frequencies used. *multi* should be at least 1, which corresponds the Nyquist frequency. (see Table 5).

Table 5. Distance vs. *multi*

multi	1	2	3	4	5	6
n vs. n	0.075	0.059	0.060	0.059	0.059	0.060
n vs. f	1.705	1.912	1.911	1.911	1.911	1.911

5.2 Discriminatory ability

Tables 6-8 show the ability of MFD to discriminate between shapes. Table 6 shows the MFD distances between the shapes of each letter from the original set. This gives us baseline values on the discriminatory ability of the MFD. The original set is the set of images obtained using scanner as mentioned earlier. Table

Table 6. Distances between letters – original set.

	m	n	u	h	l·	t	f
m	0.000	1.802	1.809	1.625	0.893	1.802	1.512
n	1.802	0.000	0.075	1.439	1.026	1.729	1.907
u	1.809	0.075	0.000	1.483	0.991	1.747	1.852
h	1.625	1.439	1.483	0.000	1.081	1.583	1.557
l	0.893	1.026	0.991	1.081	0.000	1.109	1.077
t	1.802	1.729	1.747	1.583	1.109	0.000	1.260
f	1.512	1.907	1.852	1.557	1.077	1.260	0.000

7 shows the MFD distances between letters from the original set and a rotated set. The rotated set was obtained by taking the original set and synthetically rotating each image by 27 degrees (we avoided multiples of 90 degrees since they give the exact same results as in Table 6). Rotations were done using the ImageMagick software package (©1995 E. I. du Pont de Nemours and Company).

Table 7. Distances between original and rotated letters.

	m	n	u	h	l	t	f
m	0.085	1.815	1.887	1.550	0.889	1.605	1.545
n	1.795	0.079	0.133	1.448	1.035	1.860	1.736
u	1.805	0.139	0.102	1.492	0.999	1.905	1.735
h	1.619	1.405	1.543	0.068	1.094	1.493	1.603
l	0.837	1.154	1.034	1.077	0.016	1.109	1.070
t	1.808	1.757	1.760	1.586	1.112	0.058	1.262
f	1.512	1.911	1.923	1.571	1.085	1.244	0.040

Table 8 shows the MFD distances between the original set and a scaled set of images. The scaled set was obtained by scaling the original images by 210%. Scaling was done using the "xv" program (by John Bradley). As expected, "n"

Table 8. Distances between original and scaled letters.

	m	n	u	h	l	t	f
m	0.025	1.873	1.848	2.081	1.762	1.674	1.602
n	1.797	0.023	0.083	1.441	2.342	1.847	1.808
u	1.804	0.080	0.023	1.487	2.374	1.685	1.806
h	1.621	1.324	1.333	0.022	2.017	1.582	1.601
l	0.895	1.028	0.991	1.080	0.012	1.112	1.088
t	1.810	1.730	1.745	1.582	1.382	0.025	1.267
f	1.518	1.911	1.884	1.574	1.232	0.891	0.034

and "u" match quite closely, since they are only rotated versions of each other. "h" matches "n" and "u" better than the other letters. We see that discretization (after rotation and scaling) introduces some noise and thus the distances between the same letters are not exactly zero (Tables 7, 8) as is the case in Table 6. But the results indicate that the MFD deals with the discretization effects fairly well. Distances between different letters are always much larger (10 to 100 times) than those between the same letter.

5.3   Robustness to transformation

– Translation
  No discretization noise involved. Zero error.

– Rotation
  We plot the distance vs. rotation angle in Figure 5a. The upper curve is the distance between "f" and rotated versions of "n". The lower curve is the distance between "n" and its rotated version. The rotation step is five degrees.

Note how discretization noise affects the distance (the curves are not exactly constant, but have small ripples). However, even if the noise changes each distance a small amount, the overall robustness of the MFD distance is still very good – the average magnitude of the upper curve is about 20 times that of the lower curve.

– Scale
  We plot distance vs. scale factor in Figure 5b. The upper curve is the distance between "f" and scaled versions of "n" (from 30% to 210%, with a step size of 30%). The lower curve is the distance between "n" and scaled versions of "n". The magnitude difference is also about a factor of 20, indicating that the MFD is scale invariant.

– Starting point
  No discretization noise involved. Zero error.

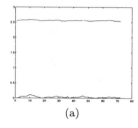   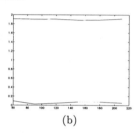

(a)   (b)

Fig. 5. "n vs. n" and "n vs. f" for various (a) rotation angles; (b) scale factors

6   Conclusions

We presented a new method of shape representation and its distance measure. We compared it with existing FD methods in terms of both computational cost and practical robustness. The main features of our method are:

1. The method is in variant to translation, rotation, scale, and starting point.

2. The method takes into account spatial discretization.

3. The computational cost for feature extraction is low, and for feature matching the cost is extremely low, making the method suitable for real-time multi-user CBR systems.

4. The representation is able to describe complex shapes while remaining relatively compact, reducing the disk space and memory required in the CBR system.

References

1. C. Faloutsos, "Efficient and effective querying by image content," tech. rep., IBM Research Report, 1993.
2. T. S. Huang, S. Mehrotra, and K. Ramchandran, "Multimedia analysis and retrieval system (MARS) project," in *Proc of 33rd Annual Clinic on Library Application of Data Processing - Digital Image Access and Retrieval*, 1996.
3. J. R. Smith and S.-F. Chang, "Tools and techniques for color image retrieval," in *IS & T/SPIE proceedings Vol.2670, Storage & Retrieval for Image and Video Databases IV*.
4. J. R. Bach, C. Fuller, A. Gupta, A. Hampapur, B. Horowitz, R. Humphrey, R. Jain, and C. fe Shu, "The virage image search engine: An open framework for image management," in *SPIE Storage and Retrieval for Still Image and Video Databases IV*.
5. H.-J. Zhang, "Retrieval and browsing: An integrated and content-based solution," in *ACM Multimedia'95*.
6. S. Mehrotra, Y. Rui, M. Ortega-B., and T. S. Huang, "Supporting content-based queries over images in MARS," in *Proc. of IEEE Int. Conf. on Multimedia Computing and Systems*, 1997.
7. Y. Rui, A. C. She, and T. S. Huang, "Automated shape segmentation using attraction-based grouping in spatial-color-texture space," in *Proc. IEEE Int. Conf. on Image Proc.*, 1996.
8. Y. Rui, S. M. Thomas S. Huang, and M. Ortega, "A relevance feedback architecutre in content-based multimedia information retrieval systems," in *Proc of IEEE Workshop on Content-based Access of Image and Vidco Libraries (to appear)*, 1997.
9. Y. Rui, T. S. Huang, and S. Mehrotra, "Content-based image retrieval with relevance feedback in MARS," in *(submitted to) Int. Conf. Image Processing*, 1997.
10. Y. Rui, T. S. Huang, S. Mehrotra, and M. Ortega, "Automatic matching tool selection using relevance feedback in MARS," in *(submitted to) Inter. Conf. on Visual Information Retrieval*, 1997.
11. M. K. Hu, *Visual Pattern Recognition by Moment Invariants, Computer Methods in Image Analysis*. IEEE Computer Society.
12. E. M. Arkin, "An efficiently computable metric for comparing polygonal shapes," *IEEE Trans on PAMI*, 1991.
13. C. T. Zahn and R. Z. Roskies, "Fourier descriptors for plane closed curves," *IEEE Trans. on Computers*, 1972.
14. E. Persoon and K. S. Fu, "Shape discrimination using fourier descriptors," *IEEE Trans. Sys. Man, Cyb.*, 1977.
15. C. T. Zahn, "A formal description for two-dimensional patterns," in *Proc Int. Joint Conf. Artificial Intelligence*.

Video Retrieval

CONTEXT-SENSITIVE AND CONTEXT-FREE RETRIEVAL IN A VIDEO DATABASE SYSTEM

Qing LI   K.M. Lam

Department of Computer Science, University of Science & Technology
Clear Water Bay, Kowloon, Hong Kong
email: {qing, kmlam}@cs.ust.hk

ABSTRACT

Video retrieval is an important topic in video database systems. Annotation-based video retrieval is a natural and an effective means for accessing video data when higher level semantics are involved, and is complementary to content-based access. In the context of MOOVIS - an experimental video database system that we have implemented, both context-oriented and feature-based meta data descriptions are organized in a structured yet flexible manner, which can facilitate to accommodate user queries that are either context-free or context-dependent. An associated set of query language facilities is currently being developed, and is to be incorporated into MOOVIS on the PC Pentium platform.

1 INTRODUCTION AND MOTIVATION

Recently, there has been much research on video retrieval in the area of video-on-demand and video databases. As large video archives (tapes, laser discs) become more and more popular, video retrieval is increasingly getting important in multimedia research area. Much of the work has been focused on so-called "content-based" retrieval [DG94, Fli+95, SZ94], which concentrates on image features such as color, shape, texture and various other raw data properties upon which *computer vision and image processing* (CVIP) techniques are used to extract and abstract low-level "objects" or "content" descriptions. Pure content-based search is, however, not sufficient to fulfil the users' need: some features of a video program cannot be extracted out from the video itself, no matter how advanced and sophisticated CVIP techniques can be. An alternative approach that has been around for a while and is equally important is the annotation-/attribute-based video retrieval. (One of the earliest prototype systems supporting this kind of retrieval is described in [MD89]; later on ones include those described in [CR95,Dav95,JH94,HM94].) Compared with content-based search, annotation-based video retrieval allows a wide range of user queries that involve *high-level* semantic features/concepts to be handled directly and in an effective manner. This type of video retrieval is thus complementary to content-based search, and is in general more natural and suitable for higher-level (semantic) queries which need to be processed efficiently.

Clearly, annotation-based video retrieval closely depends on the kinds of conceptual data (or meta-data) available, as well as the way meta-data is structured and organized.

In particular, two kinds of meta-data are noted here: *context-oriented* and *(semantic) feature-based*. Meta-data of the former kind describes/defines the search "scopes" of video data (such scopes can be a video clip, scene, and/or an entire video program), whereas the latter kind of descriptions provides high level index-terms (such as events or actions) that can be either specific to a "context" (e.g., within a scope), or general-purpose descriptions (i.e., common/sharable to several contexts). Both context-based and (semantic) feature-oriented annotation descriptions are useful and important to support in a video database, as they allow for video retrieval (and browsing) to be conducted in "context-sensitive" as well as "context-free" manners. So far, existing work on annotation-based video retrieval has focused on one type of the two search methods, but not both. Further, most annotation-based systems are not flexible enough to support for creating or modifying the annotations on the fly. We regard this as a handicap caused by their underlying meta-data models adopted. At HKUST, we have been developing a fully-fledged video information manipulation system (VIMS) [LLX96]. An important component of VIMS is an advanced object-oriented video data manager called MOOVIS[1], which is based on an extended object-oriented database model supporting *conceptual clustering* [LS92]. Among other capabilities, MOOVIS supports both context-sensitive and context-free retrieval based on its underlying versatile meta-data model facilities. In this paper, we discuss those modelling facilities in detail, and describe how such facilities are used in MOOVIS to support user queries that are either context-free or context-sensitive. We also show how user can browse the meta-data and conduct nagivational search elegantly.

2 THE MAIN FACILITIES OF MOOVIS

2.1   THE ARCHITECTURE

The architecture of MOOVIS is shown in Figure 1. At the core of the MOOVIS system is a dynamic object-oriented data model embodied by a versatile Conceptual Clustering Mechanism (CCM) [LS92,LL95], which is responsible for accommodating "semantic indexes" in the forms of cluster- and role-tree (cf. Figure 2). Such semantic indexes are defined based on the semantic contents derived from another component called VCC (for Video Classifier Component), along with possible user's input for subsequent revisions. The semantic indexes embodied by the cluster- and role-trees are stored in the EOS - a persistent object storage manager developed by AT&T Bell Lab.

2.2   CCM's VERSATILE MODELING CAPABILITIES

CCM represents a balanced model between conventional type-strong and less conventional type-weak data models [LH95]. A distinct feature of CCM is that it permits objects in a database to be aggregated dynamically into *clusters*; the objects in a cluster can play various *roles* [LS92]. Being variants of classes, clusters and roles can establish sub-cluster composition and base-/noble-role ("is_a") hierarchies, respectively. At present, these hierarchies are tree structures. Generally, however, they are sufficient for video data processing because an existing object in a video database can play many different/orthogonal roles, and similarly an object can also participate in a variety of

---

1. MOOVIS stands for a *Manager of an Object-Oriented Video Information System* [LH95].

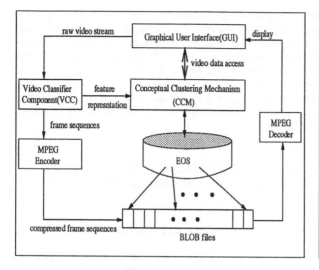

Figure 1. The Architecture of MOOVIS

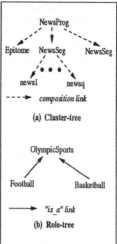

Figure 2. A cluster- and role-tree

clusters which are not at all related.

2.2.1 CLUSTERS AND CLUSTER-TREE FACILITIES

Clusters in MOOVIS corresponds to the context-oriented meta data (or *search scope* descriptions). In particular, clusters can be used to model different scopes at various granularity, such as a video clip, a video scene, and/or an entire video program. An example cluster node describing a news program consists of three segments: epitome, news, and weather forecast, may look as follows:

```
<NewsProg; {Anchorperson: "Mary": I; Date:"1 Aug. 1992": I; Timelen:20:NI; ...};
          {interactive-play(): I; broadcasting(): NI; ...}; /* method-set */
          {StartSeg: <Epitome>; MainNews:<NewsSeg>; EndSeg: <WeatherForecast>} >
```

Clusters are tied together by composition links. For example, Figure 2(a) shows a cluster-tree describing the above news program with (some of) its sub-clusters. While in a conventional object-oriented model no inheritance is supported among composition links, in MOOVIS one can selectively allow some attributes to be inherited by its children (through the 'I'/'NI' flag) [LH95]. For example, a local news which is part of the news program may share descriptions like date, anchorperson, etc. (via the 'I' flags). In short, instance variables (attributes) and member functions in a cluster node can be made public and inheritable by its subclusters.

2.2.2 ROLES AND ROLE-TREE FACILITIES

If a cluster specifies a "scope" for video data access, then a role in CCM serves as a (semantic) feature index, both inside and outside of a cluster context. In particular, roles form a separate role-tree hierarchy based on "is_a" relationships, and roles specified in a cluster (such as the StartSeg, MainNews, etc.) are not necessarily owned by that cluster exclusively. Rather, a role node in a cluster-tree can be *shared* by more than one cluster as needed. Roles can be both predefined according to prototypical kinds of video programs (such as news, drama, animation, comedy, etc.), as well as dynamically introduced on the fly to accommodate new types of video and/or ad hoc feature descriptions interested by the user. Besides the fact that roles are dynamic constructs (i.e., can be introduced dynamically), another characteristic is that member objects that play a role can be of heterogeneous types (or of different levels and granularity) [LS92,LL95]. The following illustrates an example role definition (which is defined upon another base role called Sports).

<Soccer; [base-role: Sports];
{Opponents: "Germany vs. Italy": NI; FinalResult: "1-1"; NI, ...};
{slow-play(): I; ...} /* additional methods besides those inherited from Sports */

3 CONTEXT-SENSITIVE/FREE RETRIEVAL IN MOOVIS

Based on the CCM's dynamic and versatile modelling facilities (viz., cluster- and role-trees), MOOVIS allows both context-sensitive and context-free retrieval to be conducted effectively, in addition to a natural support of browsing the meta-data of video objects navigationally, as explained below.

3.1   NAVIGATIONAL BROWSING OF THE META-DATA

Both the cluster- and role-trees can be naturally used for browsing meta-data of a set of video collections. Browsing the cluster-tree provides the end-user with an overall picture about the *structure* of a video program, whereas navigating the role-tree offers an introduction to the *semantic features* recognized/understood by the system, which can be used as high-level indexes for feature-oriented search.

To be more specific, traversing the cluster tree downward (from a cluster to its subclusters) reveals from a less detailed overview of the video program to a more detailed one. Similarly, one can traverse the role tree from top to bottom, which corresponds to moving from a more general feature to a more specific one. Hence there exists a "rough" correspondence between the two trees, as intuitively depicted in Figure 3. For example, starting from the cluster tree node Newsk1 which contains a role called basketball (cf. Figure 4), it is natural to expect that the parent node (i.e. Newsegk) may contain a role which is more general than the role basketball (e.g. Sports). The construction of the role tree nodes in MOOVIS is indeed "guided" by this philosophy. Such rough corre-

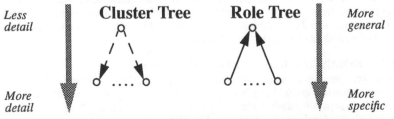

Figure 3. The correspondence between cluster- and role-tree

spondence relationships between these two kinds of trees serve as an excellent navigational means which is similar to "relevance feedback" in information retrieval (IR). This technique enables the user to browse among different clusters (i.e. video programs) and different roles (i.e. semantic features) flexibly, as illustrated in Figure 4..

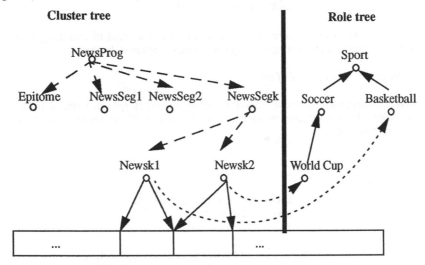

Figure 4. Navigating nodes across the cluster- and role-trees

3.2 CONTEXT-SENSITIVE RETRIEVAL

The cluster tree in MOOVIS is useful not only for browsing the structure of video programs, but also for delimiting the *search scope* of user queries. For example, the user can choose to see a video clip at any level of abstraction. Back to the news example, if the user wants to watch all the main news, he can select the tree node in the upper level of the cluster tree. When he only wants to see a portion of a sport news piece (say, about soccer), he can select the node at the bottom, and retrieve the video segment there according to an appropriate role (viz. Soccer). Structured querying facilities similar to SQL can be devised naturally to accommodate such kinds of search. In this way, the user can easily select video objects at different level of abstraction, and/or retrieve the video data from different search "scopes" or contexts. We consider below three scenarios of retrieving video data using this approach.

3.2.1. Restriction on the cluster's attributes

This type of queries allows a cluster (viz., a video program) to be retrieved based on the attribute description of the cluster. For example, suppose we want to retrieve from NewsProg all the subclusters (video clips) which are about "sports".

Using the associated query language facilities called OQL/race [FL95] for CCM, the SQL-like query statement may look like the following:

```
Select x
from NewsProg
Where
        x belongs_to NewsProg AND
        x.category ="sport";
```

Note that the roles of the clusters are not involved in this kind of searching, and is therefore similar to the conventional type of queries in relation databases.

3.2.2 Restriction on the type of roles

In this situation, queries are processed according to certain type of roles in a cluster. For example, to look for some news about soccer from NewsSegk, we can set the query to be something like:

```
Select x
from NewsProg
Where
        x belongs_to NewsSegk AND
        x has-role y AND
        y type_of soccer;
```

Note that although no (sub-)cluster of NewsSegk has any role with type "soccer" (c.f. Figure 4), due to the is-a hierarchy in the role tree, the role World Cup is a specialized type of the role Soccer, the system will thus return the cluster Newsk2 (which contains the role WorldCup) as a result.

While the **type_of** operator allows more specialized roles to be treated/viewed from a more general level, it is essentially still for exact match. However, inexact or imprecise match is sometimes also desired and useful from the end-user's viewpoint. Therefore, MOOVIS also supports another operator called **similar_to**. For example, if the user request some video scenes that are similar to soccer, then instead of using the **type_of** operator, he can use **similar_to** instead. In evaluating this query, the neighbouring nodes of soccer in the role tree (e.g. basketball) will also be used for locating a cluster that has such a role, yielding a more relaxed query internally.[2]

3.2.3 Restriction on the attributes of role

In addition to the above two cases, search can also be conducted by imposing restriction on some role's attributes. For example, suppose the user is interested in viewing all the events taken place at the New York Stadium, the following OQL/race query statement may be issued:

---

2. Of course, such relaxation needs not to be done horizontally only, but vertically as well. But this raises a question on how much to relax (i.e. how many level to go up the role tree). This is similar to the "query generalization" problems for relational databases; further discussions on this aspect are beyond the scope of this paper.

```
Select x
from NewsProg
Where
        x belongs_to NewsProg AND
        x has-role y AND
        y.venue = "New York Stadium";
```

3.3 CONTEXT-FREE SEARCH

Context-sensitive retrieval is very efficient when the user has a clear idea of where to look for. Quite often, however, the user may only have very vague idea on what program/clips to select[3], though s/he may know what *semantic features* to look for (e.g., any video scene about "horse-racing"). In MOOVIS, this type of retrieval is called "context-free" search, and is readily supported by the role-tree facilities since, as adumbrated above, roles can be utilized both within a cluster context and/or outside of a cluster context. In the latter case, roles effectively serve as semantic feature *indices* to the clusters, without which one cannot perform context-free search *effectively*. For instance, without knowing which particular video programs contain a scene about a bus accident, it is possible for a user to start a probe in MOOVIS by selecting from the role-tree a node describing bus-accident, and the system will respond by returning a list of video clusters (programs/scenes/clips) that contain such a role. In other words, *backward search* from role-tree back to cluster-tree is also allowed and supported in MOOVIS, in addition to the forward search (i.e., from a cluster to its roles).

Furthermore, there are also different scenarios where different selection restrictions can be applied. The cases are similar to those of context-sensitive search. We illustrate the main idea in the following example. Suppose we want to see some video clips about soccer in 1994, but don't know which video programs (clusters) to look for from the whole video library/database. The corresponding OQL/race statement can be used to formulate such a "context-free" query:

```
Select *
from [all] x
Where
        x has-role y AND
        y type_of soccer AND
        y.year = "1994";
```

Note that in this type of search, the search path starts from a role (denoted by y in the above example) that satisfies the user's description, relates back to any/all cluster (i.e. x) that contains y as its role, and then display the video clips of x. Note that the default case is to select only one video cluster, but the user can optionally request to select all the possible video clusters by specifying the keyword **all** in the from clause.

---

3. Alternatively, the user may not want to restrict the search to be within any particular scope.

4 CONCLUSIONS AND FURTHER RESEARCH

In this paper, we present in the context of VIMS an experimental video data manager called MOOVIS, by describing the main facilities that it has, as well as its annotation-based retrieval techniques. The underlying data model (i.e., CCM) utilized by MOO-VIS is characterized as a balanced model between type-strong and type-weak ones. Its versatile facilities embodied by the cluster- and role-tree allow us to perform both context-sensitive and context-free retrieval, in addition to navigational browsing of the structure as well as semantic features. By separating feature-oriented conceptual data (i.e., roles) from context-based conceptual data (viz., clusters) and maintaining their respective hierarchies, it allows a user to retrieve video objects based on the feature index terms either within a context or in a context-free manner. Therefore it becomes possible to accommodate both "precise" and "imprecise" (or vague) queries in a video database. Currently, we are enhancing the MOOVIS prototype (built on Sun) in terms of adding a structured query language facility. Also, the prototype is being ported to PC Pentiums where the VCC part (of VIMS) has been developed; integration of the VCC and MOOVIS is currently under way.

REFERENCES

[CR95] T.-S. Chua and L.-Q. Ruan. "A Video Retrieval and Sequencing System." *ACM Trans. on Information Systems*, Vol.13, No.4, 1995.

[Dav95] M. Davis. "Media Streams: an Iconic Visual Language for Video Representation." *Readings in Human-Computer Interaction: Toward the Year 2000*, pp. 854-866, 1995.

[DG94] N. Dimitrova and F. Golshani. "Rx for Semantic Video Database Retrieval." *Proc. of 2nd ACM Int'l Conference on Multimedia*, pp. 219-226, 1994.

[Fli+95] M. Flickner et al. "Query by Image and Video Content: the QBIC System." *IEEE Computer*, Vol.28, No. 9, 1995.

[FL95] C. Fung and Q. Li. "Versatile Querying Facilities for a Dynamic Object Clustering Model." *Proc. of 14th Int'l Conf. on OOER Modeling*, pp. 77-88, 1995.

[HM94] R. Hjelsvold and R. Midtstraum. "Modelling and Querying Video Data." *Proc. of 20th Int'l Conference on Very Large Data Bases*, pp. 686-694, 1994.

[JH94] R. Jain. "Metadata in Video Databases." *ACM SIGMOFL95D RECORD*, Vol.23, No.4, pp27-33, 1994.

[LLX96]C.M. Lcc, Q. Li and W. Xiong. "VIMS: a Video Information Manipulation System." submitted to *Multimedia Tools and Applications*, 1996.

[LH95] Q. Li and L. Huang. "A Dynamic Model for a Video Database Management System." *ACM Computing Surveys*, 27(4), pp. 602-606, Dec. 1995.

[LL95] Q. Li and C.M. Lee. "Dynamic Object Clustering for Video Database Manipulations." *Proc. of IFIP 2.6 Working Conference on Visual Database Systems*, Lausanne, March, 1995.

[LS92] Q. Li and J.L. Smith. "A Conceptual Model for Dynamic Clustering in Object Databases." *Proc. of 18th Int'l Conference on Very Large Data Bases*, pp. 337-347, Aug. 1992.

[MD89] W.E. Mackay and G. Davenport. "Virtual video editing in interactive multimedia applications." *Communications of ACM*, Vol.32, pp802-810, 1989.

[SZ94] S.W. Smoliar and H. Zhang. "Content-based Video Indexing and Retrieval." *IEEE Multimedia*, Vol.1, No.2, pp62-72, 1994.

Short Papers

Shot Break Detection and Camera Motion Classification in Digital Video

Micha Haas and Michael S. Lew and Dionysius P. Huijsmans

Department of Computer Science, Leiden University,
Postbus 9512, 2300 RA Leiden, The Netherlands
{mhaas,mlew,huijsman}@wi.LeidenUniv.NL

Abstract. In this paper we describe methods using 2D-pixel motion fields for detecting shot breaks and classifying camera motion in digital video. These flow fields can be calculated with optical flow or correlation matching. The Karhunen-Loève transform (KLT), based on statistical properties, insures extraction of optimal linear features from flow fields representing a particular motion class. Two methods for classification are discussed, and experimental results for each method are presented.

1 Introduction

There is a growing number of digital video and film databases. Therefore it is useful to develop video analysis methods such as detection of shot breaks and classification of camera or object motion. Optic flow [Horn and Schunk 1981] and correlation matching are methods used to describe 2D pixel motion within image sequences. The motion can be represented by a vector with its origin of the position in the first frame and its end at the corresponding pixel position in the second frame. Optic flow is based on the human visual system which perceives images with a small translational difference as motion. The correlation focuses on individual pixels and their displacement between frames.

A human can easily distinguish accurate flow fields for a zoom-out from those of a translation to the right. The first would have vectors pointing from the edges inwards, with a greater magnitude at the edges of the field and the second would have vectors of the same magnitude pointing to the left. Real flow fields that were used appeared more like random vectors of which it is difficult to distinguish the motion class. This is due to noise in the images and analysis methods that are susceptible to noise, and therefore it is useful to transform the flow field so that optimal features can be extracted and used to describe 2D pixel motion of a particular camera motion. This transformation is called the Karhunen-Loève Transform [Hotelling 1933; Karhunen 1947; Loève 1948] and results in a set of vectors that can reconstruct an original population with a known error. The classification can be done in two ways: (1) Reconstruct an example flow field using descriptive features of each possible motion and compare it to the example. (2) Compare coefficients used to reconstruct the original populations of the possible camera motions to coefficients used to reconstruct the example flow field. In the following sections the KLT with it's practical implementation, and classification methods with results are discussed.

2   Shot Break Detection

The terms shot/scene break/cut are ambiguous in the research literature because the notion of either a shot or scene break can arise from different sources. Movie makers, for example, have a specific definition for shot and scene where a scene is composed of one or more shots. For the purposes of this paper, we define a shot/scene cut as the break in the continuity of a camera shot. There are a wide variety of methods for automatically detecting scene cuts in the research literature[Suggested background reading: Hampapur, et al 1994; and Gudivada and Raghavan 1995]. Most, if not all, of the previous literature has been focussed on non-motion based methods, often using color histograms or color moments. These methods have the virtue that they are computationally efficient, but they do not take into account the inherent motion of the objects in the camera shots. Thus, the non-motion based methods may fail when there is significant object motion. One straightforward criterion given the 2D image motion field is to calculate the reconstruction error, that is, we displace the pixels from frame t-1 to their correspondences in frame t and take the sum of the absolute difference. If we calculated the motion field perfectly, then the error for a pair of frames within a scene will be roughly at the background noise level.

This approach brings up the question, "How well can the 2D motion field be estimated between two frames?" To answer this, we calculated the motion field using 2 different methods: correlation and optical flow [Horn and Schunk 1981].

For a typical movie, a shot break occurs every 3-5 seconds. As an example, suppose a shot break occurs within a movie every 4 seconds. At 30 frames per second, this would mean that for every 120 frames, there is one break on average. This means that if we simply wrote a program which classified every pair of frames as a scene, then it would be correct for more than 99 percent of the frame pairs. In order to remove this extreme bias, we created a test set of one hundred scene examples, and one hundred cut examples.

Regarding benchmarking with respect to the histogram methods, we first calculated the error using the difference of histograms(DOH) as shown in Fig. 1. Note that if we set the threshold for the classifier at the maximum error for all of the scene examples, this results in 9 misclassified cut examples. For the correlation and optical flow based methods, we calculated the reconstruction error as shown in Fig. 2 and Fig. 3. If we use the same thresholding strategy for the correlation method, this results in 2 misclassified cuts, and for the optical flow based method, this becomes 0 misclassifed cuts.

In Fig. 1, the scene example with the greatest error was example 8 (on the x-axis of the graph). Note that in Figures 2 and 3, the effect of example 8 has been diminished such that it is only slightly above the background noise level. This demonstates the efficacy of the pixel displacement as well as the usefulness of both template correlation and optical flow as automatic pixel motion estimators. An additional concern is whether its possible to compute the 2D pixel motion fields in real time. It should be noted that many MPEG hardware boards have real time template based block matching.

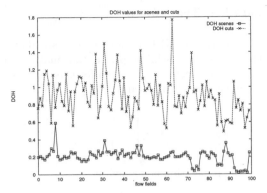

Fig. 1.

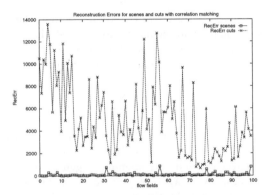

Fig. 2.

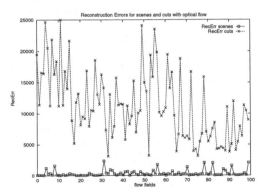

Fig. 3.

3   Karhunen-Loève Transform

The Karhunen-Loève transform (KLT) is based on statistical properties of vector representations, and has several useful properties that make it an important tool for image processing. The theory on the transform is as follows : Consider a population of random vectors of the form

$$\mathbf{x} = \begin{bmatrix} x_1 \\ \vdots \\ x_n \end{bmatrix} \tag{1}$$

The *mean vector* of the population is defined as

$$\mathbf{m_x} = \frac{1}{M} \sum_{k=1}^{M} \mathbf{x}_k \tag{2}$$

Where $E\{arg\}$ is the expected value of the argument, and the subscript denote **m** is associated with the population of **x** vectors. Recall that the expected value of a vector or matrix is obtained by taking the expected value of each element. The *covariance matrix* of the vector population is defined as

$$\mathbf{m_x} = \frac{1}{M} \sum_{k=1}^{M} \mathbf{x}_k \tag{3}$$

where T indicates vector transposition. Because $\mathbf{C_x}$ is real and symmetric, finding a set of n orthonormal eigenvectors always is possible. Let $\mathbf{e}_i$ and λ_i, $i = 1,2,...,n$, be the eigenvectors and corresponding eigenvalues of $\mathbf{C_x}$, arranged in descending order, so that $\lambda_j \geq \lambda_{j+1}$ for $j = 1,2,...,n\text{-}1$. Let $\mathbf{A}$ be a matrix be a matrix whose rows are formed by the eigenvectors of $\mathbf{C_x}$, ordered so that the first row is the eigenvector corresponding to the largest eigenvalue, and the last row is the eigenvector corresponding to the smallest eigenvalue. Suppose that $\mathbf{A}$ is a transformation matrix that maps the **x**'s into vectors denoted by **y**'s, as follows:

$$\mathbf{y} = \mathbf{A}(\mathbf{x} - \mathbf{m_x}) \tag{4}$$

Equation 4 is called the *Hotelling transform*, or *Karhunen-Loève transform*. The mean of the **y** vectors resulting from this transformation is zero; that is,

$$\mathbf{m_y} = \mathbf{0} \tag{5}$$

Another important property of the KLT deals with the reconstruction of **x** from **y**. Because the rows of $\mathbf{A}$ are orthonormal vectors $\mathbf{A}^{-1} = \mathbf{A}^T$, and any vector **x** can be recovered from its corresponding **y** by using the relation

$$\mathbf{x} = \mathbf{A}^T \mathbf{y} + \mathbf{m_x} \tag{6}$$

Suppose however, that instead of using all the eigenvectors of $\mathbf{C_x}$ we form matrix $\mathbf{A_k}$ from the K eigenvectors corresponding to the K largest eigenvalues, yielding a transformation matrix of order $K \times n$. The $\mathbf{y}$ vectors would then be K dimensional, and the reconstruction given in equation 6 would no longer be exact. The vector reconstructed by using $\mathbf{A_k}$ is

$$\hat{\mathbf{x}} = \mathbf{A}_K^T \mathbf{y} + \mathbf{m_x} \tag{7}$$

It can be shown that the mean square error between $\hat{\mathbf{x}}$ and $\mathbf{x}$ is given by the expression.

$$e_{ms} = \sum_{j=1}^{n} \lambda_j - \sum_{j=1}^{K} \lambda_j = \sum_{j=K+1}^{n} \lambda_j \tag{8}$$

The first part of equation 8 indicates that the error is zero if $K = n$ (that is, if all the eigenvectors are used in the transformation. Because the λ_i's decrease monotonically equation 8 also shows that the error can be minimized by selecting the K eigenvectors associated with the largest eigenvalues. Thus the Karhunen-Loève transform is optimal in the sense that it minimizes the mean square error between the vectors $\mathbf{x}$ and their approximations $\hat{\mathbf{x}}$.

3.1 Choosing input population

We need to calculate a covariance matrix of size $(w \times h) \times (w \times h)$. Because the dimensions of the flow fields that were used are about 160×110, the amount of memory used by the covariance matrix would be $(160 \times 110)^2 \times 4$ bytes, or 1239.04 Mb! Gradually several different ways of splitting up the flow fields into non-overlapping parts were tried so that it was possible to calculate the covariance matrix with a reasonable amount of memory. Divide the flow field in square blocks of size $p \times p$. The sizes for p that were tried were 10 and 32. Another way to fill $\mathbf{x}$ is by selecting the values of one row of the flow field. This can be extended by selecting two rows instead of one. The last scheme that was implemented implemented was sub sampling. The idea was to get a 32x32 square which was filled with the average motion of a rectangle in the flow field. The dimensions 32x32 were chosen because that was about the highest value that could be used without running out of memory, and still be able to do some testing without waiting for days on results.

4 Motion classification

In this section we examine two different methods for motion classification of an example flow field. In the first method, we compare the flow fields using linear features derived independently from each motion class. In the second method we compare the coefficients using linear features derived from the combined motion classes.

4.1   Comparing flow fields

Example input flow fields will be reconstructed six times, once for each motion class. For this method the averages, eigenvalues and eigenvectors of each separate motion are needed. These are then stored on disk so that they can be retrieved for reconstructing an example flow field. The reconstruction procedure is as follows:

$$\text{example} = \mathbf{A}_K^T \mathbf{y} + \mathbf{m_x} \qquad (9)$$

Where $\mathbf{A}$ and $\mathbf{m_x}$ are the pre-calculated eigenvalues and mean of the vector population. Because most of the information about the vector population is stored in the K eigenvectors corresponding to the K largest eigenvalues, it is possible to use only these K eigenvectors and hereby guaranteeing a minimal error between the example and it's reconstruction. To reconstruct we need to calculate the unknown vector $\mathbf{y}$ of dimension $K \times 1$. Equation 9 can be written as

$$\text{example} - \mathbf{m_x} = \mathbf{A}_K^T \mathbf{y} \qquad (10)$$

This is an over determined set of n linear equations and K unknowns($n \geq K$). The least-squares solution for $\mathbf{y}$ can be found by calculating

$$\mathbf{y} = \mathbf{A}_K(\text{example} - \mathbf{m_x}) \qquad (11)$$

The reconstruction of the example from the eigenvalues, $\hat{\text{example}}$, can now be found by substitution of $\mathbf{y}$ in equation 9. The distance from the example to the reconstruction can be calculated with the mean square error, or the normalized correlation coefficient. A visual representation is given in Fig. 4. When an example flow field has to be classified, n reconstructions are made using the different sets of eigenvectors.

4.2   Comparing coefficients

A more common and faster way of using the KLT for recognition is by comparing K coefficients used for reconstructing an example flow field to K coefficients used for reconstructing each flow field in the population. The difference with the previous method is that we now have to calculate the eigenvalues and eigenvectors of all the flow fields of all the camera motions. The next step is to calculate $\mathbf{y}$ in equation 9 for each flow field in the population. The elements of $\mathbf{y}$, $y_1, y_2, ..., y_K$ are the coefficients to the K eigenvectors of which the flow field is reconstructed by. For each camera motion these coefficients should be around a specific mean and preferably with a low variance. Coefficients of example flow fields can then be compared to each set of pre-calculated coefficients using the NCC and MSE. Before comparison, the coefficients should be normalized by dividing each coefficient by the sum of the absolute values. This normalization is necessary because the relative proportions of the coefficients are more important than the magnitudes. Comparing the coefficients is done by calculating the NCC, and the MSE.
  Fig. 5 also gives a visual representation of the steps for this method. When an example flow field has to be classified, the coefficients are calculated. These are

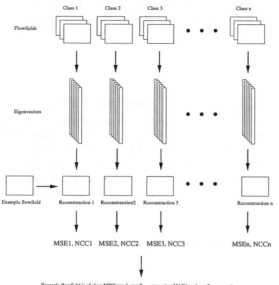

Fig. 4.

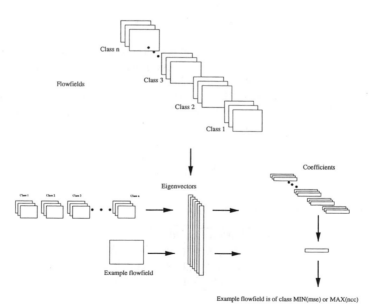

Fig. 5.

then compared to all the stored coefficients in the database by calculating the MSE and NCC. The example flow field can then be classified as the motion class of the set of coefficients that resulted in the lowest MSE or highest NCC.

5   Results

The results for motion classification were calculated using 80 training, and 125 example flow fields for each motion class. Six motion classes were included in these tests : four translations, and two zooms. As data for typical rotations with the center of rotation in the center of the frames is hard to come by, experiments with rotations clockwise and counter-clockwise were omitted. The following tables show the percentages of correct classification for the six classes in each column. The first column shows the number of eigenvectors used in the testing.

5.1   Classification by comparing flow fields

Method with squares, $p = 10$

K	left	right	up	down	in	out
1	98.4	0.0	0.0	2.4	0.0	0.0
5	100.0	0.0	0.0	1.6	0.0	0.0
10	92.9	4.8	5.6	27.0	31.7	0.0

This table shows that only the flow fields of the translations to the left were correctly classified. When the negative classifications of the remaining motion classes were examined, it became clear that these were also classified as translations to the left. The reason for these errors is in this specific methods of splitting up the flow field. When the flow field is divided into small blocks, most of the vectors in that block will have the same direction and magnitude. The eigenvectors of the motion class that describe these homogeneous blocks best, will also be able to describe the homogeneous blocks of the other motion classes. In this case that motion class is the translation to the left.

5.2   Method with squares, $p = 32$

K	left	right	up	down	in	out
1	41.3	27.8	19.0	49.2	92.9	0.0
5	68.3	14.3	3.2	88.1	39.7	0.0
10	84.1	4.8	2.4	83.3	7.9	0.0

Increasing the size of p from 10 to 32, improved the results because the blocks are now less homogeneous. The figures for zoom out however are still zero, the flow fields are classified as zoom in.

5.3 Method with 1 row

A single row is still quite homogeneous for the translations, but should be different for zooms.

K	left	right	up	down	in	out
1	52.4	7.1	15.9	27.8	98.4	3.2
5	82.5	11.9	31.0	9.5	97.6	0.8
10	88.1	5.6	28.6	4.8	88.1	0.0

This is displayed by the increased values for zoom in. Compared to the previous table, this one doesn't show any significant improvement.

5.4 Method with 2 rows

K	left	right	up	down	in	out
1	32.5	11.1	25.4	36.5	79.4	52.4
5	42.1	23.8	52.4	11.1	92.9	24.6
10	48.4	19.8	48.4	7.1	97.6	21.4

Taking two rows as input clearly shows an overall improvement, but this method still is not useful for classification.

5.5 Sub sampling, $p = 32$

K	left	right	up	down	in	out
2	83.3	74.6	85.7	63.5	95.2	88.1
3	83.3	73.0	83.3	55.6	98.4	83.3
5	79.4	73.0	84.1	55.6	98.4	64.3

This table clearly shows that the sub sampling method gives the best result.

5.6 Classification by comparing coefficients

To test the classification by comparing coefficients, only the sub sampling method to split up the flow fields was used.

5.7 Sub sampling, $p = 32$

K	left	right	up	down	in	out
2	96.0	64.3	99.2	88.9	100.0	100.0
3	96.8	74.6	99.2	86.5	100.0	99.2
5	96.8	77.0	99.2	89.7	100.0	99.2

It is clear that these results are the best so far. The only problem is with the translation to the right. A close examination of the test set showed that about each third frames had a larger translation than the others. The flow fields corresponding to these frames were not classified correctly, because they looked like random vectors. The cause of this problem was the rate at which the frames were digitized. For some reason the frame grabber did not write sufficient frames to disk, and 2D pixel motion between frames was larger than the 'allowed' displacement to calculate the flow fields correctly. The rates for translation to the right improved to 93.7% when the tests were redone with adjusted parameters to calculate the flow fields.

6   Conclusion

In this paper we have shown that motion based shot break detectors had lower error rates than a typical histogram based shot break detector. Furthermore, motion field information can be used for accurate motion classification. Different camera motions have been successfully classified in the experiments, but the training phase can be computationally intensive. To increase the usability of the methods that have been discussed, it is necessary to have a method that calculates flow fields, or parts of it, in real time. This is already possible and affordable with the available MPEG hardware which uses motion information to compress digital video. Motion classification can be extended by adding more motion classes such as rotations. Also combinations of motion classes could be detected, or object versus camera motion classification.

7   References

Hotelling, H., "Analysis of a Complex of Statistical Variables into Principal Components", "Journal of Educ. Psychol., vol. 27, pp. 417-441, 1933.

Karhunen, K., "Uber Lineare Methoden in der Wahrsceinlichkeitsrechnung", Ann. Acad. Sci. Fennicae, Ser. A137, 1947.

Loève, M., Fonctions Aleastoires de Second Ordre", Processus Stchastiques et Mouvement Brownien, Hermann, Paris, 1948.

Horn, B.K.P. and B.G. Schunk, "Determining Optical Flow", Artificial Intelligence, vol.17, pp. 185-203, 1981.

Hampapur, A.,R. Jain and T. Weymouth, "Digital Video Segmentation", ACM, pp. 357-364, 1994.

Gudivada, V. N., and V. V. Raghavan, "Finding the Right Image, Content-Based Image Retrieval Systems", IEEE Computer, pp. 18-62, Sept. 1995.

2D Pixel Trigrams for Content-Based Image Retrieval

D.P. Huijsmans, S. Poles, M. Lew
Computer Science Department, Leiden University
P.O. Box 9512, 2300 RA Leiden
The Netherlands

Abstract. The problem of finding similar images and images with a similar sub-image given a search image or part of a search image is addressed in this article by using 3x3 local pattern statistics in thresholded gradient images of scanned portraits normalized for scale, orientation, position and lighting. Pattern frequencies sorted on magnitude are closely linked to a spatial frequency ordering. The 2D trigram feature vector is formed by a weighing of the pattern frequencies. Several weighing functions were applied to a database of 3014 image files: the results indicate that a sort of band pass approach, suppressing both ends of the sorted pattern frequency distribution works best. The method works well on full image comparison and will be applied to sub-image search in the near future.

1 Introduction

The Leiden Imaging and Multi-media group set out to select, create and implement features and algorithms for content-based image retrieval. The first problem tackled is copy location in a noisy environment due to the photo and scanning process. One of the best feature found for copy location [see Huijsmans, Lew 1996] was the use of horizontal and vertical projections in gradient space. The second problem tackled is sub-image search. The way we would like to organize sub-image search is twofold:

- first compare features of the sub-image with features of the full-image to select a candidate set of full-images that according to the features could contain the searched sub-image

- second use a pixel by pixel shifted comparison method to locate the best matching positions in the candidate set. Rank the full-image candidate set according the best match and register the best matching position.

In this case projections are largely unsuited for the initial selection of the candidate set because the projections of the search sub-image can not selectively be recovered from the projections of the full images.

2   Finding copies in a portrait database

Copy location in a database of 19th-century portraits, so called "carte de visite" pictures made by the millions between 1860 and 1914,makes sense and is challenging. Studio photographers typically produced a dozen copies on carton from a same glass negative for costumers that distributed these photo's among relatives and friends. Since only about 1 in 20 photo's was annotated at the back with information like the depicted person, the date the photograph was taken etc. genealogists would like to trace back un-annotated copies to a possibly annotated picture in one of the bigger collections. Since the separate copies were kept under different circumstances they often developed differences due to different fading, staining, cutting, coloring to name but a few. Manually this task of locating extra copies of the original dozen among 50,000 such pictures is close to impossible.By scanning in the bigger collections (our aim is to scan in at least 50,000 portraits over the next 4 years) we can automate this search problem.

3   Normalization phase

All scanned images are normalized with respect to scale, orientation, position and lighting as described in [Huijsmans, Lew 1996]. After normalization the images are scaled down to 37.5 dpi, gradient filtered (Sobel magnitude 3x3) and thresholded to binary images with threshold value 8 (about 3 sigma noiselevel).

4   Features for sub-image location

In this research the feature exploited for characterizing image content is the statistic vector of frequency of occurrence of 3x3 spatial B/W patterns in thresholded gradient space. The idea of using elementary local patterns for image matching was derived from a character trigram approach in text searching [Chudacek 1984]. Generalizing the trigram method to images is not as straightforward as it seems, due to the presence of noise, which makes exact matching almost impossible. A 2D analog of the trigram is the 2-dimensional B/W pattern around a center pixel. In a 3x3 binary image this pattern can be any of the $2^9 = 512$ patterns since any of the 9 pixels in the pattern can take on 2 values (Black/White). Image content can be characterized by the frequencies of the 3x3 pattern. We expect that the characterization of the sub-image will be more selective using the 3x3 pattern approach than the row and column projections. Like in the text searching, the least frequent patterns may have the highest selective power. To see how selective the 3x3 pattern statistics are, we made a number of measurements using the Leiden portrait database. The versions used for these measurements contains front and back sides of 572 and 1507 19th century B/W studio portraits.The thresholded gradient representation were used to obtain statistics about the 2 completely different image classes (the faces on the front and the studio advertisement and annotations at the backside of the studio portraits).

5 Frequency distribution

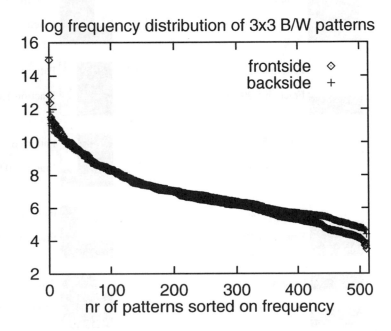

Fig. 1. 2D Trigram pattern sorted frequencies on a logarithmic scale: results obtained from first 1154 back and front side files

In fig. 1 the frequency distribution of 3x3 B/W patterns in thresholded gradient space for the Leiden portrait database is given for the front and the back sides. The ratio of the most- versus least common pattern is as high as $2 * 10^5$. The sorting on 3x3 B/W patterns on frequency closely correspond to a sorting on spatial frequency as can be seen from the 10 most common (lowest spatial frequency) patterns in figure 2 and the 10 least common (highest spatial frequency) patterns in fig. 3.

6 Optimal weight function

Since the pattern frequency varies enormously we thought about the best way to exploit this characteristic. With the results of equal weighing as a base reference one can devise more optimal weighing schemes exploiting the selectivity of the specific patterns and taking noise into account. Since the selectivity of the low frequency patterns is greatest we first applied two weighing methods that amplify the low frequency (but high spatial frequency) pattern contributions: both an inverse and anti-linear weighing function were applied. However the less often

Most Common Pattern – Visual Representation

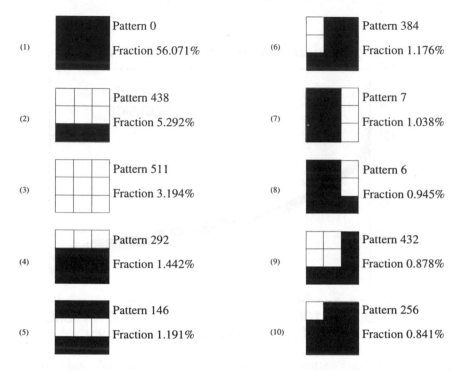

Fig. 2. low spatial frequency texture fractions measured in first 1154 back and front side files

a pattern occurs on average in an image, the greater the effect of noise contributions will become. This means that to avoid too high a noise contribution, the weight of the lowest frequency patterns should be kept low as well. Two methods with low weights on either end of the sorted frequency range were applied: one is a variation on the anti-linear weighing (that did better than the inverse weighing) and the other one is a crude band pass filter suppressing the contribution of the black and white pattern on the high end and the rare patterns on the low end. The anti-linear with cutoff weighing function is zero at the lowest Fmin and highest Fmax occurring pattern and tops at the average expected frequency Fa. The band pass weighing function is zero outside a lower Fl and upper Fu frequency pattern and 1 in between: the upper cutoff was determined by the highest frequency below all black and all white (fractions below 0.02); the lower cutoff by the demand that the expected frequency of a specific pattern would be at least 10 per image, this set the lower cutoff at fractions below 0.001. Applying the band pass method reduced the number of contributing patterns to about 75. Our evaluation criterion on the effect of applying different weighing functions was the error in ranking the predetermined test-set pairs highest. In figure 4 the

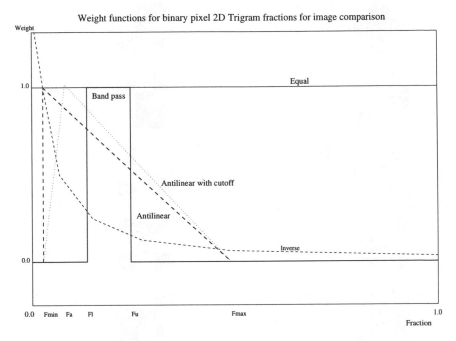

Fig. 3. weighing methods applied to frequency sorted pattern distribution

applied weight functions for the different weighing schemes in comparing the 2D Trigram feature vectors are graphically depicted.

7   Matching results for copy location

Figure 5 gives an overview of the matching results for the Leiden portrait database test-set [see Huijsmans, Lew 1996] for several methods using the 3x3 pattern statistics vector using different weights. Both the anti-linear and anti-linear with cutoff weighing scheme performed almost equally well, so only the results of the anti-linear one is given. The results of the inverse weighing is below the weighing with equal weights. The Anti-linear and Band pass weighing scheme is clearly better than the method with equal wieghts, although the Band pass only uses 13The performance figures are based on the rankings of test-set pairs in a total of 3014 image files (1507 back and front sides).

The test-set contains rescanned images (c000300front and back), faded copy pairs (c000000f; c000010f and c0000273f; c000093f and c000094f; c0000140f and c0000401f; c000026f and c000103f), a watercolored and trimmed pair (c000409f

Least Common Pattern – Visual Representation

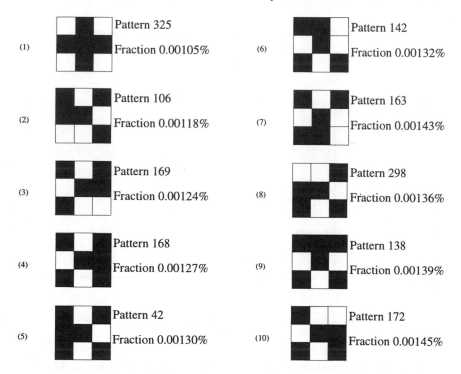

Fig. 4. high spatial frequency texture fractions measured in first 1154 back and front side files

and c000412f), a same person different pose pair (c000095f and c000094f), a same studio plus props but different person pair (c000008f and c000028f) and a number of regularly occuring backsides (c000102b, c000256b, c000275b and c000554b) that have more than 1 counterpart in the database.

8   Raising the performance by block decomposition

The performance for the test-set is still lower than we wanted to achieve for copy location. By subdividing the images in 2x2 blocks, each with its 3x3 pattern statistics vector, the performance of copy location was substantially raised to all perfect (all ranks 1). Although adding more spatial layout structure to the feature vectors is not a problem for copy location, it is a problem for our final goal sub-image location. Especially when the sub-image is located across borders of the decomposed images its location may be missed when using the block feature vectors.

Testset Pair	Equal	Inverse	Antilin	bandpass	Antilin2x2	Bandpass2x2
c000300f-c*00300f	1	1	1	1	1	1
c000026f-c000103f	1	1	1	1	1	1
c000140f-c000401f	>60	>60	10	7	1	1
c000093f-c000094f	46	>60	1	10	1	1
c000095f-c000094f	6	>60	21	8	1	1
c000008f-c000028f	1	2	1	1	1	1
c000409f-c000412f	4	>60	6	2	1	1
c000000f- c000010f	1	4	1	2	1	1
c000010f- c000273f	1	1	7	4	1	1
c000300b-c*00300b	1	1	1	1	1	1
c000102b-	1	1	1	1	1	1
c000256b-	1	1	1	1	1	1
c000275b-	1	1	1	1	1	1
c000554b-	1	1	1	1	1	1

Fig. 5. Performance results:rank of test-set counterparts when comparing with 3014 files

9   WWW demo program

By using pointer *http://ind156b.wi.leidenuniv.nl:8086/intro.html* the methods described here can be evaluated directly via our WWW content-based image retrieval demo.

10   References

[Chudacek 1984]: J. Chudacek: niet grammaticale benadering van het probleem van de verwerking van natuurlijke talen in de computer : in NGI-SION informatica symposium proc. 1984 (330-339).

[Huijsmans,Lew 1996]: D.P Huijsmans, M.S. Lew: Efficient Content-based image retrieval in digital picture Collections using projections : (Near)-Copy location. Comp. Science Dept. Leiden Techn. Report 96-07. Also to appear in the proceedings of the 13th ICPR Vienna, 1996.
This article was processed using the LaTeX macro package with LLNCS style

Two-Stage Polygon Representation for Efficient Shape Retrieval in Image Databases

Lun Hsing Tung, Irwin King, Ping Fu Fung and Wing Sze Lee

{lhtung, king, pffung, wslee}@cse.cuhk.edu.hk
Department of Computer Science and Engineering,
The Chinese University of Hong Kong,
Shatin, New Territories, Hong Kong

Abstract. We propose a two-stage polygon representation for polygon shape matching in image databases. The first stage performs qualitative measure of shape by using the Binary String Descriptor to quickly find equivalent classes of polygons. The second stage performs quantitative measure of shape by using a Multi-Resolution Area Matching which operates on the subset of shapes belonging to the same equivalent class by a coarse-to-fine area matching strategy. We describe these techniques and demonstrate how this two-stage representation works for a simple shape image database.

1 Introduction

Query-by-shape is a fundamental operation in an image database system. It provides intuitive way to access an object by its outline. Hence, shape representation, indexing and matching are important issues for image databases.

Considerable work has been carried out on shape manipulation problem. The Freeman Chain Code method is proposed in [5, 6] which use a string to record the turning direction of the boundary pixels of a digitized shape. The shape matching task is performed using substring matching techniques. In [10], an improved shape moment method is proposed which compares shapes using their shape moments but with an improvement on the efficiency of computing shape moments. In [9], a shape is represented by a list of rectangles (a rectangular cover) and the similarity between shapes are measured by the similarity between their rectangular covers. In [4], preprocessed template shapes are placed inside another shape. The template shapes are then grown subject to an artificial potential field defined by the edges of the template shape and the one to match. Matching is carried out by finding the template shape that has the maximum growth. In [12, 13], polygons are normalized and the Euclidean Distance between the coordinate lists of polygons are used as the similarity measure between polygons.

Methods for the shape matching problem can be classified into two categories. The first category use model-driven approach, in which the target shape is compared individually against each model shape in the database. This approach suffers from inefficiency as the matching process requires every stored shape to be compared with the target shape. The second category use data-driven approach, in which shapes are mapped into some multidimensional index structures and matching is conducted by performing searching in the index trees. The efficiency of this approach highly depends on the efficiency of Point Access Method (PAM, data structures that support storage and retrieval of points in a multidimensional space) used. Roughly speaking, a large number of dimension is required when mapping shapes into multidimensional index structures and PAMs suffer from inefficiency when the number of dimension involved is large.

In this paper, we propose a method which performs shape matching using an combination of model-driven approach and data-driven approach. It is a model-driven approach augmented with data-driven method for reducing the number of shapes needed to be compared and thus improves the efficiency of model-driven based polygon matching. We combine two techniques in polygon matching task: Binary String Descriptor (BSD) [2] and Multi-Resolution Area Matching (MRAM) technique. Table 1 gives a summary on the characteristics of these two techniques. Our idea is to perform polygon matching in two stages:

1. perform a coarse but fast polygon classification
2. perform a precise polygon matching within a subset of polygons produced previous step

In the first stage, polygons are represented by BSD (Section 2) and are partitioned into different equivalent classes with respect to their Standardized Binary Shape Descriptors (SBSD) (Section 2.2). The second stage of polygon matching is carried out within an equivalent class produced in first stage. In this stage, polygons are represented by Multi-Resolution Area Information (MRAI) (Section 3.1) and similarity measure between polygons is performed using coarse-to-fine area based matching (Section 3.2). How these two techniques are incorporated into image database systems is presented in Section 4. We have implemented a simple database system to evaluate our approach and the result of our experiments is discussed in Section 5. Conclusion is made in Section 6.

2   Binary String Descriptor

In our present work, instead of handling arbitrary shapes, we only handle closed, simple and non-degenerate polygons.

Definition 1. A polygon is represented by an ordered list of vertices $P = \{V_1, V_2, \cdots, V_n\}$, where n is the number of vertices of the polygon and $V_i \in \mathbb{R}^2$.

Definition 2. A polygon is simple if no two edges of the polygon cross each other.

Definition 3. A polygon is non-degenerate if $\nexists 1 \leq i \leq n$ such that $V_i, V_{(i+1) \bmod n}, V_{(i+2) \bmod n}$ are collinear.

2.1 Basic idea

A BSD [2] is a binary string recording the convexities and concavities of the vertices of a polygon. Let '0' denotes a convex vertex (interior angle less than π) and '1' denotes a concave vertex (interior angle larger than π).

Definition 4. A Binary String Descriptor (BSD) is a string $\{0, 1\}^n$, where n is the number of vertices of the polygon the descriptor is associated with.

Figure 1 shows several polygons and their BSDs. Note that the BSD is scale and orientation invariant since the measurement of convexity and concavity of a vertex is independent of these properties. However, the specific instance of the BSD of a polygon depends on the selection of the *anchor vertex* (the vertex of the polygon at which we start recording the BSD).

2.2 Standardizing Binary String Descriptor

A polygon can be represented by more than one BSD depending on the sequence of vertices being recorded. For example, a polygon represented by BSD '0010' can also be represented by '0100', '1000' or '0001', depending on the anchor vertex (Figure 2). The idea of standardizing BSD is introduced in [2] in order to obtain a unique BSD for a given polygon.

Given a BSD $B = \{0, 1\}^n$, a rotated BSD B_i, for $1 \leq i \leq n$, is another BSD resulted by rotating the bits of B such that the ith MSB of B becomes the MSB of B_i. Let $M(B_i)$ denotes the magnitude of B_i regarding it as a binary integer.

Definition 5. The standardized Binary String Descriptor (SBSD) of B is B_j such that $M(B_j) = \min_i M(B_i), 1 \leq i \leq n$.

Note that SBSD inherits the scale and orientation invariant properties from BSD and it is independent of the selection of anchor vertex.

2.3 Number of equivalent classes for n-gons

BSD function is a many-to-one mapping, i.e. more than one polygon may have the same BSD. Two polygons having the same SBSD are said to be in the same equivalent class. For polygons with n sides, there are 2^n possible BSDs. However, some of them are invalid and some are the same after standardization. For n-gons, the number of equivalent classes (E) is given in [2] as:

$$E = \frac{1}{n} \sum_{m \in D_n} m X_n(m) - (\lfloor \frac{n}{2} \rfloor + 2)$$

where D_n is the set of divisors of n,

$$X_n(m) = 2^{\frac{n}{m}} - (X_n(m_1) + \cdots + X_n(m_k))$$

and $m_1, \cdots, m_k$ are the multiples of m belonging to $D_n \backslash \{m\}$.

Table 2 shows the number of equivalent classes for polygons with sides from 3 to 16. It indicates that the BSD may not be a good method for polygon classification when the polygons being handled are with small number of sides since the numbers of equivalent classes are relatively small in these situations. For example, all triangles will be in the same equivalent class.

3   Multi-Resolution Area Matching

Once the equivalent class is found, the subset of polygons will then be matched by MRAM. We will now describe how multi-resolution area information (MRAI hereafter) of polygons is computed and how similarity between polygons is measured using MRAI.

3.1   Computing MRAI

A polygon, which is normalized to have a unit bounding box (Section 4.1), is first scan-converted onto a frame buffer with $W \times W$ pixels. MRAI is computed using a pyramid structure approach with Quadtree [14] area coding:

1. MRAI is recorded starting at level 0.
2. At level 0, the whole frame buffer is regarded as a cell. The portion of area covered by the polygon is recorded.
3. At level k, cells are obtained by quartering every cell of level $k - 1$. The portion of area covered by the polygon in each level-k cell is recorded. There are 4^k cells at level k.

The MRAI at each level is concatenated into a complete MRAI vector. The size of this vector depends on K, the maximum resolution level to be recorded, and is given as $L = \sum_{i=0}^{K} 4^i = \frac{4^{K+1}-1}{3}$.

Figure 6 shows an example of computation of MRAI. In this example, the size of the frame buffer is 16 pixels by 16 pixels large and MRAI is recorded up to resolution level 2. Figure 6(a) shows the cell partitioning of resolution level 0. The area information recorded at level 0 is $\langle \frac{180}{256} \rangle$. Likewise, Figure 6(b) shows the cell partitioning of resolution level 1 and the area information recorded at level 1 is $\langle \frac{46}{64}, \frac{46}{64}, \frac{45}{64}, \frac{43}{64} \rangle$. The same operation is applied at resolution level 2. By concatenating the area information of the three levels, we obtain the complete area information as: $\langle \frac{180}{256}, \frac{46}{64}, \frac{46}{64}, \frac{45}{64}, \frac{43}{64}, \frac{6}{16}, \frac{14}{16}, \frac{6}{16}, \frac{8}{16}, \frac{10}{16}, \frac{16}{16}, \frac{16}{16}, \frac{16}{16}, \frac{5}{16}, \frac{16}{16}, \frac{16}{16}, \frac{13}{16}, \frac{8}{16}, \frac{16}{16}, \frac{13}{16}, \frac{1}{16} \rangle$.

3.2   Measuring similarity using MRAI

We use the L_p distance to measure the similarity of two polygons at a specific level of resolution. Given polygon A and B, with their MRAI, the similarity of these two polygons at resolution level k is:

$$S_k(A, B) = \left(\sum_{i=1}^{4^k} |A_{ki} - B_{ki}|^p \right)^{\frac{1}{p}}$$

where $S_k(A, B)$ is the similarity measure of A and B at resolution level k, A_{ki} and B_{ki} are the portion of covered area in level k cells of polygon A and B respectively, and $p = 2$ in our implementation.

Matching of two polygons can be done in stages, that is, perform similarity measuring from coarse resolution (level 0) to fine resolution (the maximum resolution level K, where $K = 3$ in our implementation).

Definition 6. Two polygons A and B are said to be similar at level k if $S_k(A, B) \leq \delta_k$ where δ_k is a predefined threshold value for level k similarity measure.

Definition 7. Two polygons are said to be matched if they are similar at all levels, i.e. the two polygons are similar at level $0, \cdots, K$.

4 Polygon matching in image database

4.1 Database population

When an image is added into an image database, some preprocessing tasks are carried out. First of all, user has to define a number of polygons on the input image for future queries, if this image should be involved in query-by-shape operation. This task can be automated, by employing some shape segmentation algorithms such as [1, 15, 8, 11, 7], or the shape can be outlined by user manually. Each defined polygon will then go through the following preprocessing:

1. **Removal of collinear vertices** For any three successive vertices V_i, V_j and V_k of a polygon, V_j is removed if the three vertices are collinear such that the resultant polygon will be non-degenerate.
2. **Orientation standardization** We compute the BSD, B, of a polygon and then standardize B to obtain the SBSD, B_j, using the algorithm in Section 2.2. The representation of the polygon is then changed to $\{V_j, V_{j+1}, \cdots, V_n, V_1, \cdots, V_{j-1}\}$. After the re-arrangement of vertices, the coordinates of $V_1, \cdots, V_n$ are translated to place V_j at the origin and then rotated with respect to V_j such that the edge (V_j, V_{j+1}) is aligned with the y-axis.
3. **Scale normalization** We find out the bounding box of a polygon, then scale the bounding box to a unit square and transform the coordinates of $V_1, \cdots, V_n$ according to the same scaling factor.
4. **Polygon smoothing** Along the perceived edges of the polygon, there may be many jerks and trivial edges (e.g. when automatic shape segmentation algorithm is employed). We reduce the number of sides of the polygon by removing such disturbances and make the polygon smooth. A polygon $P' = \{V'_1, \cdots, V'_m\}$ is a smoothed version of polygon $P = \{V_1, \cdots, V_n\}$ if $m < n$ and $\exists f$ such that $f(V_1, \cdots, V_n) \rightarrow (V'_1, \cdots, V'_m)$. One of the goals of polygon smoothing is to find a minimum m that maximizes the common area of P' and P.

After the above preprocessing steps, we should have a smoothed, orientation standardized, and scale normalized non-degenerate polygon and it is ready for further manipulation. For each preprocessed polygon defined in an image, we compute its SBSD and MRAI as stated in Section 2 and Section 3. A tuple ⟨SBSD, MRAI, image⟩ is then added into database for future queries and retrievals.

4.2   Query-by-shape

This section describes how query-by-shape can be carried out using our approach. Two kind of shape queries, namely *matching queries* and *similar queries*, are considered. We will describe how to initiate a shape query and how to process these two kind of queries.

Initiating a query To initiate a shape query, user may either specify a polygon by sketching it out or by selecting a shape from the database. For sketched shapes, automatic shape segmentation algorithm and shape preprocessing techniques, mentioned in Section 4.1, have to be employed in order to obtain a polygon. This polygon is regarded as the *target polygon* in remaining discussion. We then compute the SBSD and MRAI of the target polygon.

Matching query Matching queries refers to queries like "find me images containing objects having this shape (a target polygon)". A matching query is carried out in following steps:

1. Select the set of polygons $Q = \{p_i \mid p_i \in P \ \wedge \ SBSD(p_i) = SBSD(T)\}$ where P is the set of polygons in the database and T is the target polygon.
2. Select the set of polygons $R = \{p_i \mid p_i \in Q \ \wedge \ matched(p_i, T)\}$ where $matched(p_i, T)$ denotes the predicate which measures the similarity between p_i and T using the algorithm proposed in Section 3.2.
3. The set of images in the database containing polygons in R is the result of the query.

Similar query Besides matching query, users of image database need to perform similar query like "find me 10 images containing objects that are most similar to this shape (a target polygon)". A similar query is carried out in the following steps:

1. Select the set of polygons $Q = \{p_i \mid p_i \in P \ \wedge \ SBSD(p_i) = SBSD(T)\}$ where P is the set of polygons in the database and T is the target polygon.
2. **for** $i = 0$ **to** K **do**
       sort Q in descending order of $S_i(p_j, T)$ where $p_j \in Q$
       $Q \leftarrow \{p_j \mid p_j \in Q, 1 \leq j \leq N_i\}$ ﹐
       /* $K = 3, N_0 = 100, N_1 = 50, N_2 = 25, N_3 = 10$ */
       /* in our implementation */
   end for

3. The set of images in the database containing polygons in Q is the result of the query.

5 Experiments

A simple database system is implemented to carry out experiments on the proposed approach. This simple system consists of three components:

1. a polygon generator which generates testing data (produces random polygons with uniformly distributed SBSD).
2. a database builder which takes the output of the polygon generator, normalizes the polygons as described in Section 4.1, computes the SBSD and MRAI of the polygons, and then stores them in simple database files.
3. a matching engine incorporating our approach which allows users to select the target polygon from a list of templates and performs similar queries within a simple database using the algorithm proposed in Section 4.2.

Note that the databases used in this simple system is simply flat files with no indexing and buffering. Figure 6 shows an example of similar matching query performed on the simple database system.

Empirical tests are conducted on a Sun SPARCstation 10. Table 3 lists some performance statistics of the experiments. The column "time for building database" shows the time used by database builder in constructing simple databases. The column "average query time" shows the average time used for a query to be carried out on different simple databases. Simple databases of polygons with sides from 3 to 8 are used and each database contains 9000 polygons with the same number of sides.

The time needed to construct the databases are roughly the same since the numbers of polygons to be processed are all 9000 and the computation of MRAI is independent of the number of sides. The average query time decreases when the number of sides increases. This is because when the number of sides is small, there are fewer equivalent classes thus many polygons will be mapped into the same equivalent class as the target polygon and more detailed comparisons must be carried out when queries are conducted. For example, when the number of sides of polygons is 3, all the polygons in the database will be in the same equivalent class as the target polygon and thus, every polygon has to be compared to the target polygon when queries are conducted. When the number of sides increases, the number of equivalent classes also increases, which results in a reduction of polygons needed to be compared to the target polygon when queries are conducted since less polygons are mapped into the same equivalent class as the target polygon.

6 Conclusion

We proposed a two-stage method for matching closed, simple and non-degenerate polygons using a combination of model-driven approach and data-driven approach. This method can be use to provide query-by-shape facility in image databases. Our approach incorporated both Binary String Descriptor and Multi-resolution Area Matching techniques for qualitative and quantitative measure of polygons.

References

1. D. H. Ballard. Generalizing the Hough Transform to Detect Arbitrary shapes. *Pattern Recognition*, 13(2):111–122, 1981.
2. B. Bhavnagri. A Method for Representing Shape Based on an Equivalent Relation on Polygons. *Pattern Recognition*, 27(2):247–260, 1994.
3. E. Bribiesca and A. Guzman. How to Describe Pure Form and How to Measure Differences in Shapes Using Shape Numbers. *Patter Recognition*, 12:101–112, 1980.
4. J. H. Chuang. A Potential-Based Approach for Shape Matching and Recognition. *Pattern Recogntion*, 29(3):463–470, 1996.
5. H. Freeman. Boundary Encoding and Processing. In *Picture Processing and Psychopictorics*, pages 241–266.
6. H. Freeman. Analysis of the Precision of Generalized Chain Codes for the Representation of Planar Curves. *Pattern Analysis and Machine Intelligence*, 3(5):533–539, Sept. 1981.
7. P. F. Fung, W. S. Lee, and I. King. Randomized Generalized Hough Transform for 2-D grayscale object detection [to be appeared in ICPR'96].
8. J. Illingworth and J. Kittler. The Adaptive Hough Transform. *IEEE Trans. Pattern Anal. Machine Intell.*, 9:690–698, 1987.
9. H. V. Jagadish. A Retrieval Technique for Similar Shapes. In *Proc. of the ACM SIGMOD International Conference on the Management of Data*, pages 208–217, May 1991.
10. J. G. Leu. Computing a Shape's Moments from its Boundary. *Pattern Recognition*, 24(10):949–957, 1991.
11. H. Li, M. Lavin, and R. LeMaster. Fast Hough Transform, a hierarchical approach. *Computer Vision, Graphics and Image Processing*, 36:139–161, 1986.
12. R. Mehrotra and J. E. Gray. Feature-Based Retrieval of Similar Shapes. In *Proc. 9th International Conference on Data Engineering*, pages 108–115, 1993.
13. R. Mehrotra and J. E. Gray. Similar-Shape Retrieval in Shape Data Management. In *IEEE Computer Magazine*, pages 57–62, 1995.
14. H. Samet. *The Design and Analysis of Spatial Data Structures*. Addison-Wesley, 1990.
15. L. Su, E. Oja, and P. Kultanen. A New Curve Detection Method: Randomized Hough Transform (RHT). *Pattern Recognition Letters*, 11:331–338, 1990.
16. W. H. Tsai and S. S. Yu. Attributed string matching with merging for shape recognition. *IEEE Trans. Pattern Analysis Mach. Intell.*, 7:453–462, 1985.

Table 1. Characteristics of BSD and MRAM.

	BSD	MRAM
Characteristic	Qualitative	Quantitative
Strategy	Angle-based, Coarse	Area-based, Coarse-to-fine
Speed	Fast	Slow
Properties	Scale and orientation invariant	Scale and orientation sensitive

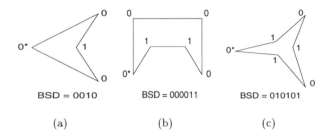

BSD = 0010   BSD = 000011   BSD = 010101

(a)   (b)   (c)

Fig. 1. Several polygons and their BSDs. The anchor vertex is marked with "*".

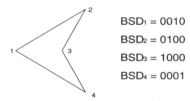

$BSD_1 = 0010$

$BSD_2 = 0100$

$BSD_3 = 1000$

$BSD_4 = 0001$

Fig. 2. Different BSDs for a polygon with different anchor vertices.

Table 2. N-gons and number of their distinct equivalent classes.

n	3	4	5	6	7	8	9	10	11	12	13	14	15	16
E	1	2	4	9	15	30	54	101	181	343	624	1173	2183	4106

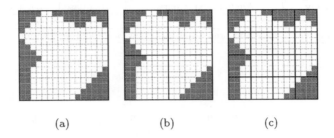

(a)   (b)   (c)

Fig. 3. Computing Multi-Resolution Area Information (MRAI). (a) Resolution level 0 with 1 cell. (b) Resolution level 1 with 4 cells. (c) Resolution level 2 with 16 cells.

Table 3. Experiment results.

N-gon	Number of equivalent classes	Polygons per equivalent class	Total number of polygons	Time for building database	Average query time
3	1	9000	9000	339.42 sec	2.18 sec
4	2	4500	9000	340.22 sec	1.86 sec
5	4	2250	9000	350.03 sec	1.74 sec
6	9	1000	9000	366.88 sec	1.65 sec
7	15	600	9000	362.30 sec	1.60 sec
8	30	300	9000	364.62 sec	1.58 sec

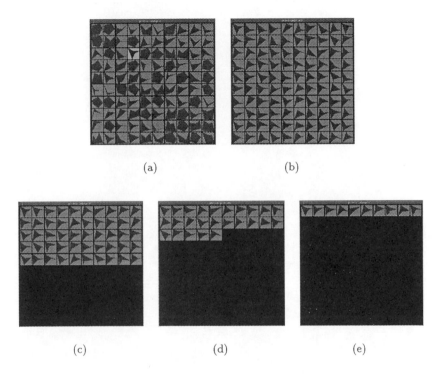

(a)   (b)

(c)   (d)   (e)

Fig. 4. Example of similar matching query. (a) the highlighted polygon is selected from a list of templates as the target for query-by-shape. (b) the 100 candidates after level 0 Multi-resolution Area Matching. (c) the 50 remaining candidates after level 1 Multi-resolution Area Matching. (d) the 25 remaining candidates after level 2 Multi-resolution Area Matching. (e) the 10 most similar polygons to the target after level 3 Multi-resolution Area Matching.

A Comparison between Different Modal Matching Based Similarity Indexes

Fabio Dell'Acqua[1], Paolo Gamba[1] and Alessandro Mecocci[2]

[1] Dipartimento di Elettronica, Università di Pavia, I-27100 Pavia, Italy
[2] Facoltà di Ingegneria, Università di Siena, I-55300 Siena, Italy

Abstract. In this work we present the application of modal matching to visual search in an image database by means of a user-defined sketch. Similarity evaluation for scarcely sampled shapes is outlined, as well as the problems related to modal matching between differently sampled objects. Four different definitions of possible similarity indexes are presented and discussed.

1 Introduction

While our society evolves from a word-driven to an image-driven communication environment, also stored informations are now passing from a collection of words (*documents*), to a collection of digital data (*images*). Correspondingly, image and video databases are now widespread, and many commercial as well as research projects have been started in this area (for a summary, see [1].

However, stored informations need to be retrieved in an efficient way while allowing the user to interact with a query system that exploits the characteristics of the objects to be extracted. That's why new typologies of query, more and more suitable to cope with the human psychology and the intrinsic structure of the data have been developed.

In this research direction, one of the key problems in database image retrieval is shape recognition. Shape analysis allows to search of objects whose characteristics are difficult to be expressed by words. Moreover, shape search, as well as color and texture search, provides a very intuitive and user-friendly interface to non-technical users, who may consider more easy to draw a sketch of the object than to describe it by words.

In the last years many techniques have been developed to achieve shape recognition ([2]-[4]). More recently, to solve the problems which affect many methods (sampling error, parameterization error, and nonuniqueness), a modal matching approach has been proposed [5], where the deformation modes of a shape are computed and used as a basis for correspondence and recognition. In [5], these modes are computed as the solutions of a generalized eigenvalue problem.

Modal matching need to be further optimized for similarity search between differently sampled shapes. Scarcely sampled shapes, for instance, are defined by only a few N points, and this helps to keep low the computational burden of the method. However, as a consequence of the FEM method in the modal matching technique, the precision of the eigenmodes and eigenvalues of the problem is also proportional to N. Therefore, modal matching involving scarcely sampled shapes should be improved to be more effective.

In this paper we present the application of modal matching to the visual search in an image database; this leads to the comparison between scarcely and optimally sampled shapes (the user-defined sketches and the database images). Different similarity index are introduced and compared, evaluating their effectiveness; some investigations on the choice of the shape of the basis functions are also made.

2   The Modal Matching Technique

The modal matching technique is based on the representation of an object by means of N points, generally (but not only) from its boundary. Each point is considered as a concentrated mass element (or *node*), bounded to its neighbors by elastic relations. The ensemble of all points follows the *dynamic equilibrium equation*:

$$\mathbf{M}\frac{\partial^2 \mathbf{U}}{\partial t^2} + \mathbf{D}\frac{\partial \mathbf{U}}{\partial t} + \mathbf{K}\mathbf{U} = \mathbf{R} \quad in \ \mathbb{R}^2 \tag{1}$$

where $\mathbf{U}$ denotes the vector of displacements at each node, $\mathbf{R}$ is the load function, $\mathbf{M}, \mathbf{K}$ and $\mathbf{D}$ are the mass, stiffness and damping matrices defined by the material matrix $\mathbf{C}$, that expresses the material stress-strain law, by the mass density ρ, and by the interpolation matrix $\mathbf{H}$, that relates the basis functions to $\mathbf{U}$.

Equation (1) is solved introducing N Gaussian basis functions

$$g_i(\mathbf{x}) = \exp(-\|\mathbf{x} - \mathbf{x}_i\|^2 / 2\sigma^2) \tag{2}$$

each centered on a node, and a FEM (Finite Element Method) procedure. The displacement is expressed in terms of the solutions of the eigenvalue matrix equation:

$$\mathbf{K}\Phi = \Omega^2 \mathbf{M}\Phi \tag{3}$$

where both $\mathbf{K}$ and $\mathbf{M}$ are computed using, among the others, the matrix

$$\mathbf{A} = \mathbf{G}^{-1} = \begin{bmatrix} g_1(\mathbf{x}_1) & g_2(\mathbf{x}_1) & \cdots & g_N(\mathbf{x}_1) \\ g_1(\mathbf{x}_2) & g_2(\mathbf{x}_2) & \cdots & g_N(\mathbf{x}_2) \\ \cdots & \cdots & \cdots \\ g_1(\mathbf{x}_N) & g_2(\mathbf{x}_N) & \cdots & g_N(\mathbf{x}_N) \end{bmatrix}^{-1} \tag{4}$$

To overcome as far as possible the problems related to the inversion of $\mathbf{G}$, we do not solve (3), but

$$\mathbf{K}'\Phi' = \Lambda^2 \mathbf{M}'\Phi' \tag{5}$$

$$\lambda_i = \omega_i \sqrt{\frac{\rho\sigma^2}{\beta}} \tag{6}$$

$$\mathbf{K}' = \frac{1}{\pi\beta} \begin{bmatrix} \mathbf{G} & 0 \\ 0 & \mathbf{G} \end{bmatrix} \mathbf{K} \qquad (7)$$

$$\mathbf{M}' = \frac{1}{\rho\pi\sigma^2} \begin{bmatrix} \mathbf{G} & 0 \\ 0 & \mathbf{G} \end{bmatrix} \mathbf{M} \qquad (8)$$

$$\Phi = \begin{bmatrix} \mathbf{G} & 0 \\ 0 & \mathbf{G} \end{bmatrix} \Phi' \qquad (9)$$

$\beta = E(1-\nu)/((1+\nu)(1-2\nu))$, ν is the Poisson ratio, E the material's modulus of elasticity.

With respect to (3), the choice of (5) leads to different (but related) eigenvalues and eigenvectors, and we loose the intuitive meaning of each ϕ_i' (for example, the first three eigenvectors no longer represent two translations and a rotation). However, one has the advantage of a greater robustness of the algoritm. In fact, in fig. 1 we report the value of σ (computed for a simple linear shape as a function of the number N of points) that leads to errors in the numerical evaluation of (3) or (5): the figure shows that the new formulation allows a wider range of σ to be used.

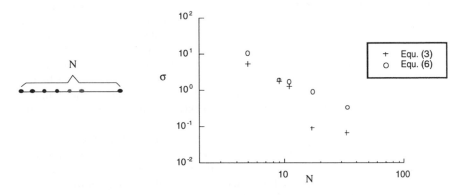

Fig. 1. Given a segment of unitary length, represented by N points, for each value of N the figure shows the correspondent value of σ that cause the matrix M or M′ to be ill-conditioned (according to standard LINPACK mathematical routines).

Once modal analysis has been completed, the modal matching procedure continues by finding correspondences between points in similar shapes through the comparison of the nodal displacements due to each mode. To assure a better correlation, an alignment step if the shapes have a very different orientation and a reordering of the modes can be also established [6]. Finally, a reliable measure of similarity is obtained by means of the strain energy required to stretch one of the shapes to fit to the other.

3   Scarcely Sampled Shapes and Modal Matching

The Modal Matching technique can be easily applied in image database management; for example, the user chooses one of the images, even distorted, and query for similar ones in the archive [8]. The search is performed by a comparison of the previously stored and pre-analyzed shapes with the chosen object. However, we would like to let the user draw a sketch of the desired object, and compare this shape with the stored ones. The advantage of modal analysis in this case is related to the ability to deal with the (mean) poor quality of these sketches: even if the shape is only roughly drawn, lower modes (that represent the lower details of the image) should be sufficient to retrieve good quality results. Nevertheless, some problems arise: in particular, since sketched shapes are introduced by hand, they appear generally scarcely and non-regularly sampled (the user usually picks feature points of the shape), while stored images are usually optimally sampled. Therefore, we must face the problem of modal matching of differently or very differently sampled shapes.

3.1   The choice of the basis functions

First of all, we need some considerations about basis functions: Gaussian basis functions are surely the best choice to build the $\mathbf{K}$ and $\mathbf{M}$ matrices with small computational effort, but only once a suitable choice of the parameter σ has been found. For the same figure, in fact, different values of σ define actually different structures, with different deformation modes. The larger is σ, the more the nodes are bounded one to the other; with smaller σ, instead, deformations have a more local behavior. Moreover, the range of σ is limited: it can not be too small, since in this case each point behaves as if it is alone; on the other hand, it can not be too large, otherwise matrix $\mathbf{M}'$ quickly becomes ill-conditioned, and the equation (5) has no more real solution.

For a given arbitrarily shaped object and a given sampling, we found that the best choice for σ is $\sqrt{A/N}$, where A is the figure's area, and N the number of sampling points. This value assumes that sampling is uniform in $\mathbb{R}^2$. If, instead, the figure is sampled only on its boundary, a suitable alternative definition could be the mean sampling distance. Both this choices allow to overcome the problems about $\mathbf{M}'$; this matrix never becomes ill-conditioned. However, we stress that the same figure, differently sampled, produces different modes, since they are computed with different σ. As long as we do not have any a priori knowledge about the objects to study, this is a unavoidable drawback. As an example, in fig. 2, 3 the first deformation modes of the same, but differently sampled, shape are reported.

3.2   Mode Reordering

Since different σ means different modes, after modal analysis, it is necessary a mode correspondence and reordering step. This is done after a pre-alignment of the shapes by a fast moment-of-inertia method [7]. Then, once figures have been

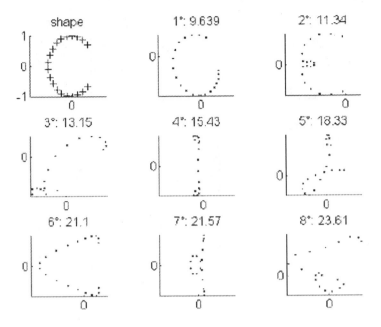

Fig. 2. Deformation modes of a 'C' shape represented by means of 20 points.

aligned, mode correspondence can be achieved by comparing the displacements caused by each mode at the M points of a regular grid around the shapes. The comparison is performed over the whole set of modes of both figures, since with scarcely or differently sampled shapes correspondent modes of different figures may be in very different positions.

The mode correspondence algorithm relies on the **V** matrix, whose ij-th element v_{ij} is defined as

$$v_{ij} = 1 - \frac{1}{M} \sum_{k=1}^{M} \frac{\left| \mathbf{\Delta}_k^i \cdot \mathbf{\Delta}_k^j \right|}{\left\| \mathbf{\Delta}_k^i \right\| \left\| \mathbf{\Delta}_k^j \right\|} \tag{10}$$

where $\mathbf{\Delta}_k^j$ is the j-th modal displacement at the k-th element of the grid. Mode reordering is achieved by searching for the smallest value in each row, assuming that rows represent the modes of the less sampled shape.

Table 1 reports the reordered modes for differently sampled 'C' shapes (see fig. 4). We observe that the initial sequence of modes is generally changed very much.

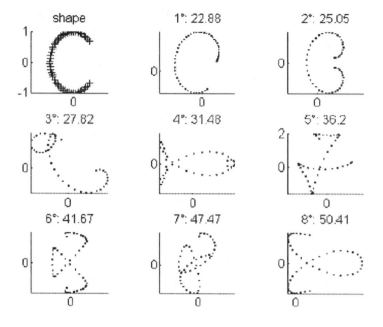

Fig. 3. Deformation modes of a 'C' shape represented by means of 50 points.

Table 1. Mode order (after reordering) for differently sampled 'C' shapes.

	1	2	3	4	5	6	7	8	9	10	11	12	13	14	15	16
C_{20}	1	2	3	4	5	6	7	8	9	10	11	12	13	14	15	16
C_{30}	1	2	3	4	5	7	44	8	50	10	12	31	13	14	15	16
C_{40}	1	2	59	4	5	7	54	9	8	41	52	31	51	13	15	50
C_{50}	63	2	58	4	5	8	54	9	53	70	37	31	51	33	12	50

3.3   Similarity Evaluation

After mode reordering, we need a similarity index to define how much the compared shapes are similar. A first idea comes from the same mode reordering procedure: in quite different figures, modes tend to be associated with other modes in similar or even quite different positions, and, accordingly, comparing different figures, mode order tends to be upset. This means that a similarity index can be related to the distances of the corresponding modes, i.e.

$$i_1 = \frac{1}{2N} \sum_{i=1}^{2N} (i - j) \qquad j \, / \, \min_j v_{ij} \qquad (11)$$

where N is the node number for the less sampled figure.

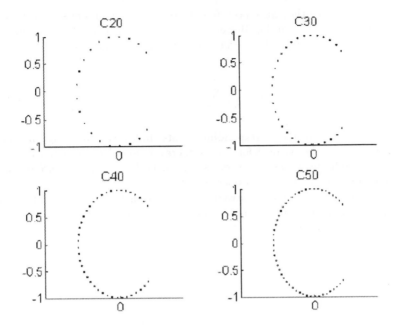

Fig. 4. Differently sampled 'C' shapes: $C_{20}, C_{30}, C_{40}, C_{50}$.

However, situations have been found where different figures preserve the same mode order. This is due to the fact that the algorithm is compelled to associate most similar modes, regardless of how different they actually are; so, it may occur that most similar modes, even from different figures and very different themselves, are by chance corresponding in increasing eigenvalue ordering. So, we can say nothing when mode order is left unchanged, but figures with different mode order upset are certainly different: i_1 is, more appropriately, a good *dissimilarity* index. Obviously, this feature can be very useful in speeding up visual search.

A better similarity choice could be to consider the differences between corresponding modes, and a second similarity index can be defined as

$$i_2 = 1 - \frac{1}{2N} \, \text{trace}(\mathbf{V}') \tag{12}$$

where $\mathbf{V}'$ is the $2N \times 2N$ submatrix extracted from $\mathbf{V}$ after the mode reordering.

However, for small N, modal correspondences proved to be an unreliable index of how similar the figures are; the variability of experimental values has shown to be too large to ensure a suitable evaluation. More precise measures can be achieved instead by nodal correspondences. The N' corresponding points of the shapes to be compared are obtained by means of the comparison of the modal displacements; once they have been found, we can use a similarity index based on the strain energy as in [5]. However, a simpler energy similarity evaluation method could be based on the distance between the associated points of the two figures, i.e.

$$i_3 = \frac{1}{N'} \sum_{i=1}^{N'} \|\mathbf{x}_i - \mathbf{x}'_i\|^2 \tag{13}$$

where $\mathbf{x}_i$ and $\mathbf{x}'_i$ are the corresponding points. Index i_3 is actually an energy index, related to the mean deformation energy required to stretch one of the shapes to match the other only on corresponding nodes. It is more noise-sensitive than strain energy index, but also less cpu-time consuming.

Finally, it can be useful to introduce a correction to index i_3 and take into account the robustness of point associations, to overcome errors due to unreliable point matchings. Therefore, we introduced the index i_4

$$i_4 = \frac{1}{N'} \sum_{i=1}^{N'} w_{ii} \|\mathbf{x}_i - \mathbf{x}'_i\|^2 \tag{14}$$

where $\mathbf{W}$ is a weight matrix similar to $\mathbf{V}'$, but computed starting from corresponding nodes instead than modes. Moreover, two more indexes have been studies and results shown in the following section, namely

$$i_5 = \frac{1}{N''} \sum_{i=1}^{N''} w_{ii} \|\mathbf{x}_i - \mathbf{x}'_i\|^2 \tag{15}$$

$$i_6 = \frac{1}{N'''} \sum_{i=1}^{N'''} w_{ii} \|\mathbf{x}_i - \mathbf{x}'_i\|^2 \tag{16}$$

where N'' is the number of points such that $P\left(\|\mathbf{x}_i - \mathbf{x}'_i\|^2 \le d_{max}\right) = 0.9$, $d_{max} = \max_i \|\mathbf{x}_i - \mathbf{x}'_i\|^2$, and N''' is the corrispondent of N'' when considering also the weights w_{ii}.

We are looking forward to consider another index, a possible i_7, in whose the choice of elements to put into the set N' is based on absolute distances, instead of weighed distances. This is expected to carry some improvements in the sense of more reliable elimination of less likely point matchings. These latter, in fact, have usually farthest absolute distances; we fear that multiplication of those distances by possibly low reliability coefficients might in some cases hide their actual precariousness and let them be accepted even if so few likely. By performing choice of matchings to eliminate before multiplying distances by reliability coefficients we may evade this obstacle. So far, this improvement is not certain at all, but experiments are in progress.

4 Database search results

The previously defined similarity index have been used to speed up the visual search in two simple image databases, one with elements that are manually introduced alphabetical letters, and an other with stilized objects. Evens if the program is not completely optimized, since it is written in MATLAB language and runs on a standard PC, results are very encouraging.

Table 2. Similarity indexes i_1, i_2 and i_3 for the 'C' shapes.

	i_1				i_2				i_3			
	C_{20}	C_{30}	C_{40}	C_{50}	C_{20}	C_{30}	C_{40}	C_{50}	C_{20}	C_{30}	C_{40}	C_{50}
C_{20}	0.00	4.58	12.08	21.05	0.00	0.55	0.64	0.72	0.0000	0.0038	0.0033	0.0568
C_{30}	4.575	0.00	8.20	19.18	0.55	0.00	0.50	0.60	0.0038	0.0000	0.0012	0.0030
C_{40}	12.08	8.20	0.00	17.56	0.64	0.50	0.00	0.44	0.0034	0.0012	0.0000	0.0014
C_{50}	21.05	19.18	17.56	0.00	0.72	0.60	0.44	0.00	0.0568	0.0030	0.0014	0.0000

Table 3. Similarity indexes i_4, i_5 and i_6 for the 'C' shapes.

	i_4				i_5				i_6			
	C_{20}	C_{30}	C_{40}	C_{50}	C_{20}	C_{30}	C_{40}	C_{50}	C_{20}	C_{30}	C_{40}	C_{50}
C_{20}	0.0000	0.0042	0.0026	0.0522	0.0000	0.0029	0.0027	0.0089	0.0000	0.0037	0.0029	0.0102
C_{30}	0.0042	0.0000	0.0016	0.0027	0.0029	0.0000	0.0010	0.0020	0.0037	0.0000	0.0011	0.0017
C_{40}	0.0026	0.0016	0.0000	0.0014	0.0027	0.0010	0.0000	0.0010	0.0029	0.0011	0.0000	0.0011
C_{50}	0.0522	0.0027	0.0014	0.0000	0.0089	0.0020	0.0010	0.0000	0.0101	0.0017	0.0011	0.0000

In Table 2, 3 the values of all indexes for the 'C' shapes of fig. 3 are reported. We note that i_2 presents the best results, since it gives almost equal values for all the comparisons, that refer to the same figure, only differently sampled. Index i_1, instead, presents constantly increasing values from C_{20} to C_{50}, while a better behavior is shown by i_3 and i_4, that, nevertheless, give both too high results for the comparison between C_{20} and C_{50}. More precise results, in this sense, could be obtained by means of i_5 and i_6, that both show a better behaviour. Therefore, a useful choice could be to exploit i_2 for an initial screening step in the search procedure, where we want to discard as much as possible different shapes, but also to maintain similar ones, even very differently sampled.

For the further, and final, step, we need instead, as we pointed out in Section 3.3, a node-based index, since i_1 may give wrong results, and i_2 is based on mode correspondences, that proved to be not completely reliable. Therefore, the final step in our search procedure is the ordering of the results by means of i_4, i_5 or

i_6 (that are better, by definition, than i_3). Table 4 shows the value of the two indexes used in our method for a limited subset of the database.

Table 4. Similarity indexes i_4, i_2 for some alphabetical letters.

	i_4					i_2			
	'C'	'O'	'Q'	'X'		'C'	'O'	'Q'	'X'
'C'	0.00	0.64	0.75	0.78		0.00	0.22	1.66	17.25
'O'	0.64	0.00	0.60	0.74		0.22	0.00	1.16	2.71
'Q'	0.75	0.60	0.00	0.70		1.66	1.16	0.00	7.16
'X'	0.78	0.74	0.70	0.00		17.25	2.71	7.16	0.00

In fig. 5 and 6, finally, two examples of results of a visual query in the complete databases are reported.

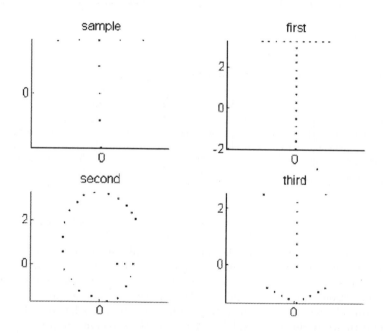

Fig. 5. An example of results of a visual query: the sample and the first three more similar shapes in the database.

In the first example, the correct sequence of alphabetical letters is obtained.

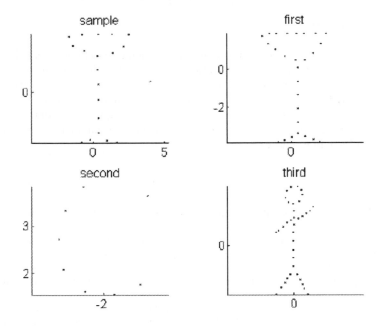

Fig. 6. An other example of results of a visual query: the sample and the first three more similar shapes in the database.

However, our results are far from definitive: in the second example, for instance, a 'C' appears between the two best answers.This is due to very close values of i_4: further improvements to our method are expected from the use of i_7.

However, we studied extensively the behaviour of the algorithm and of the similarity index on our databases: the results can be summarized in the following considerations. First of all, it should be mentioned that the letter database consists of 29 images and it was studied by means of nearly 500 trials, while the other one consists of 25 images and was tested with 100 trials. We found that, after the entire shape search procedure, the mean percentage of discarded objects is 60%, while the error percentage (the searched object has been discarded in one of the search steps) is a merely 2%. In 70% of the trials the first figure is the most similar (according to a human evaluation) to the sketch, but in 95% of cases it is among the first three, and in 97% among the first four ones. The remaining 3% almost corresponds to the error percentage considered above, and this shows that the algorithm tends to perform well or to completely fail, almost without any intermediate possibility.

5   Conclusions

In this work we have studied the application of modal matching to visual search in a simple image database. Considerations related to the choice of the parameter σ for unconstrained search, as well as different definitions of a similarity index for shapes with different deformation modes due to different sampling have been presented. The results show that a screening among shapes can be obtained by a mode reordering labor index, while refined answers to visual queries are achieved by a node matching index.

References

1. *IEEE Computer*, Special Issue on Content-Based Image Retrieval Systems, Sept. 1995.
2. Scott, G., Longuet-Higgins, H.: An algorithm for associating the features of two images. Proc. Royal Soc. of London B **244** (1991) 21–26
3. Pentland, A., Sclaroff, S.: Closed-form solutions for physically-based shape modeling and recognition. IEEE Trans. Pattern Analysis and Machine Intelligence **13** (1991) 715–729
4. Kirby, K., Sirovich, L.: Application of the Karhunen-Loeve procedure for the characterization of human faces. IEEE Trans. Pattern Analysis and Machine Intelligence **12** (1990) 103–108
5. Sclaroff, S.: Modal matching for correspondence and recognition. IEEE Trans. Pattern Analysis and Machine Intelligence **17** (1995) 545–561
6. Sclaroff, S., Pentland, A.: Modal matching: a method for describing, comparing and manipulating digital signals. Tchnical Report, MIT Media Laboratory Vision and Modeling TR-311 (1995).
7. Ballard, D., Brown, C.: Cumputer Vision. Prentice-Hall, 1982.
8. Pentland, A, Picard, R.W., Sclaroff, S..: Photobook: tools for content-based manipulation of image databases. Proc. SPIE Conf. on Storage and Retrieval of Image and Video Databases II **2185** (1994)

IFS Based Indexing in Image Databases [*]

M. Nappi, G. Polese, and G. Tortora

Dipartimento di Informatica ed Applicazioni "R.M. Capocelli"

Università degli Studi di Salerno

Abstract. We present a new Image Indexing method and an implemented system to perform Content Based retrieval in heterogeneous Image Databases. The method is based on the Theory of Iterated Function Systems (IFS), already exploited for image compression, and it uses a training set of images to build the set of indexing features. The index structure is represented through a reduced vector of features on which we use R-Tree to efficiently access images in the database.

Keywords: Content Based Retrieval, IFS, Contractive Function, DFT, R-Tree.

1 Introduction

The considerable growth of multimedia systems and applications has required the construction of appropriate data models and new indexing techniques to better manipulate complex multi media data. Particular attention has been paid to the construction of indexing techniques that allow to query multi media databases by using a query format similar to the one of the stored data [3, 9, 12]. In this context, we have constructed a new indexing technique, based on The Fractal Theory of Contractive Functions, to allow efficient retrieval in Image Databases (IDB). Starting from a training set of heterogeneous images, we construct an appropriate set of Contactive Functions (CFs), and use their frequencies inside images to derive the index structure. Performances are then improved by using Discrete Fourier Transform [14] to reduce index dimensionality, and R-Tree to speed up access to the data. The approach can be classified as a Query by Example, it can yield false alarms but limited false dismissals [4]. For brevity, in the rest of the paper we will refer to this technique as FIDI, which stands for Fractal Image Database Indexing. We have constructed a prototype system implementing the technique and run several experiments to assess it. The paper is organized as follows. In section 2 we review the basic concepts of IFS Theory, whereas in section 3 we explain how we used them to perform image indexing. Section 4 describes the method. In section 5 we show experimental data from a sample of medical images, portraits, landscapes, etc, and provide performance evaluation according to well known evaluation methods. Finally, conclusions and future developments are given in section 6.

[*] Correspondence to: M. Nappi and G. Polese, Dipartimento di Informatica ed Applicazioni (R.M. Capocelli) Università di Salerno, 84081 Baronissi (Sa) Italia, tel. +39–89–965391, fax +39–89–965272, email: {micnap, giupol}@dia.unisa.it

2   Principles of IFS Theory.

IFS Theory [2, 11] relies upon the concept of a Contractive Function (CF). This can be defined as a function $f : X \to X$ on a complete metric space (X, h) such that there exists a constant s for which the following condition is satisfied:

$$h(f(x), f(y)) \leq sh(x, y) \forall x, y \in X. \tag{1}$$

where h is the metric function and the real number s is the contractive factor for f. From Banach's fixed point theorem we know that each CF converges to a point $x_f \in X$, independently from the starting point on which it is applied. These theoretical results can be used for image coding, since we can solve the problem of finding the set of CF that better approximates the points of a given image. Such a set is called Iterated Functions System (IFS). The IFS of an image can be constructed by using Jaquine's algorithm [11], in which images are first partitioned into regions, and then encoded by finding the CFs transforming image regions (which in this context are called domains) into similar image regions (here called ranges). This transformations have the following general form:

$$w_i \begin{bmatrix} x \\ y \\ z \end{bmatrix} = \begin{bmatrix} a_i & b_i & 0 \\ c_i & d_i & 0 \\ 0 & 0 & \alpha_i \end{bmatrix} \begin{bmatrix} x \\ y \\ z \end{bmatrix} + \begin{bmatrix} e_i \\ s_i \\ \beta_i \end{bmatrix}, \tag{2}$$

where its coefficients represent characteristics as the geometric contraction, the isometric transformation, greyscale factors, etc. Thus, IFS coding provides a compact but still rich representation of an image.

3   Image Indexing with IFS

An efficient image indexing technique should guarantee properties such as scale invariance, isometric transformation invariance, stability and compactness [7]. In this section we introduce a new image indexing technique, based on CFs, and show how it meets the requirements above. We will see that these requirements are satisfactorily met, thanks to the intrinsic properties of IFS representations of images. In fact, the IFS representation of graphical objects does not change significantly if they only differ by scale, rotation, etc [13].

The present implementation of the FIDI system allows queries by image content through the Query by Example paradigm. The content of an image is represented through a vector of features, computed from elementary functions of the IFS representation for the image. Such a vector embeds important characteristics of the original image which makes it possible to efficiently perform content based retrieval through vector comparison. Each vector component represents the frequency by which a linear Contractive Function appears inside the IFS representation of the associated image.

One important issue to be addressed is the choice of the appropriate number of vector components, i.e. the appropriate set of features. We will discusss this issue from both IFS compression and image indexing point of views. As we already know, in order to preserve image quality during encoding, both in terms of Signal to Noise Ratio (SNR) and subjective parameters, it is advisable to keep the basic set of features sufficiently broad. However, increasing the set of features also increases the computing time for the IFS compression. Thus, a good tradeoff between the size of the basic set of features and the required computing time must be reached. Jacquine's technique preserves a good image quality also if we considerably reduce the size of the basic set of features. At the end, we will only use a small subset of these features. We will also see that in the case of IFS indexing with FIDI we can achieve more a considerable reduction in the number of features. As an example, let us consider the 8-bit 512×512 Lena Image, that we have encoded by using two basic sets of features with different size. The first set had cardinality of about 100 millions, whereas the second one had 100 thousand features. In both cases we gained the same compression factor, with a bit rate of 0.36 bits per pixel (bpp), whereas the SNR was 33.05 decibel (db) and 29.06 db respectively. Thus, the perceptive quality is acceptable also with the second basic set size.

Effective IFS indexing with FIDI also requires the selection of a reduced set of indexing features. We have seen that this number should be below 1000 to achieve satisfactory performances, since we have to compute Fourier transform and Euclidean distance, as we will see. One way to keep the number of features low is by setting a high value of the shift domain and a reduced number of bits to represent α and β coefficients which appear in (2).

We gained acceptable performances by setting a shift domain value of 16 pixels and quantizing α and β with 2 bits. To ensure contractivity α was set to a real value in the range]-1,1[. As for β, for 8 bit images we set it to an integer in the range [0,255]. Once we have set the shift value, as a consequence we will have also derived the set of domains that will be used to derive the IFS representation of the images. They are represented through the cartesian coordinates of their upper left corner.

4 The Method.

The construction of an image index with FIDI requires the following steps:

- Select a Training Set of Images;
- Select N Indexing Features, i.e. a set of representative CFs;
- Build N-dimensional Feature Vectors for images to be stored in IDB and reduce them to the K-dimensional space ($K < N$) using DFT;
- Build R-Tree on reduced vectors.

Each domain should be associated to a reduced set of CFs that better characterize it with respect to the training set of heterogeneous images. Since we have chosen 2 bits to represent both α and β coefficients, the total number of CFs that we can select is limited to 16×N, if N is the number of domains. At this point, we will be using the training set of images to select four among the most appropriate values of α and β on each domain, which will provide the four most appropriate CFs for the domain. We first compute α and β values for each image, and then compute four central values on each domain. At this point we have built the space of CFs, and as a consequence we have also determined the cardinality of our feature vector. Thus, we are ready to perform indexing on images to be stored in the database.

Given an image to be indexed, our goal is to build a feature vector for this image. As we already know, each vector component is associated to a specific CF. We will compute the frequency by which this CF appears inside the image and store it as the value for the corresponding vector component. Thus, we first use Jaquine's algorithm to subdivide the image into several ranges and then select, for each of them, the most appropriate CF over the $16 \times N$ possible candidates. This will be the one that minimizes the mean square error (MSE).

As an example, let us consider Figure 1. Depicted in figure (a) is Lena's image, whereas in figure (b) a Lung CT scan. Each figure is splitted in two parts, on the left we have the original image with a feature (e.g. a domain) highlighted, whereas on the right part we have indicated the frequency by which that feature appears inside the image.

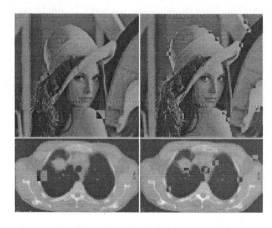

Fig. 1. On the left side lena and a lung CT Scan with an highlighted feature; on the right the frequency by which it appears inside images

As for computational complexity, so far it is given by the complexity for IFS coding, which depends on the granularity of the domains used for partitioning the original image. However with the recent introduction of classification schemas and parallel algorithms the computing time has been made considerably efficient[5, 8].

We can use Discrete Fourier Transform (DFT) [14] to map feature vectors on the domain of frequencies. As we already know, in the domain of frequencies it is sufficient to keep few coefficients without loss of significant information about the original signal [14]. However, we have to make sure that such transformation does not corrupt the result of possible queries. To this aim, we can use Parseval's theorem [14], which shows that any transformation of this type, on a pair of points from the n-dimensional to the k-dimensional space, does not increase their Euclidean distance [1].

As for the total complexity, other than IFS coding, which we have described above, we have to consider DFT computation, and similarity search. DFT complexity is constant since the cardinality of the feature vector is constant. The complexity of similarity search corresponds to the time for computing the Euclidean Distance plus the time for scanning the Database. The former is constant because DFT considerably reduces the space on which the distance will be computed. Database scanning is linear in the number of images populating the Database, if we use sequential scanning. However, we have improved this by using R-Trees [10].

5   Performance Evaluation of FIDI

The prototype system implementing FIDI runs on an IBM RS/6000 workstation, model 320. It has been implemented using C language on UNIX operating system. This section presents experimental results and performance evaluation obtained by testing the system on an database with 14,000 images chosen from commercially available photo clips, medical and art images.

Frequently used evaluation criteria are the *recall* and the *precision* [15]. We have chosen an extension of the former, namely the *normalized recall*, introduced in [6]. Basically, it extends the *recall* to deal with approximate match, so that it can be used in image retrieval. In order to assess performances of FIDI, with respect to Human perceptual similarity, we have selected a sample of 15 heterogeneous images. For each of them, we have first manually selected the 20 most similar images from the database, and then contrasted them with the corresponding images automatically retrieved by using the prototype system. For each query, we computed the following measures [6]:

- *AVRR* is the average rank over the set of relevant images retrieved by the system;
- *IAVRR* is the ideal AVRR. In our case it coincides with the AVRR when the system perfectly retrieves the 20 most relevant images.

We run experiments on a subset of 2000 images, randomly selected from our IDB. The results are shown in Table 1. The first column represents the number of images, whereas the second and the third columns report the *AVRR* and *IAVRR* respectively, averaged over the 15 test queries. The ratio and the difference of *AVRR* and *IAVRR* give a measure of the effectiveness of FIDI.

In our experimentation, we used DFT to reduce the cardinality of the feature vector from an initial value of 1000 to a final value of 20. In fact, in our DFT we have used 10 coefficients, and since these are complex numbers we have to retain 20 values. Experimental results have shown that this cut-off frequency is fairly adequated to achieve good perfomances both in terms of computing time

Table 1. Performance of FIDI using *normalized recall* on 15 queries.

Size of db	AVRR	IAVRR
2000	4.8	2.8

and false dismissals. Having chosen Euclidean distance as a similarity measure, a query with FIDI will retrieve the points in the 20-dimensional space that fall within a hyper-sphere of radius t, where t is the selected tolerance.

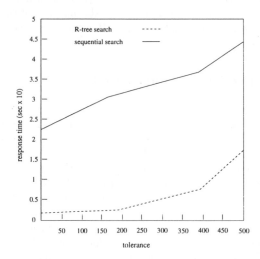

Fig. 2. Averange (over 30 queries) retrieval response time as function of the tolerance for sequential and R-tree search.

The experiments revealed the superiority of the R-tree over sequential scanning search. Figure 2 plots the response time averaged over a set of 30 queries. We notice that whatever tolerance factor we chose R-tree search always outperforms sequential scanning.

Figure 3 plots the average retrieval response time for the sequential and R-tree search using $t = 220$ as a tolerance factor. It is evident that the perfomance gap between the two different scanning techniques widens as the number of stored images grows. Finally, we present two examples of image retrieval, where the first query represents a woman's face, and the second one a lung CT scan. By setting $t = 320$ for each query FIDI has retrieved 248 images. For sake of brevity, in Figures 4 and 5 we reported only four most significant retrieved images.

So for example, if a user wants to retrieve about 30 images, t must be less than 180. By running an experiment with this value of t on a sample of 40 queries we have observed a miss rate of 0.5 dismissals over 1200 retrieved images).

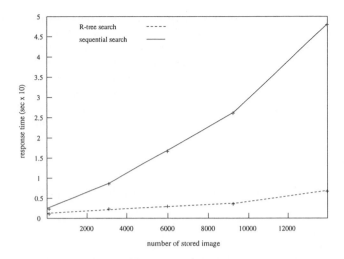

Fig. 3. Averange retrieval response time for a fixed tolerance ($t = 220$) as a function of IDB size, using sequential and R-tree search.

Fig. 4. Example of retrieval: on the left side the query image, on the right side a sample of most similar retrieved images

6 Conclusion

In this paper we proposed a fractal based image indexing technique (FIDI) for image retrieval in IDB. We have then provided experimental results and have evaluated FIDI performances in terms of computing time and retrieval precision. In future work we aim to further investigate several issues. First, the implementation of an advanced visual interface to allow Query by Sketch other than QBE.

Fig. 5. Example of retrieval: on the left the query, on the right a sample of most similar retrieved images

In particular, the adoption of this query paradigm entails further investigation in order to extend the method to deal with vector indices of sketch images. Such vectors will probably miss some of the features, hence we need to devise an appropriate comparison method between these incomplete vectors and the ones for the stored images, which are completely specified. We would also like to examine other orthonormal transformations, in addition to DFT. In particular, we are interested in deeper theoretical investigations on relationships amon different CFs, in order to detect the most appropriate sort of vector components.

References

1. R. Agrawal, C. Faloutsos, Efficient Similarity Search In Sequence Databases *FODO 93* Evanston, Illinois Oct. 13-15, 1993.
2. M. Barsnley, Fractals everywhere, *New York: Academic Press*, 1988.
3. S.K. Chang, and C. Yan, Iconic indexing by 2-D strings,*IEEE Trans. Patt. Anal. Mach. Intell.*, Vol. PAMI-9, pp. 413-428, May 1987.
4. *IEEE Computer: Finding the right image*, Special Issue on Content Based Image Retrieval Systems, Vol. 28, N. 9, September 1995.
5. G. Della Vecchia, R. Distasi, M. Nappi, M. Pepe, Fractal Image Compression Algorithms on a MIMD Architecture, *High-Perfomance Computing and Networking –HPCN'96, H. Liddell, A. Colbrook, B. Hertzberger, P. Sloot (Eds.) Lecture Notes in Computer Science*, vol. 1067, pp. 961-963, Springer Verlag, 1996.
6. C. Faloutsos, W. Equitz, M. Flickner, W. Niblack, D. Petkovic, R. Barber Efficient and Effective Querying by Image Content, *to appear in Journal of Intelligent Inf. Systems.*
7. C. Faloutsos, R. Barber, M. Flickner, W. Niblack, D. Petkovic, and W. Equitz, Efficient and effective querying by image content, *Journal of Intelligent Information Systems*, Vol. 3(3/4), pp. 231-262, July 1994.
8. Y. Fisher, Fractal compression: Theory and application to digital images, *Springer Verlag*, New York 1994.
9. W. I. Grosky, P. Neo, and Rajiv Mehrotra, A pictorial index mechanism for model-based matching, *Data and Knowledge Eng.*, 8:309-327, 1992.
10. I. Kamel, C. Faloutsos, On Packing R-Trees, *Second Int. Conf. On Information Knowledge Management CIKM*, November 1993.
11. A. E. Jacquin, Image coding based on a fractal theory of iterated contractive image transformations, *IEEE Trans. Image Proc.*, vol. 1, pp. 18-30, Jan. 1992.
12. S. Y. Lee, F. J. Hsu, Spatial Reasoning and Similarity Retrieval of Image Using 2D C-String Knowledge Representation, *Pattern Recognition*, Vol. 25, No. 3, pp. 305-318, 1992.
13. M. Nappi, G. Polese, G. Tortora, An Image Indexing Technique based on Contractive Functions, *Journal of Computing and Information (JCI)*, vol. 2, No. 1, pp. 957-978, 1996.
14. A.V. Oppenheim, R. W. Schafer, *Digital Signal Processing*, Prentice-Hall, Englewood Cliffs, N.J., 1975.
15. G. Salton and M. J. McGill, *Introduction to Modern Information Retrieval*, McGraw-Hill, 1983.

ImageMiner^{TM} —

Intelligent Retrieval for Images and Videos

P. Alshuth, Th. Hermes, J. Kreyß and M. Röper

Center for Computing Technology
University of Bremen, Germany

Mailing address: P. O. Box 330 440, D-28334 Bremen
E-mail: {petera,hermes,kreyss,roeper}@informatik.uni-bremen.de

Abstract. The large amount of available multimedia information (e.g. videos, audio, images) requires efficient and effective annotation and retrieval methods.
The System ImageMiner, which was developed at the University of Bremen in the AI group, is designed for content-based retrieval of single images.
As videos become a more important role in the frame of multimedia, we want to make videos available for ImageMiner. The first step is the detection and extraction of *shots* from a video using a histogram based method. The second step is to combine the images in a shot to a single image. This image describes the shot (*Mosaicing*-technique) and can be analyzed with ImageMiner.

1 The ImageMiner-System

In order to retrieve images it is more sophisticated and usual for human beings to use natural language concepts, e.g. *mountainlake*, than syntactical features, e.g. *red region left up*. This leads to a content-based image retrieval. Furthermore, it is unreasonable for any human being to make the content description for thousands of images manually.

ImageMiner combines methods and techniques from computer vision and Artificial Intelligence to generate content descriptions of images in a textual form automatically. The text retrieval can be done by an ordinary text-retrieval system. We use the IBM[1] SearchManager for AIX[2]. The system is implemented on IBM RS6000[3] operating under AIX.

The two dominating goals of this system are an automatic processing of the images and a comfortable user interface with a query vocabulary to formulate higher order queries by using concepts.

Therefore the ImageMiner-System is divided into two modules; one for the image analysis to build up the database and a second one for the retrieval.

---

[1] IBM is a trademark of International Business Machines Corporation.

[2] AIX is a trademark of International Business Machines Corporation

[3] RISC System/6000 is a trademark of International Business Machines Corporation

The image analysis module consists of three submodules for the feature extraction based on low-level image processing methods and a fourth one for the object recognition. They are shortly described in the next section (2).

Including videos into the ImageMiner-system makes it necessary to add another module, which performs the video analysis. It consists of two submodules. The first submodule divides the video into "shots" (see section 3). A shot is a short scene with a common content. The second submodule is responsible to create a single "still image" (Mosaic-Image) from a scene. The so-called *Mosaicing-Technique* is described in section (5).

The single mosaic image could be analyzed from the ImageMiner-system using the same procedures and methods as described in section (2).

2   Image Analysis

The image analysis module consists of three submodules for the extraction of the low-level features (color, texture and contour) and a fourth module for the object recognition.

Each module extracts segments containing the relevant feature information. With this information a textual description of the image is created. At this stage of the analysis there are no objects extracted.

This is done by the object recognition module. It is based on the previous generated annotations and combines the information about the extracted feature segments with the domain knowledge. The domain knowledge is stored inside a thesaurus.

2.1   Color based Segmentation

A grid with arbitrary elements of homogeneous size divides the image into so-called grid elements. For every grid element in the image, a color histogram is computed. The dominant color within the histogram defines the color of the grid-element.

In the next step, grid elements with the same dominant color are grouped and the circumscribing rectangles are determined. An overlap between segmented rectangles is allowed.

The rectangles are called color-rectangles, with attributes such as size with respect to the underlying grid size and the classified color.

2.2   Texture based Segmentation

The image is divided into grid elements, using the same arbitrary grid as already mentioned in the previous section. Based on [HSD73], second-order statistics are used to obtain texture feature vectors.

For each grid element the cooccurence matrix with four orientations (horizontal $0°$, vertical $90°$ and the two diagonals $45°$ and $135°$) is determined. From this calculation five significant features are used: The angular second moment, the contrast, the correlation, the variance, and the entropy.

From these 20 values (5 for each direction) the averages are calculated. The average values are given into a neural net which classifies the textures. This net is a backpropagation net trained with a standard backpropagation learning algorithm. For the landscape domain there are 8 output neurons. They symbolize the eight textures (sky, cloud, sand, forest, grass, stone, snow, and ice) which are defined for the landscape images.

Grid elements with the same texture are grouped together with the calculation of the surrounding rectangle and they are called texture rectangles.

2.3   Contour based Shape Detection

For images where no color and no texture information (Greyscale images, Technical drawings) is available, there has to be another source of information.

An important feature in the image are the edges of an object. It is possible to extract image contours from the detected edges. From the object contour the shape information can be derived.

Therefore, the first step in the shape analysis is the edge detection. The image is processed with two convolution kernels that approximate the first derivation of a gaussian function. For a detailed description of this method see [Can86].

Edge detection also provides edge points that are caused by noise. Noise may also be the reason for incomplete edge points of the objects. Edge points have to be connected to form an object or region contour. A contour point-connecting algorithm is used to produce closed contours. This method is fully described in [Zha94].

The result are the points which circumscribe an image region. From these closed regions shape parameters like the coordinates of the center, the size, etc. can be extracted from this information.

2.4   Object recognition

The object recognition is done in two steps:

1. Bridge the gap between the low level information (obtained in the last three sections) and the atomic entities of the high level information, i.e. the primitive objects described in a thesaurus.
   The result of this first step is the generation of an hypothesis concerning the primitive objects.
2. Combining of the primitive objects according to the compositional semantics of more complex objects also described in a thesaurus. A hypothesis used in the description of the analyzed images becomes a thesis.

Inherent in the information about color, texture, and contour of the image analysis phase is the information about the topological relations between the different segments. These neighbourhood relations are distinguished by three cases: overlaps, meets, contains, and their inverse relations. One fundamental assumption in the ImageMiner-System is that these relations restrict the recognition of objects; i.e. a (primitive) object is built upon segments which are in this neighbourhood relation. By this assumption the process of object recognition can be treated as the process of graph transformations, i.e. the process of graph rewriting.

In the ImageMiner-system a graph parser - the so called GraPaKL - is used to solve the object recognition phase. The underlying graph grammar formalism and the parser algorithm are described [Kla94].

The grammars are compiled out of the knowledge representation in the thesaurus. In this sense the model of our recognizable world is represented within the thesaurus.

3   Shot-detection

The analysis of videos needs an efficient way to group continous images to shots. Fig 1 illustrates the whole video at a glance. The pixels look different between two shots.

Fig. 1. An icon presenting a sequence of shots; starting with the first frame in front.

We use a histogram comparing method, which makes use of the difference in the intensity histograms of two frames. $H_i(j)$ denotes the histogram of the ith frame and j is one of the G levels.

$$SD_i = \sum_{j=1}^{G} \mid H_i(j) - H_{i+1}(j) \mid$$

A new shot is detected if the difference *SD* is larger than a given threshold. Normaly grey levels would be used to build the histogram. As the image exists only in color pixels (15 or 24 Bit RGB image), we have to transform the color pixels to a grey scale image. To reduce this process we use the color information with the two most significant bits of each color component [ZKS93]. The graph of the frame-to-frame histogram differences is shown in fig 3. A shot is detected at bars with high level.

Fig. 2. Another example for an icon presenting a sequence of shots; starting with the first frame in front.

After the shot detection is finished we can build all frames of one shot to a mosaicing image.

4   Mosaicing Technique

The basic idea of the mosaicing technique is the creation of a single image for each detected shot in the complete video sequence. This image contains the full information about the scene.

To create such Mosaic-Image all the images in the shot have to be aligned with respect to the coordinate transformation (motion) from image to image.

The following sections describe the major ideas of this procedure and the algorithm and the first results obtained with this approach.

4.1   Coordinate transformation

We are considering two images (frames) taken at the time t and $t' = t + 1$. The coordinate transformation maps the image coordinates from the first frame $\mathbf{X} =$

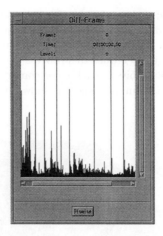

Fig. 3. Histogram differences: a shot is detected at bars with very high levels

$[x, y]^T$ to a new set of coordinates $\mathbf{X}^0 = [x', y']^T$ at the time t', corresponding to the second frame.

The approach to find the related coordinates relies on the assumption of the transformation models. The most common models and their transformations are shown in table 1 taken from [MP95].

Model	Coordinate tranformations from X to X'	Parameters
Translation	$X' = x + b$	$b \in R^{2x1}$
Affine	$X' = AX + b$	$A \in R^{2x2}, b \in R^{2x1}$
Bilinear	$x' = q_{x'xy}xy + q_{x'x}x + q_{x'y}y + q_{x'}$ $y' = q_{y'xy}xy + q_{y'x}x + q_{y'y}y + q_{y'}$	$q_i \in R$
Projective	$X' = \frac{AX+b}{C^T X + 1}$	$A \in R^{2x2}, b, C \in R^2$
Pseudoperpective	$x' = q_{x'x}x + q_{x'y}y + q_{x'} + q_\alpha x^2 + q_\beta xy$ $y' = q_{y'x}x + q_{y'y}y + q_\alpha xy + q_\beta^2$	$q_i \in R$

Table 1. Image coordinate transformation models

The implemented algorithm, which was introduced by S. Mann and R. Picard from the MIT Media Lab [MP95]. is based on the projective flow model. It determines the eight paramters which are necessary to take into account all possible camera motions (zoom, rotate, pan, and tilt).

4.2 Projective Flow Method

The brightness constancy constraint equation contains the optical flow velocities u_f and v_f. They contain the information how two successive images are related to each other.

$$u_f E_x + v_f E_y + E_t \approx 0 \tag{1}$$

E_x and E_y are the spatial derivatives and E_t is the temporal derivative of intensity (brightness) for each point in the image. u_f and v_f is the optical flow in the horizontal (vertical) direction.

To solve the underestimation problem (one equation for two unknown parameters), it is common practice to compute the flow over some neighbourhood. This means at least two pixels, but it is also possible to use the whole image, like it is done in this approach.

Using the projective flow model for the transformation we can compute the new coordinates $X' = [x', y']^T$, by

$$X' = \frac{A[x,y]^T + b}{C^T[x,y]^T + 1} = \frac{Ax + b}{C^T x + 1} \tag{2}$$

where $A \in R^{2 \times 2}$ and $b, C \in R^{2 \times 1}$ are the parameters to describe the transformation. The optical flow, which can be derived from the above equation is the model velocity with its components u_m and v_m.

Minimizing the sum of the squared differences between the flow velocity and the model velocity and expanding the result into a Taylor series using only the first three terms, results in a formulae corresponding to the bilinear model.

$$
\begin{aligned}
u_m + x &= q_{x'xy}xy + q_{x'x}x + q_{x'y}y + q_{x'} \\
v_m + y &= q_{y'xy}xy + q_{y'x}x + q_{y'y}y + q_{y'}
\end{aligned} \tag{3}
$$

Including this two terms for the model velocity into the brightness constancy equation (1) leads to a set of eight linear equations with eight unknown parameters.

As result we receive the eight approximate parameters $q_k(k = 1...8)$, which have to be related to the eight exact parameters for the projective flow model.

4.3 The "Four-Point-Method"

We use 4 points in the first frame. This could be the four edges of the image $[\mathbf{s} = (s_1, s_2, s_3, s_4)]$. For this points we apply the approximate parameters to determine their position in the second frame.

$$
\begin{aligned}
r_{kx} &= u_m + s_{kx} \\
r_{ky} &= v_m + s_{ky}
\end{aligned} \tag{4}
$$

The result is a new vector $\mathbf{r} = [r_1, r_2, r_3, r_4]$. The components are the coordinates of the four selected points calculated with the model flow u_m, v_m. The correspondence between $\mathbf{r}$ and $\mathbf{s}$ gives four linear equations:

$$\begin{bmatrix} x'_k \\ y'_k \end{bmatrix} = \begin{bmatrix} x_k, y_k, 1, 0, 0, 0, -x_k x'_k, -y_k x'k \\ 0, 0, 0, x_k, y_k, 1, -x_k y'k, -y_k y'_k \end{bmatrix} \tag{5}$$

$$[a_{x'x}, a_{x'y}, b_x, a_{y'y}, b_{y'}, c_x, c_y]^T$$

where $1 \le k \le 4$ defines the number of the point. Taking all four points into account, we have 8 linear equations for the eight unknown parameters. The solution of the equations is $\mathbf{P} = (a_{x'x}, a_{x'y}, b_x, a_{y'y}, b_{y'}, c_x, c_y)$, whose components are the parameters for the projective flow model.

5   Results

This section shows the results of the mosaicing procedure. Fig. 4 shows three frames of a shot detected with the histogram based shot recognition. The shot consists of 200 individual frames.

Fig. 4. Three individual frames of a shot with 200 frames

The result of the mosaicing procedure with all 200 single frames is shown in Fig.5.

This image was analyzed with the ImageMiner-System. The recognized objects for this image are shown in Fig. 6.

Another example shows Fig. 7. This detected shot consists of 308 indiviual frames.

6   Conclusion

In this paper we have presented an extension to the ImageMiner-System, which makes the content information of a video sequence available for the retrieval by identifiying the scenes with a similar content (Shot detection) and by creating a single image for each shot (Mosaicing Technique).

Fig. 5. Mosaiced Image for a shot with 200 frames

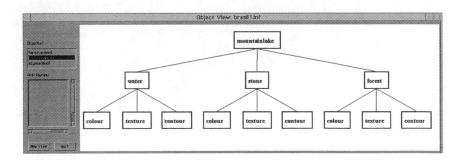

Fig. 6. Results of the object recognition for the mosaiced image

Fig. 7. Three individual frames of a shot with 308 frames

Fig. 8. Another example for a mosaiced Image for a shot with 308 frames concerning to Fig.7

References

[Can86] J. Canny. A computational approach to edge detection. *IEEE Transactions on Pattern Analysis and Machine Intelligence*, 8(6):679–698, 1986.

[HSD73] R.M. Haralick, K. Shangmugam, and I. Dinstein. Textural Features for Image Classification. *IEEE Transactions on Systems, Man, and Cybernetics*, SMC-3(6):610–621, 1973.

[Kla94] Ch. Klauck. *Eine Graphgrammatik zur Repräsentation und Erkennung von Features in CAD/CAM*. DISKI No. 66. infix-Verlag, 1994.

[MP95] S. Mann and R.W. Picard. Video orbits of the projective group: a new perspective on image mosaicing. Technical Report 338, MIT Technical Report, 1995. submitted for publication.

[SAG95] H.S. Sawhney, S. Ayer, and M. Gorkani. Dominant and multiple motion for video representation. In *Proceedings of ICIP*, 1995.

[Zha94] J. Zhang. *Bereichsbasierte Verfahren zur Straßenerkennung für die autonome Führung von Fahrzeugen*. PhD thesis, Universität Karlsruhe (TH), Fakultät Informatik, 1994. Fortschrittsberichte VDI, Reihe 10, Nr. 298.

[ZKS93] H.J. Zhang, A. Kankanhalli, and S.W. Smoliar. Automatic partitioning of full motion video. *Multimedia Systems*, 1(1):10–28, 1993.

Analysis and Evaluation of Search Efficiency
for Image Databases

W.W.S. So, C.H.C. Leung and Z.J. Zheng
Victoria University of Technology, Ballarat Road,
P.O. Box 14428, MCMC, Melbourne 8001, Victoria, Australia
Email: {simon, clement, zheng}@matilda.vut.edu.au   Fax: +61 3 9688 4050

Abstract

The problem of image identification by content from an image database is viewed as a search space reduction problem where different paradigms and approaches are employed to progressively reduce the search space. Unlike information recovery, such reduction cannot in general be used to pinpoint exactly all and only those images that are needed by a query. In this paper, three main search space reduction strategies are evaluated: high-level descriptive approach, low-level signatures comparison, and user-level picture keys. The effectiveness of these approaches are studied and quantified. Based on these strategies, it is possible that highly effective query models may be built. In combination, they offer the potential to drastically reduce the search space for image content identification through the use of ranking and relevance feedback techniques.

1. Image Contents Characteristics

Effective image identification by content from an image database requires a radically different approach from that of searching a structured database. While a brute force exhaustive search generally works for the latter, no equivalent procedure exists for identifying all the meaningful features and objects in an image database. In identifying images by content from an image database, images will fall into one of two categories: those whose existence the user is aware of (image recovery), and those whose existence the user is not aware of (image discovery). In essence, image database [Jain93, Gros92] and multimedia search is concerned with reducing the search space into a smaller subset. In the process of targeting possible candidates, search space reduction strategies must be correctly employed to minimise recall and precision errors.   In this paper, several methods for achieving search space reduction in image databases are examined. Since each method has its strengths and weaknesses, a combination of different approaches may be used to efficiently reduce the search space to a reasonable size.

Image contents may be categorised into complex contents and primitive contents [Leun95] with different methods for their extraction. Primitive contents are low-level contents which can usually be extracted automatically (eg. textures, colours, boundaries, and primitive shapes). Colour histogram, moment/centroid, segmentation, and other primitive features can be used to form the *signatures* of the images. Complex contents are extracted manually or semi-automatically, and they correspond to patterns within an image which are considered meaningful by human users. They cannot normally be extracted fully automatically and are often qualitative in character.

2. Limiting Search Using Quantitative Index

Primitive contents such as colours, textures and shapes can be numerically computed to form a representation of the image. These may take the form of a set of numerical quantities, which may be represented as vectors or histograms. The signatures of all images in the databases may be indexed using these signatures. Ideally, similar images should have a close match in the signature scale, while dissimilar ones should exhibit very different signatures.

The indexing scheme proposed in [Zhen95] consists of two vectors, each of which has six components. An illustration of these vectors is given in Figure 1. Conceptually, these vectors may be amalgamated into a single vector consisting of 12 components. These 12 components are designed to provide a quantitative characterisation of an image using purely automatic algorithms. Although such algorithms do not directly support the extraction of complex contents, they should play a part in helping to limit the search process in producing images which are similarly characterised.

Indexing vectors:
(0.50, 0.46, 0.37, 0.04, 0.09, 0.05)
(0.50, 0.49, 0.32, 0.05, 0.09, 0.05)

Figure 1. Indexing Vectors for Baboon

The extent of search reduction, however, depends on the probability distribution of the image collection over the appropriate vector space used for their characterisation. In general, for a k-dimensional space, if we denote the probability density of image distribution over the neighbourhood of $\mathbf{x} = (x_1, \ldots, x_k)$ by $f(x_1, \ldots, x_k)\,d\mathbf{x}$, and if the search space is characterised by

$$m_1 \leq x_1 \leq M_1,$$
$$m_2 \leq x_2 \leq M_2,$$
$$........$$
$$m_k \leq x_k \leq M_k,$$

then a search with argument $\mathbf{x}$ and nearness ε, will result in all images lying within the index region

$$R = \{\, \mathbf{y} : |x_i - y_i| \leq \varepsilon \,\},$$

which gives a conditional search reduction of

$$\rho\,(\mathbf{x}) = \frac{\displaystyle\int_R f(x_1,\ldots,x_k)\,d\mathbf{x}}{\displaystyle\prod_{i=1}^{k}(M_i - m_i)}\,.$$

The unconditional search reduction is therefore

$$\rho = \int_\Omega \rho\,(\mathbf{x})\,d\mathbf{x}\,,$$

where Ω represents the entire search space. The density $f(x_1,\ldots,x_k)\,d\mathbf{x}$ could be incrementally measured and stored in the image database. The range constants $\{\,m_i\,\}$ and $\{\,M_i\,\}$ may be estimated from the collection as

$$\tilde{m}_i = \min\,\{\,x_i\,\}$$
$$\tilde{M}_i = \max\,\{\,x_i\,\}$$

where the minimum and maximum are taken over the entire image collection. From [Fell71], it can be shown that these estimates will converge to their true values:

$$E(\tilde{m}_i) \approx \frac{M_i - m_i}{n+1} + m_i \to m_i\,,\ \text{as}\ \ n \to \infty$$

$$E(\tilde{M}_i) \approx \frac{nM_i}{n+1} \to M_i\,,\ \text{as}\ \ n \to \infty$$

where n is the number of images in the database (sample size). The maximum and minimum values may be stored as a special search space boundary record in the image database, and would need to be updated as images are inserted and deleted from the database. Although insertion updating may be comparatively straightforward, deletion updating may involve searching the entire index. Such a record consists of $4k$ fields, and is shown in Figure 2.

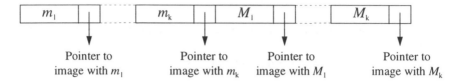

Pointer to
image with m_1

Pointer to
image with m_k

Pointer to
image with M_1

Pointer to
image with M_k

Figure 2.   Search Space Boundary Record

When a new image is inserted, its index vector is computed. Let its values be z_1, ..., z_k. The boundary record is retrieved and comparisons are made between z_i and m_i as well as M_i for $i = 1, ..., k$. If

$$m_i \leq z_i \leq M_i,$$

for all i, in which case the boundary record will remain unchanged. If this is not true, then both the appropriate m or M value and the associate pointer in the boundary record will need to be updated to refer to the newly inserted image. It is possible that several values of the boundary record may be altered as a result of a single image insertion. In the case where an existing image I is deleted from the database, the amount of work involved in correctly updating the boundary record is considerably more elaborate. Let the index vector of image I be w_1, ..., w_k, which has been previously computed when the image was inserted and is available in the database. As before, comparisons are made between w_i and m_i as well as M_i for $i = 1, ..., k$. If

$$m_i \leq w_i \leq M_i,$$

for all i, then no action is required. If this is not the case, then all the index vectors in the entire database will need to be searched to determine the value of the field to be updated. Suppose $w_i = m_i$ and the corresponding pointer points to I. If the image for which the next corresponding smallest value is I' with associated value m_i', then m_i will be replaced by m_i' and its pointer will now point to I' instead. Such an exhaustive search for updated values tends to be inefficient, and it causes considerable delay for image deletion. It is much better to use an additional supplementary record which has the same structure as the boundary record and contains all the relevant information relating to the next level of extreme boundary values together with the associated pointers. In this way, the deletion process can be accomplished much more quickly while maintaining the boundary record up-to-date. The supplementary record may be updated at a later stage when there is less activity on the database.

If the estimation of the density f proves to be impractical, then the uniform distribution may be employed to determine the search reduction, which in this case, simplifies to

$$\rho = \frac{(2\varepsilon)^k}{\displaystyle\prod_{i=1}^{k}(M_i - m_i)} \quad .$$

For a given search reduction factor ρ, the nearness ε may be adjusted to provide the required level of reduction:

$$\varepsilon \leq \frac{1}{2}\sqrt[k]{\rho \prod_{i=1}^{k}(M_i - m_i)} \quad .$$

Many techniques may be used to generate signatures, and different signatures may be used together for search space reduction. Invariance properties are highly desirable for signatures. In particular, a robust signature scheme should be invariant at least with respect to rotation and scaling. Since all the signatures of the image repository are pre-computed, the computational cost of this search method is only confined to numerical comparison.

Although this method is primarily used for low-level contents, recent reports have shown that it is able to provide an effective index [Geve96]. In many applications which contains only single or well-defined objects, this method is advantageous. However, it does not appear to work well for complex or natural objects, but could be very valuable if used in conjunction with higher-level methods.

3. Picture Keys

Although signatures provide a convenient way to represent images, it has limited use for complex contents. Instead a pictorial summary of the complete image should be maintained. These may be viewed as *picture keys* [Leun95], which are much smaller than the original image and are designed to capture the salient features and characteristics of the image.

Many techniques can be used to implement picture keys. Shrinking the resolution of images into miniatures or reducing the pixel depths from colour images to grey-scale or even binary images are obvious ways of producing picture keys. Image compression [So96] seems to offer a particularly promising approach. Lossy compression with high compression ratio is acceptable in this instance as long as the compressed images are legible. If certain objects in an image are considered to be in the foreground, different compression ratios for the foreground and background may be adopted. Progressively better image quality can also be used to aid identification by using a series of compressed picture keys with increasing image clarity. Figure 3 illustrates the possible formation of picture keys.

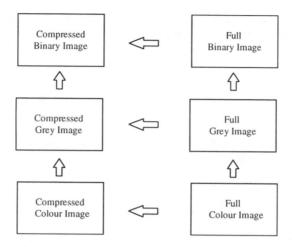

Figure 3. Possible Formation of Picture Keys

Classification schemes used in conjunction with picture keys furnishes a particularly effective way to rapidly reduce the search space. For example, images for cartoons and man-made objects are quite different from images of natural scenes. High degree of colour contrast and well-defined geometric shapes can be detected in images of cartoons and man-made objects while irregular, complex and fuzzy shapes such as trees are observed in images of natural scenes. Hence, one of the classification schemes would be based on the detection of such characteristics in images.

Although picture keys provide a powerful mechanism for interactive browsing, they tend to be relatively difficult to manipulate. The computational cost to prune the search space through picture keys is higher than signatures.

4. Picture Descriptions

Although image retrieval using visual contents is the logical and direct method for content-based image retrieval [Gudi95], they are not always able to provide substantial reduction in the search space. They also suffer from the problem of *input specification*, since specifying target image characteristics using pictures is not always the most efficient: one may have to scan in an image, sketch an object, or start from an image already in the database. Query specification using English like descriptions which capture the salient features and objects within an image still appears the most effective way of achieving a drastic search space reduction. However, the use of keywords or captions to search images is very restrictive, as they are limited in their expressive power. In particular, relationships between objects within an image cannot be easily represented; consequently, inappropriate search techniques imported from information retrieval such as proximity search may be forced upon the system in order to extract relationships, often with a high degree of uncertainty. Highly structured data model such as the Ternary Fact Model [Leun95] appears to offer a promising way to overcome these problems and is able to capture the complex relationships among objects in the images. This approach provides an indexing mechanism and storage structure for image objects, object attributes and relationships among different objects within an image which are not expressible using conventional techniques. In this method, one could either use *controlled vocabulary* or *uncontrolled vocabulary*. In both cases, the use of some form of thesaurus is inevitable to assist query refinement and term substitution.

An indication of the search reduction achievable using a descriptive approach for complex contents may be obtained by making use of the data collected in [Leun91]. The most ideal situation for a given descriptive query is to be able to locate all the relevant images and nothing else, so that the best search reduction possible *r*, in percentage terms, is

$$\frac{\text{Number of irrelevant images in database}}{\text{Total number of images in database}}$$

which is related to the generality factor γ [Salt83] as $1-\gamma$. Clearly, the search reduction is a function of the individual query, and different queries tend to result in different search reduction factors. It needs to be acknowledged that, while the concept of relevance is critical to the search reduction measure, it can only be determined manually (subjectively) for each query. In using an image database consisting of 196 images extracted from a total of 38,000 images based on the French Revolution, a set of 21 specific descriptive queries are used to determine image relevance, from which the maximum search reduction may be calculated (Table 1).

Query	Max Search Reduction (%)	Query	Max Search Reduction (%)
1	86%	12	84%
2	93%	13	99%
3	98%	14	97%
4	94%	15	99%
5	95%	16	99%
6	97%	17	99%
7	96%	18	98%
8	99%	19	99%
9	97%	20	98%
10	98%	21	99%
11	82%		

Table 1.

The set of relevant images are determined by browsing through each image in the entire collection of 196 images against the given queries. The mode of these data gives a 99% reduction, while the mean gives 96%. Even the minimum gives a 82% reduction. Although based on a small database size and a limited set of queries, these data suggest that the descriptive approach offers the potential to deliver a highly substantial search reduction. However, whether these high search reduction figures are realisable will depend on the query language and model used to support the descriptive approach.

5. Search Query Optimisation

The order of search strategies will affect the efficiency of the overall retrieval operation. In some instances, a large collection of possible candidates can be eliminated quickly by a particular indexing method so that the speed of the filtering process is dramatically increased. In other instances, the search method may already be determined by the input method. Using different combinations of search strategies, query plans should be formulated and their computational cost and complexity should be evaluated before embarking the search.

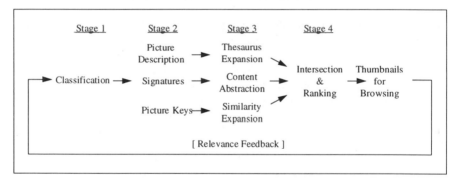

Figure 4. Stages For Search Strategies

Conceptually, our search strategies to achieve space reduction are carried out in four stages as shown in Figure 4. The first stage is the reduction of images by classification. This is a global operation designed to drastically reduce the search space at the outset. The subjects of target images as well as the types can be used to prune a large collection of images into a subset which forms the universe of search space in the next stage. Multiple classes may be selected to allow maximum inclusion of the possible target images which also cater for more complex relationships among images.

Classification by itself is designed for relatively crude but effective pruning, and is not sufficient for handling images at a fine level of details. The second and third stages are employed for the refinement of image contents through signatures, picture keys and picture descriptions. These consist of processes of relaxation for image content followed by the intersection of each domain. The subsets of intersection are then ranked to indicate the level of relevance among the target images. Specifically, *thesaurus expansion* is used for picture description to provide generalisation of terms. This relaxation through thesaurus is designed to accommodate richer vocabularies as well as to avoid an overly narrow description of images. *Content abstraction* can be used for the signatures. Since signatures are often quantitative in nature, they are too precise for any practical use. Abstraction in signatures is designed to make the specification less precise. For examples, 80% of red in image contents can be translated into the specification of "mostly red". A vector for a particular signature can be relaxed to include its neighbourhood. *Similarity expansion* for picture keys are used to group related images. The codebook of the compressed image, for example, can be further generalised into rougher categories for possible matching. Thesaurus expansion, content abstraction and similarity expansion are designed to relax the search criteria. Each operation will produce a subset of images for further processing.

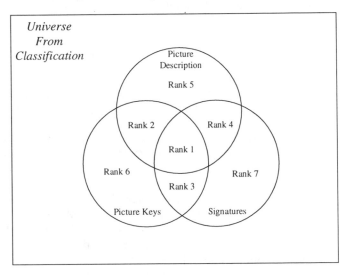

Figure 5. Intersection and Possible Ranking

The fourth stage in our search strategies is intersection and ranking. Figure 5 illustrates the intersection of each domain and the possible ranking of images. The intersection of all three domains are deemed to be the most relevant and identified as the images having top rank. Images of only matched signatures will take the last rank because they are the least reliable measure. In some queries, not all types image contents are specified. The strategies of ranking still remains the same but with missing ranks. For example, if picture keys are not specified, the resulting ranks will be 4, 5 and 7.

Once the images are properly ranked, they are presented in thumbnails images for quick browsing. Relevance feedback will be used to further refine the query results. If the user persistently favour certain domains of images, the ranking process can be dynamically altered to better tailor the needs of individual queries.

6. Summary and Concluding Remarks

Finding images from an image database on the basis of their contents requires a combination of paradigms which are very different from conventional database approaches. It presents new challenges in terms of query specification, content indexing, and search refinement. The identification process will involve both automatic and manual schemes, and the outcome of the associated processes, in general, will not deliver exact results. In this paper, three main search space reduction strategies are evaluated: high-level descriptive approach, low-level signatures comparison, and user-level picture keys. The effectiveness of these approaches are studied and quantified. Based on these strategies, new query models may be designed, which will be radically different from the traditional SQL or text-based approaches. In combination, these strategies offer the potential to significantly reduce the search space to manageable levels.

References

[Fell71]   W. Feller, An Introduction to Probability Theory and its Applications, Vol. 2, Wiley, 1971.

[Gros92]   W. Grosky, and R. Mehrotra, "Image Database Management", in M.C. Yovits (ed), *Advances in Computers*, Vol. 34, San Diego, CA: Academic Press, 1992, pp. 237-291.

[Jain93]   R. Jain (ed), *NSF Workshop on Visual Information Management Systems*, ACM SIGMOD RECORD, Vol. 22, No. 3, September 1993, pp. 57-75.

[Leun91]   C.H.C. Leung, and J. Hibler, *Architecture of a Pictorial Database Management System*, Technical Report, University of London, 1991.

[Leun95]   C.H.C. Leung, and Z.J. Zheng, "Image Data Modelling for efficient Content Indexing," *Proc. International Workshop on Multimedia Database Management Systems*, New York, August 1995, IEEE Computer Society Press, pp. 143-150.

[Gudi95]   V.N. Gudivada, and V.V. Raghavan, "Content-Based Image Retrieval Systems," *IEEE Computer*, Vol. 28, No. 9, September 1995.

[Geve96]   T. Gevers, and A. Smeulders, "Evaluating color- and shape-invariant image indexing for consumer photography", *Proc. International Conference on Visual Information Systems,* Melbourne, February 1996, pp. 293-302.

[Salt83]   Salton, G. and M. McGill, *Introduction to Modern Information Retrieval*, McGraw-Hill, 1983.

[So96]   W.W.S. So, C.H.C. Leung, and Z.J. Zheng, "Picture Coding For Image Database Retrieval," *International Picture Coding Symposium*, Melbourne, March 1996, pp. 69-74.

[Zhen95]   Zheng, Z.J. and C. H. C. Leung, "Quantitative measurements of feature indexing for 2D binary images of hexagonal grid for image retrieval," *Proc. IS&T/SPIE Symposium on Electronic Imaging: Science & Technology,* San Jose, California, Vol. 2420, 1995, pp. 116-124.

Content Based Image Retrieval Model in an Object Oriented Database

Chabane Djeraba, Ian Savory, Max Barere, Steve Marchand

IRIN, IRESTE

2 rue de la Houssinière, BP 92208 - 44322 Nantes Cedex 3, France. E-mail :
djeraba@irin.univ-nantes.fr

Abstract

In this paper, we present an image retrieval system based on the content. The content of images include both low level features such as colors, textures, and high level features such as spatial constraints and shapes of relevant regions. Based on object technology, the image features and behaviors are modeled and stored in a database. Images can be retrieved by examples (show me images similar to this image) or by selecting properties from pickers such as a sketched shape, a color histogram, a spatial constraint interface, a list of key words and a combination of these. The integration of high and low level features in the object-oriented database is an important property of our work.

Keywords

Retrieval, extraction, images, relevant regions, texture, color, shape, databases, object concepts, matching.

1. Introduction

The explosion of multimedia information (images, video, audio) in several domains such as criminal investigation, surveillance flights, observing satellites, and others, has created a need of new tools to locate images based on their content. The image retrieval by content is required to use efficiently the data contained in the image databases and to assist the final users, even those unfamiliar with the database, to find relevant images.

Over the last years, research in content-based retrieval of multimedia information has made significant progress. They have resulted in the development of systems. Some of them are text-based retrieval systems or attribute-based retrieval [Gud 95] such as MMI [Gob 92]. Their direct advantage is their image semantic content. However, the extraction process becomes tedious and increases rapidly the time cost of the database creation. Other systems, such as Virage [Jai 95], Visualseek [Smi 96], [Haf 95], [Sri 95], Qbic [Fal 93], Photobook [Pen 94], Trademark [Kat 91], and others are based on image analysis. The image features are extracted automatically or semi-automatically, using segmentation subsystems. Although, the automatic segmentation subsystems are interesting for specific application domains, they remain generally very difficult to apply in any application domain where the regions extracted have not real world meaning. Commercial systems supporting these functionalities, such as Virage implemented on Object Store and commercialized by Virage Inc. Corporation, or Ultimedia Manager from IBM, QBIC from IBM, and the Visual Intelligence Blade from Illustra Information Technologies, Inc., are beginning to emerge.

Our motivation is to : - integrate the text-based and image analysis approaches, in order to allow powerful queries based on both low (i.e colors, textures, shapes) and high level features (real world concept) of images, - provide both similar image and user specification queries, - make the queries, and more generally the system framework extensible and independent of an application domain, - support knowledge (relationships between image features) extraction from data images, - support efficiently the previous functionalities in an object-oriented database.

In this context, we designed and implemented an image retrieval system that considers two kinds of features. The first one may be extracted semi-automatically. It includes significant shapes (region-of-interest ROF) and key words. The second one may be extracted automatically. It includes textures, colors, and spatial constraints. We introduced : - a data model based on the object technology supported by an object-oriented database system, - a useful query interface, and - a domain-independent framework. An important difference of our system comparing to others, is the image queries of symbolic regions (Show me images that contains regions of such colors and/or such texture and/or such shape and/or such spatial constraints). The regions considered are symbolic, so they have real world meaning (i.e. mountain, river, forest, sun, person, etc.). Another difference is the powerful mathematical representation and the real world meaning of the shape. A shape corresponds to a significant region, and its representation is based on powerful mathematical formulas (Fourier descriptors) that makes it independent of the rotation, translation and scale. To the question (Show me the images that contain a cup shape), the system may return images that contain similar shapes independently of the scale, the rotation and the translation of the cup. Finally, the framework of the data model is based on object technology that make it evolving and flexible.

In this paper, we start by presenting the framework of the image retrieval system (section 2). The system is based on two parts, the first one extracts, models and stores, based on object-oriented concepts, image features (section 2.1) in the database. In this section, we highlight more particularly the significant regions and shapes, because they are two important features of our model. The second one supports the user queries (section 2.2). Finally, we present our conclusion (section 3).

2. Framework

We designed and Implemented a prototype system, called RECI (Retrieval and Extraction by Content of Images) with two important components : database features (index) and image retrieval (Figure 1.). In the first one, methods, aided by the user, identify relevant regions in images, and compute features describing color, texture and shape data of these regions. In the second one, images can be retrieved by selecting properties such as a color, a sketched shape, a texture of image regions, or a combination of these. RECI includes a visual query tool that lets users to form a query by painting, sketching and selecting textures, colors and shapes.

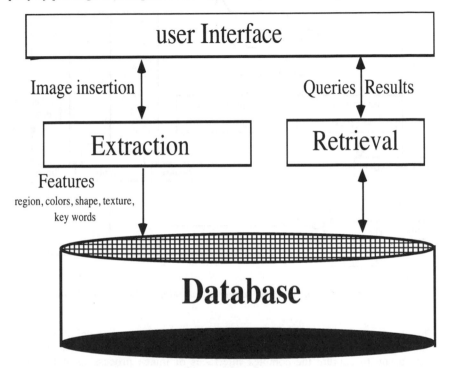

Figure 1: Framework

2.1 Database features

The content of images are stored when the images are inserted in the collection. The storage process takes two ways. In the first one, the image values are stored in files (i.e. gif, jpeg, ... formats) outside the database. In the second one, the extracted content of images is inserted in the database.

In the second way, the user may insert a set of key-words that characterize, in his point of view, the image. After the storage of images and key-words, the system extract automatically the dominant texture and color of the image, and then the user, generally an expert of the application domain, may extract semi-automatically the shape of relevant regions, using a visual tool. The relevant regions are pixel zones that have real world meaning in the perception of the user. When the user identifies and surrounds, by a closed border (shape), the real world (relevant) regions, such as rivers, persons, animals, mountains, etc., the system extracts automatically their colors and textures, and stores the regions, their automatic extracted features (color, texture) and their semi-automatically extracted features (shapes, set of key-words) in the database, using the object-oriented model of the database management system O2.

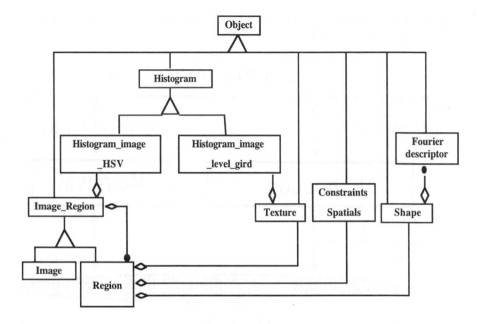

Figure 2: Object-oriented model : aggregation relationships in OMT formalism

The object-oriented model, and particularly the object-oriented model of a database management system, has several interesting common advantages. First, it is well appropriate to capture the complex interfaces of image processing and analysis services in a modular form which is easy for application developers to use. Secondly, it simplifies the encapsulation of data and save developers many details of particular image hardware, because image processing software often involve special hardware with appropriate interfaces. Thirdly, it addresses the need for extensibility by offering mechanisms for extending existing code. This is a result of the texture, color and shape software nature which frequently evolves. Fourthly, object oriented interfaces make platform dependencies more explicit, and so, they simplify the development for heterogeneous platforms, because content based image retrieval should, ideally, run on different platforms and tolerate multimedia hardware variations within platforms. Finally, content based image retrieval systems are less constrained by existing software, that is why we are relatively free to exploit new techniques such as object-oriented modeling. The content based image retrieval presents the opportunity to start with a new area, comparing to other domains in which software developers face the need to maintain compatibility with earlier applications.

2.1.1 Shape

The shapes are the first important features. they represent the borders of user relevant regions. The relevant regions are significant and well defined in the application domain, so they correspond to a high level of abstraction. Ideally, extracted significant regions would be automatic, but this is either difficult or impossible, when the approach is independent of specific application domains.

The automatic extraction approach is possible for specific domains such as museum, bio-medical, etc. A system, such as QBIC, has successfully used fully automatic unsupervised segmentation methods based on a background model to recognize regions in a specific class of images.

Figure 3: Examples of possible automatic extraction of significant regions

The alternative approach, manual extraction, is tedious particularly, when the images are generated at an ever-increasing rate, and the image regions have complex borders. Although these disadvantages, we opted in RECI, in the context of a short-term approach, for manual extraction of the shape without discarding, in the middle-long-term, semi-automatic approaches for generic application domains and automatic approaches for specific application domains. The semi-automatic approach is less specific than the fully automatic approach, and more specific than the manual extraction approach. We can combine several methods such as flood-fill, used in several photo-editing tools, and snake methods. Flool-fill methods start from a single pixel and repeatedly add adjacent pixels whose values are under a special value that depend of the application domain. Snake methods consider the user-drawn curve and automatically align it with nearby image edges.

In our long-term approach, we have to study the evolving of semi-automatically extraction, and when possible automatically extraction for specific application domain, of relevant regions using segmentation processes. This functionality makes the query component more powerful comparing to the current semi-automatically approach. So when the image is inserted in the collection, the system triggers the segmentation process, such as the segmentation process developed by [Mou 90], and returns a set of regions. If a region corresponds to a real world object, but its border is not clearly closed, the user, generally an expert of the application domain, must have the possibility to close the rest of the border, using a visual manual tool for example, to obtain a region that has a real world meaning. But there is a price to pay for this functionality. When the images are complex or contain lot of real world objects, the segmentation, even if it is semi-automatic, is not simple. So one of the problem still unsolved with content based retrieval is the segmentation of natural and complex scenes.

Figure 4: An image after the segmentation process

The last two figures summarize the problems of automatic segmentation and pattern recognition of regions.

In our system, the shapes are represented by a matrix of pixels contained in the region. The matrix of pixels consists of elements equal to 1 if the pixel is a part of the region, and 0 if not. Another method, that is considered in our system, uses the Freeman Codes to represent the border of the region. This method permits the deduction of Fourier descriptors which are accurate and have better semantic than Freeman code to describe the shape of the region.

If the Freeman code of a region shape is composed of a start point (x, y) and a list of elements a1, a2, .., an where ai is an element of {0,1,2,3,4,5,6,7}, then the Fourier descriptors can be deduced. The advantages of Fourier descriptors are : - the reduction of the number of useful values, so they permit to find particular points in the contour such as the extreme points. - they represent mathematically the shape independently of the region orientation, and permit a tolerance of elastic deformations between structures by taking into consideration certain coefficients. The descriptors of Fourier are a set of attributes (an, bn, cn, dn) where :

$$a_n = \frac{T}{2n\Delta\tau\Delta}\sum_{p=1}^{k}\frac{\Delta x_p}{\Delta t_p}[\cos(\frac{2\pi n t_p}{T}) - \cos(\frac{2\pi n t_{p-1}}{T})]$$

$$b_n = \frac{T}{2n\Delta\tau\Delta}\sum_{p=1}^{k}\frac{\Delta x_p}{\Delta t_p}[\sin(\frac{2\pi n t_p}{T}) - \sin(\frac{2\pi n t_{p-1}}{T})]$$

$$c_n = \frac{T}{2n\Delta\tau\Delta}\sum_{p=1}^{k}\frac{\Delta y_p}{\Delta t_p}[\cos(\frac{2\pi n t_p}{T}) - \cos(\frac{2\pi n t_{p-1}}{T})]$$

and $$d_n = \frac{T}{2n\Delta\tau\Delta}\sum_{p=1}^{k}\frac{\Delta y_p}{\Delta t_p}[\sin(\frac{2\pi n t_p}{T}) - \sin(\frac{2\pi n t_{p-1}}{T})]$$

Each index «n» of the attributes an, bn, cn, dn represents a step of the contour definition. For n = 0, the descriptors of Fourier represent the barycenter of the region. For n = 1, the descriptors of Fourier represent an ellipse. While n increases, the shape obtained approaches the original shape. Example :

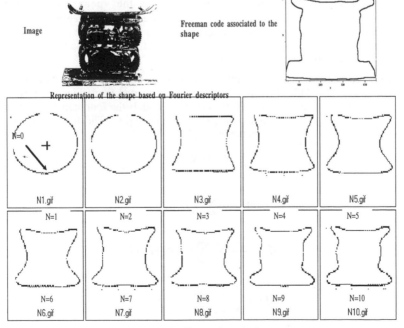

Figure 5: Shape description.

Firstly, the user draws the shape using the visual tool. Secondly, the content of the shape is automatically filled.

In the object oriented modeling, we have the class Shape which is characterized by a set of attributes and methods. The first one models the coordinates of a pixel in the original image, it locates the shape in the original image, the second one models the Freeman code in the form of a list of values. The third one models the value (n) necessary to accurate the mathematical description of the shape. The final attribute models the length of Freeman code. The methods return respectively the code of Freeman, Fourier descriptors, the value of n, and the length of Freeman code.

2.1.2 Texture

The texture is an important aspect of human visual perception, and it is the second important feature extracted automatically from image regions. Some practical experiences on texture modeling permit us to see the difficulties to find a generic texture model that may be independent of the application domain. So, in our short-term approach, we model at least two simple classes of textures that may be extended, in our long-term approach using object technologies, by other texture classes regarding to the application domains.

When two patterns differ only in scale, the magnified one is coarser. The variance measures the dispersion of the difference of gray-level with a certain distance. The contrast measures the vividness of the texture and is a function of the gray-level difference histogram. The directionality measures the «peakedness» of the distribution of gradient directions in the image. For example the region may have a favored direction. The detail of formulas are presented in [Sav 96]. It is not a powerful texture representation, but may be interesting for retrieval process when mixing it with other features (colors, shape, key-words).

In the first class, the texture of the region is represented by statistic formulas based on four moments (M1, M2, M3, M4). In the object oriented modeling, we define the class Texture structured by a set of attributes that models the four statistic moments : M1, M2, M3, M4 and the number of pixels of the region. The four moments are computed respectively by four methods M1, M2, M3, M4.

$$M_1 = \frac{1}{N} \sum_i \sum_j f(i,j) \,,$$

$$M_2 = \frac{1}{N} \sum_i \sum_j ijf(i,j) \,,$$

$$M_3 = \frac{1}{N} \sum_i \sum_j i\Delta j \, \Delta f(i,j) \,,$$

$$M_4 = \frac{1}{N} \sum_i \sum_j i^3 j^3 f(i,j)$$

f(i, j) is the value of the pixel in ith line and jth column.

In the second class, the texture of the region is represented by the histogram of the gird differences. We consider a distance as a segment between two points. The corner of the direction of the distance and the length of the distance is dependent of the application domain. Based the histogram, the system computes the coarseness, the variance, the contrast, the entropy and the directionality.

2.1.3 Color

The color is the third important image feature extracted automatically from an image or a region. In the first step of the extraction process, based on raster format, the region or image color is extracted and represented in the RGB model, and the mean and variation of each component of RGB model are computed.

Based on the RGB model, the color is transformed and represented in the HSV model, characterized by three means H, S and V. The HSV model is more suited than the RGB model, in which certain ambiguities appear between colors (sućh as Yellow and Green).

In theory, the results are different when using different distances, but our first experimentation showed that there are no significant differences between that distances in the first result images, the differences appear after the first result images (after the 5-10th image). Based on the sorted distances, the result images are ordered and sorted by similarity. Generally, we stop at the 15th distance, corresponding to the 15th image returned by the retrieval sub-system of RECI.

In the object-oriented modeling, we define two classes of colors RGB and HSV. The first one, called RGB-histogram is structured by three attributes red, green and blue and two methods. Each attribute takes as values an object structured by two attributes : the variation and the mean of the color. The two methods compute respectively for each color (red, blue or green) the mean and the variation of the color. The second class, called HSV histogram, contains a structure part that includes the histogram of colors and a set of distances, and the method part that includes the methods that compute the attributes of the structure part. The color of a region is represented by a histogram of 165 colors. Each element of the histogram represents the number of pixels that have the suited color. So, comparing the colors of two regions is equivalent to compute the distance between the histogram of the regions target and source. Before submitting the query, the user may select the distance.

2.1.4 Spatial relations

The spatial relations modeled until now are not very powerful, they just locate the relations between image regions, and compute the distance between two points of that regions. We consider each region in a minimal rectangle. The distance considers left and top points of each rectangle.

The gravity center of the region is (x_i, y_i) : $x_g = \dfrac{\sum x_i}{n}$ et $y_g = \dfrac{\sum y_i}{n}$

The gravity center computed by of the first harmonic (N=0) of Fourier descriptors confirmes the results obtainted by these formulas.

The image is subdivised in 9 areas of identical dimension, each one is identified by an identifier. The position of a region is deduced from the position of the gravity center in one of these 9 areas. The localisation is finally stored in the database.

2.2 Image Retrieval

2.2.1 Queries

The user may request and combine three types of queries: color, texture and shape queries.

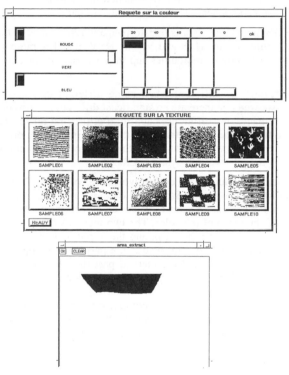

Figure 6: Visual interface query

To formulate the color query, the user has to select at most five colors. To represent the quantities of the different colors, we use an intuitive scrolled scale. Each qualifier is assigned to a range of values. This solution may be interesting when the user has a good appreciation of the region colors he looks for, but it is tedious when this appreciation is not accurate, that is why the user may select a region from an existing image by defining the borders, and the system extracts automatically the colors of this region. These colors are then matched with image regions of the database to find the most similar images. We call this mechanism, retrieval by selection.

To formulate the texture query, the user has a palette of a set of textures (black and white) at his disposal to define the texture. To formulate the shape query, the user draws the shape which undergoes a transcription into the model.

The database is then scanned to retrieve the images with regions that correspond to the shape, texture and color specified by the user. So the system matches the values of the colors, the texture or the shape with the values of the regions that are stored in the object-oriented database.

2.2.2 Matching

In the retrieval process, features (colors, shapes, textures) of the query specification are compared with features of the image database to determine which images match correctly (similar) with the given features. The matching process is based on distance computing between target and source region images. For pragmatic reasons, before triggering the retrieval process, the distance used is selected by the user out of five distances. histogram distance L1 and Euclidean distance L2 are the simplest one, histogram intersection distance, moment distance L1 and quadratic distance are generally more efficient when the result images are voluminous, but they are more complex. For example, quadratic distance is time consuming comparing with the first two distances. Technical details about that distances are presented and compared in [Far 97].

We consider H and I the histograms of respectively target image (query image) and source image (image database). they are defined by an array (vector) (hc1,hc2,hc3,...,hcn), in which each element hcj represents the number of pixel of the color cj in the image. N is the number of pixels in the image.

The distance between two histograms of colors H and I is represented by :

Distance L1 $d_{L1}(H,I) = \sum_{l=1}^{n} |h_{cl} - i_{cl}|$

Euclidean distance L2 $d_{L2}(H,I) = \sqrt{\sum_{l=1}^{n} (h_{dl} - i_{dl})^2}$

Distance between moments

$d_{mom}(H,I) = \sum_{i=1}^{r} w_{i1}|E_i - F_i| + w_{i2}|\sigma_i - \varsigma_i| + w_{i3}|S_i - T_i|$

"Ei" the mean of H, "Fi" the mean of I, σ_i the variation of H et ς_i the variation of I, "Si" the moment of degree 3 of H, and "Ti" the moment of the degree 3 of I.

Quadratic distance $d_A(H,I) = \sqrt{(H-I).A.(H-I)^T}$.

H(M) and I(N) are respectively the histograms of colors of images M and N defined by the vectors *(h1, h2, ... hi ....., hn)* and *(i1, i2, ... ii...., in)* where each element hi or ii represents the number of pixels that have the color I in the images M and N. This distance is the most one because it appreciates correctly the color similarity, but it is time consuming comparing with other distances (I.e L1)

Histogram intersection distance $d_I(I, M) = \sum_{j=1}^{n} \min(I_j, M_j)$

When mixing several features, such as colors and shapes, the result distance is equal to the somme of feature distances. The result images are presented in a sorted way, the littlest distance corresponds to the most similar image.

In the similarity matching, classical indexing methods such as B-trees are not well suited, because the similarity is defined in a high-dimensional space (for example, HSV histogram, texture and features), and the problem is more complex when considering retrieval processes that combine similarity matching with spatial constraints between image regions. So, fast access data structures of high-dimensional features have to considered.

3. Conclusion

We have shown that the system presents a platform for the storage and content-based retrieval of multimedia information. The system has resulted in a prototype with two major steps extraction and queries. We combine manual, semi-automatic and automatic approaches in order to extract region images (colors, textures, shapes). Regions, which are extracted semi-automatically, are significant and relevant for the final user. Shapes are represented by powerful mathematical formulas, so the representation of the shape is independent of the rotation, scale and translation. The features extracted are modeled, using object technology, in the database management system O2. The object modeling has several advantages such as the simplification of the encapsulation of data that save developers many details of particular image hardware or software. This make the framework portable and extensible. The system has being implemented on IBM Risc 6000/Aix platform using the programming language C, and O2C language of the object-oriented database management system O2.

References

[Fal 93]   Faloutsos C., Flickner M., Niblack W., Ptrovic D., Equitz W., Barber R. «Efficient and Effective Query by Image Content». Research report, IBM Alameda Research Center, 1993

[Far 97]   Fargeaud P. «Retrieval and Extraction by Content of Images (RECI) in an Object Oriented Database» Report of CNAM, Nantes, France, 1997.

[Gob 92]   Goble C., al. «The Manchester Multimedia Information System». In Oroc. of VLDB-92.

[Gud 95]   Gudivada V.N. and Raghavan V., «Content-based image retrieval systems», In IEEE Computer, pages 18-22, September 1995.

[Haf 95]   Hafner J., al. «Efficient Color Histogram Indexing for Quadratic Distance Functions». In IEEE Transaction on Pattern analysis and Machine Intelligence, July 1995.

[Jai 95]   Jain R. "Infoscopes : Multimedia Information Systems", Virage Inc. and University of California at San Diego, 1995.

[Meh 95]   Mehrotra R. And Gary J. E. «Similar-shape retrieval in shape data management», In IEEE Computer, pages 57-62, September 1995.

[Mou 90]   Moulet «Segmentation process for both fixed and animed images», PhD these, IRESTE, Nantes University, 1990.

[Orp 93]   Orphanoudakis S. C. «I2C a system for the indexing and retrieval of medical images by pictorial content», In Image and Vision Computing, vol. 11, pages 501-503, Butterworth-Heinemann Ltd, October 1993.

[Pen 94]   Pentland A., Picard R. W., Sclaroff S. «Photobook: Tools for Content-Based Manipulation of Image Databases», in Proc. of SPIE-94, pages 34-47, Bellingham, Washington, 1994.

[Pet 93]   Petrakis E. G. M., Orphanoudakis S. C. «Methodology for the representation, indexing and retrieval of images by content», In Image and Vision Computing, vol. 11, pages 504-521, Butterworth-Heinemann Ltd, October 1993.

[Sav 96]   Savory I. «Retrieve Images by Textural Content», Report of Master degree in Computer Sciences, Nantes University, 21 June 1996.

[Smi 96]   Smith J. R., Chang S. F. «Visual SEEK : a fully automated content-based image query system», ACM Multimedia'96, November 1996.

[Sri 95]   Srihari R. K? «Automatic Indexing and Content-Based Retrieval of Captioned Images», In IEEE Computer, pages49-56, September 1995.

[Zhe 94]   Zheng Z. J. «An efficient sheme of simple network detection for binary images of the hexagonal grid». In Proceedings of IEEE TENCON-94, Singapore, 1994.

Interactive Search Method for Ambiguous Target Image

Masaomi Oda

ATR Human Information Processing Research Laboratories
2-2 Hikaridai Seika-cho Soraku-gun Kyoto 619-02 Japan
Tel; +81-774-95-1033, Fax; +81-774-95-1008, E-mail; oda@hip.atr.co.jp

Abstract. We propose an image retrieval system by which an ambiguous target image can be retrieved. The advantages of this system were examined using a facial database. An ambiguous image, such as a favorite face, was chosen as the target image. In the system, similar faces to the prototype, which was created by repeated retrieval over some period of time, were used to estimate the goal image. One of the main aims was to evaluate the method's ability to lead the retriever to the goal image without measuring the psychological preference of the retriever directly. It was found that ambiguous facial image retrieval is possible without subjective labels in the data, but with the presentation of faces similar to the prototype for the next candidates.

1 Introduction

A retrieval system is a common computer function, and many studies have been conducted on it. Oddy pointed out that even in a document retrieval system the following problems exist [1]. The retriever often can not express his/her request clearly, the request is changed dynamically, and the interaction between the system and the user is detective and dialogic. Also, in an image retrieval system, these phenomena will easily occur because the user does not always have a clear image and can not always explain the image verbally. For image retrieval systems, many methods without verbal keys have been studied [2-5].

A lot of retrieval systems have been designed aiming at maximum efficiency with minimal retriever input considering subjective sensitivity. Many have assumed that a clear target image exists in the retriever's mind. When a final target can be estimated from scant information, this method will be correct.

On the contrary, we define an ambiguous image, whereby the retriever can not get a clear image but has a concept in his/her mind. For example, most shoppers do not have a clear idea beforehand of what new clothes to buy, but they can make decisions while shopping. This is the same in the case of electronic shopping. Therefore, requiring an explanation of the target image either verbally or by drawing a picture is not an appropriate method for ambiguous image retrieval.

For an ambiguous target image, the adaptability to changes in the target image is more important than the efficiency of the retrieval, because the goal image is clarified through the retrieval process. To satisfy the retriever's demand, a mechanism that improves based on the retriever's changing desires is necessary.

We propose an image retrieval system by which an ambiguous target image can be retrieved. The advantages of this system were examined using a facial database. An ambiguous image, such as a favorite face, was chosen as the target image. In the system, similar faces to the prototype, which was created by repeated retrieval over some period of time, were used to estimate the goal image. One of the main aims was to evaluate the method's ability to lead the retriever to the goal image without measuring the psychological preference of the retriever directly.

2   System architecture

We arranged the requests for the ambiguous image retrieval system as follows.
(1) As the target image of the user is not initially clear, but becomes clear in the retrieval process, a dynamically changing process is necessary for the system.
(2) As the target is an ambiguous image, the system does not force the retriever to use keywords. The system should not request the users' rational analysis of the mind's image.
(2) The user must be satisfied with the retrieved image. A quick search is an important factor for the system, but it is not sufficient in itself. The user must be feel that he/she has attained the best possible image.
(4) Although a quick search is not a sufficient overall condition for the system, efficient retrieval is necessary.
(5) An easy interface is necessary for novice users. The user has to be able to use the system directly without a searcher, because an ambiguous image in the user's mind will be hard to transmit to a searcher.

To satisfy the above mentioned criteria, a system architecture was constructed. Image clarification is performed under human and system interaction. Image data are presented on a computer display. The retriever selects some of the images, those that compromise his/her target image, e.g., a favorite face. The system estimates what kind of image the retriever has in mind by using the selected data. The most desirable data for the retriever at this time are presented as the next candidates. By including the images in the next candidates, which are out of the criteria for the estimation, the retriever can change his/her mind or can prevent a sub-optimal goal image. The retriever can reevaluate selected faces at any time and can remove faces at that time. The one face which is most similar to the average of the selected faces is displayed among the next candidates, because the retriever can recognize the prototype that he/she is creating by this time. This mechanism is an application of the context dependency effect, which means that the concept creation is influenced by the order of the stimuli in the human's mind [6]. This principle enables the smooth convergence of image creation.

In the experimental system, similarity was used to estimate the next candidates [7]. The similarity was calculated by two criteria; the variance of each feature and the Euclidean distance from the average of selected faces. Faces included in some hypercube regions centered on the prototype in the feature space were selected as candidates. The regions were varied from large to small according to the extension of the retrieval.

A line-drawn version and photographic version were prepared for our experiments. In the line-drawn version, facial features concerned with shapes and positions (e.g., eye shape, mouth position) were used. Sixty thousand images were used in the database. In the photographic version, the KL expansion technique [8,9] was applied, and coefficients of eigenvectors were considered as features of a face. Two thousand five hundred photographs (100 original faces and 2400 morphed faces) were used.

3 Verification of system effectiveness

The effectiveness of the system was verified by experiments on the following points: The retriever can reach the goal image, and the goal image is fit for the task demanded. The retrieval experiments were conducted using a favorite face as an example of an ambiguous target image. The retrieval was conducted twice separated by another facial experiment of 20 minutes.

In the line-drawn version, twenty subjects were asked to retrieve 10 favorite image data from 60,000 data in about 7 minutes. They were involved in two types of experiments. Under the Context-Driven (CD) condition, eight similar and two random faces were presented by using a context dependency mechanism. To evaluate the results of the CD condition, an experiment of the Random-Presentation (RN) condition was conducted. Under the RN condition, 10 different faces were presented at every selection stage. The system does not support the subjects' selection under the RN condition. Only compromised faces are selected by the subjects without the influence of the context dependency mechanism.

In the photographic version, another twenty subjects were asked to retrieve the 10 favorite image data from 2500 data in about ten minutes. The experiments under the CD and RN conditions were conducted for the subjects.

At the end of each retrieval session, the subjects were asked to identify the most satisfactory face from among the 10 selected faces and to orally explain why they judged it to be the best among those faces.

Moreover, to investigate the accuracy of the selected face as being a truly favorite face, we compared the results of the retrieval method in the photographic version with

Table 1. Results of favorite face retrieval in the line-drawn version

	CD	RN
Retrieval Time	6'16"	7'32"
Retrieval Number	190	479
Selection Number	34.2	16.5
Variance	0.148	0.450

Table 2. Results of favorite face retrieval in the photographic version

	CD	RN
Retrieval Time	9'49"	9'56"
Retrieval Number	415	451
Selection Number	16.7	15.6
Variance	37.9×10^3	85.6×10^3

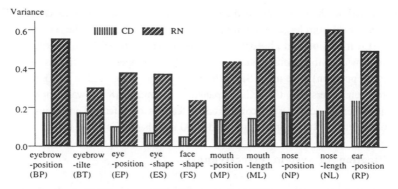

Fig. 1. Variance of line-drawn facial features for favorite faces
the album search method. The subjects were asked to select five favorite faces from 50 original photographs of the opposite gender.

3.1   Verification of goal image

The retriever had to retrieve at least 10 favorite faces from the database. The main results of the experiments in the line-drawn version are shown in Table 1. As he/she continues the retrieval and evaluation, the selected face image is converged to a favorite face. In the line-drawn face retrieval, an individual feature, like the shape of the eye, the position of the nose, etc., was used. If the retriever liked large eyes, the finally selected face was expected to have large eyes. Therefore, we could assume that the variance of features would be small.

Although the strategies used to find the goal image differed among retrievers, the goal image was found for all cases. Whatever face was selected at first to reach a similar goal face in the two experiments was examined. The final goal was confirmed to be a favorite face and not the result of enforcement by the system. Under the RN condition, all selected faces can be considered as favorites because the subjects are not influenced by the system. Therefore, the results were verified by comparing them with results under the RN condition. All variances of features were smaller under the CD condition than under the RN condition (Fig. 1).

While the same assumption could be applied to photographic data, the same result could not necessarily be expected, because the KL expansion technique was used for feature expression and the features expressed by the coefficient of the eigenvalue could not be understood by humans.

The main results of the experiments in the photographic version are shown in Table 2. The same results were derived in the photographic version (Fig. 2). Especially, the younger coefficients, which were ordered by the largeness of eigenvalues, had larger effects than the older ones. The variances of features under the CD condition were 37.9×10^3 and 85.6×10^3 under the RN condition. Although the number of faces seen is almost the same in both conditions, the variances under the CD condition were less

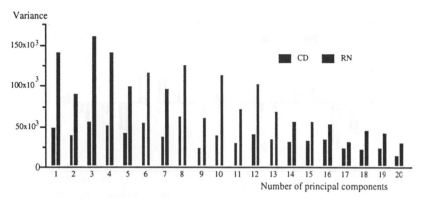

Fig. 2. Variance of photographic facial features for favorite faces

than 1/2 of those under the RN condition.

These results show that the system supports the retriever in collecting favorite faces according to the selected face. It was clarified that ease of retrieval could be accomplished not only with simple line-drawn data but also with photographed face data.

3.2 Fitness for the task demand

(1) Features values

For each of the facial features, we calculated the mean of the parameter values among the 10 faces in the final set produced by each subject for each retrieval task. The mean values of each feature are shown in Fig. 3 for the line-drawn version and in Fig. 4 for the photographic version. The results showed that the values indicate similar distribution between the CD condition and the RN condition.

We might suspect that the variances were small, but that the selected faces were actually favorite ones for the subjects. However, a comparison of the mean feature values of each condition eliminates this suspicion. This is because each feature value in the line-drawn version and each coefficient in the photographic version took similar

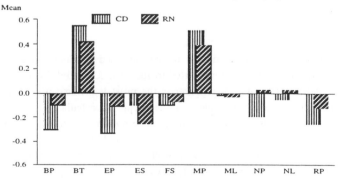

Fig. 3. Mean values of line-drawn facial features for favorite faces

Mean

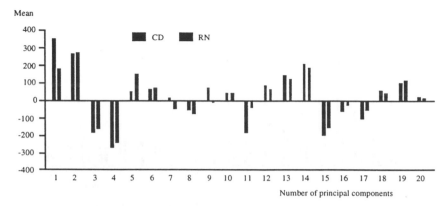

Number of principal components

Fig. 4. Mean values of photographic facial features for favorite faces
under both conditions and the subjects could select their favorite faces with no
restriction by the system under the RN condition. This showed that the subjects could
retrieve favorite faces even under the CD condition.

(2) Comparison with album searched faces

In the photographic version, the subjects were asked to select 5 favorite faces from
50 original photographs of the opposite gender after the experiment. A face which
includes an element of the original faces must have a high possibility of being the
favorite face, because there was a high linear relation as the function of the morphed
rate between the morphed face and the original face [10]. We investigated the hit
number of the most satisfactory face derived from the retrieval method with the selected
5 faces derived from the album search method. The results showed that 70% of the
subjects selected the same element of the original face in the most satisfactory face
under the CD condition as in the album searched faces. On the other hand, 55% of the
subjects selected the same element of the original face under the RN condition. These
results showed that retrieval under the CD condition was more effective in retrieving
the favorite face than that under the RN condition.

4. Discussion

It is important for the goal image to be obtained without measuring the
psychological preference of the retriever fitted to the task demanded. To consider the
psychological characteristics of each retriever is the most legitimate way, but this is
very difficult as each retriever's preferences are different. To calculate faces similar to
the prototype created by selected faces means the estimation of a future prototype in
small steps. Features used in the photographic version could not be recognized by the
retriever. Nevertheless, these features were useful for ambiguous image retrieval.
Although the method could not necessarily guarantee the convergence of the goal
image, a human can dynamically improve the goal image. The context for image

clarification was made from the selection of faces by the retriever, and this influenced the retriever in selecting from the next candidates. Even though the selection was performed under the influence of the context, the final goal was stable for each retrieval. This suggests that a retriever's image is stable whenever he/she can not perceive it as a pictorial image in his/her mind.

A similar retrieval method was applied using the GA technique [11]. In that system, the existence of a clear image was assumed. The retriever was asked to rate the presented faces at the start. The rated information was used and the most similar face was derived by the system. However, the fluctuations of the retriever's mind cannot be followed in the system's retrieval.

Although the face images in the database were high in subjective similarity to each other, the target image was successfully found. The small variety of face types might have helped the retriever easily select the first face. If data of a huge variety, e.g., covering all kinds of races, were expected, the first selection from the randomly presented faces would have been difficult. Preparing a menu of typical faces is effective for avoiding such difficulty. After the selection of the target type, this mechanism will work well.

In our experiment, the task was to select 10 favorite faces. However, in ordinary retrieval conditions, the retrievers will select one favorite face. We examined the case when the most satisfactory face was selected in the photographic facial retrieval. The results showed that the most satisfactory face was derived at 160 faces under the CD condition, and at 261 faces under the RN condition. As the final retrieval number was 415 and 451 under the CD and the RN conditions, respectively, the most satisfactory face was selected at 0.4 and 0.6 in the total retrieval period of each condition. The time periods for finding the most satisfactory faces were significantly different between the two conditions. This showed the effectiveness of the retrieval mechanism under the CD condition. Under the CD condition, when a favorite face was found, similar faces were presented as the next candidates. Therefore, the retrieval number might not increase so much even if the number of data were large. On the other hand, the retrieval number under the RN condition might increase according to the number of data. The effect of the CD mechanism will be clearer in a large database. After the most satisfactory face was derived, the retrieval was continued. This phenomenon means that the user wanted to feel that he/she had attained the best one. If the optimal face was presented alone, the user was not satisfied with it. The interactive method is necessary for ambiguous image retrieval.

The system architecture is applicable to other types of image databases, but the features of the image data must be selected carefully so as to fit the retrieval objective. In conjunction with the results of other experiments [12], it was clarified that the salient features of a face are different for different task demands (e.g., happy, fierce, similar). The important features can be investigated by using this system in advance [13]. The interactive learning method [14] will also be useful to derive important features.

5. Conclusion

A method of ambiguous image retrieval was proposed and its advantages were investigated. In particular, it was found that ambiguous facial image retrieval is possible without subjective labels in the data, but with the presentation of faces similar to the prototype for the next candidates.

References

1. R.N. Oddy, Information retrieval through man-machine dialogue, Journal of documentation, 33, 1-14, 1977.
2. J.W. Shepherd, An Interactive Computer System for Retrieving Faces, in H.D. Eliss, M.A. Jeeves, F. Newcombe and A. Young, Aspects of face processing (Martinus Nijhoff), 398-409, 1986.
3. T. Kato, H. Shimogaki, T. Mizutori, K. Fujimura, TRADEMARK, Multimedia Database with Abstracted Representation on Knowledge Base, Proc. of 2nd International Symposium on Interoperable Information Systems, 245-252, 1988.
4. S.K. Chang, C.W. Yan, D.C. Dimitroff, T. Arndt, An Intelligent Image Database System, IEEE Trans. on Software Engineering, Vol. 14, No. 5, 681-688, 1988.
5. A. Gupta, T. Weymouth, R. Jain, Semantic Queries with Pictures: The VIMSYS Model, Proc. of the 17th Int. Conf. on Very Large Data Bases, 69-79, 1991.
6. M. Oda, Context Dependency in the Formation of Image Concepts and Its Application, IEEE Int. Conf. on Systems, Man, and Cybernetics, 1673-1678, 1991.
7. M. Oda, Human Interface for an Ambiguous Image Retrieval System, The 6th International Conference on Human-Computer Interaction, 1995.
8. L. Sirovich and M. Kirby, Low-dimensional procedure for the characterization of human faces, J. Opt. Soc. Am. A, Vol. 4, No. 3, 519-524, March 1987.
9. S. Akamatsu, T. Sasaki, H. Fukamachi, and Y. Suenaga, A robust face identification scheme - KL expansion of an invariant feature space -, SPIE Vol. 1607 Intelligent Robots and Computer Vision X, 71-84, 1991.
10. M.Oda, S. Akamatsu, H. Fukamachi, Similarity judgment of a face by K-L expansion technique based on a comparison to human judgment, Proc. CVVC'94, 25-30, 1994.
11. C. Caldwell, V.S. Johnston, Tracking a criminal suspect through face-space with a genetic algorithm, Proc. of Int. Conf. on Genetic Algorithm, 416-421, 1991.
12. M. Oda, T. Kato, An Evaluation of Feature Saliency of Faces for Improving the Ambiguous-face Retrieval System, 15th International Symposium on Human Factors in Telecommunications (HFT'95), 415-417, 1995.
13. T. Kato, M. Oda, Indirect Measurement of Feature Saliency in Face Processing, ITE,Vol.49, No.8, pp.1068-1077, 1995.
14. T.P. Minka, R.W. Picard, Interactive learning using a society of models, MIT Media Lab. Technical Report No.349.

Planar Shape Databases with Affine Invariant Search

S. Startchik, R. Milanese, C. Rauber, T. Pun

Dept. of Computer Science, University of Geneva, Switzerland

E-mail: startchi@cui.unige.ch

Abstract

This paper describes the use of viewpoint-invariant representations for shape-based retrieval in image databases. In particular, we focus on a class of man-made 3D objects, whose planar surfaces contain some distinctive patterns. For this class of objects we introduce a representation scheme for parametric curves, whose reference frame is constructed using consecutive sets of points that are invariant to affine and projective transformations. In particular, we employ intersections between line segments, bitangents, and cusp tangents. In order to reduce the computational complexity of this representation, we propose an ordering algorithm for the invariant points, which reduces the number of reference frames for each curve to the number of invariant points. We then propose a two-step retrieval method. First, an indexing procedure compares the query shape to all shapes of the database using only the first-order moments of the invariant points. Once a small set of candidate shapes has been selected, the Euclidean distance between the two curves in the invariant reference frame is used to compute a detailed similarity measure. Experimental results are reported for a database of trademark patterns subject to affine transformations.

1. Introduction

In recent years, the use of computer vision and image processing techniques has been proposed to support content-based shape retrieval in image databases. A few major approaches can be identified in the existing literature. The first one consists of representing each image in the database as a feature vector, which stores information about the colour distribution of the image, some texture and shape descriptors, and possibly some spatial relations among the most prominent regions of the image. This approach is employed, for instance, in QBIC [2] and Virage [15]. One disadvantage of these systems is that they impose a pre-defined set of features, which may not be the most appropriate ones to characterize the database at hand. Various types of statistical tools have been proposed to best represent the images composing a database. Examples are principal component analysis, which has been employed in Photobook [10] and correspondence analysis [6]. Another approach to image representation for content-based retrieval is based on image transformations, such as wavelets [5]. It has been shown that, by appropriately choosing a set of basis functions and a quantization scheme, very compact and discriminative representations can be obtained, enabling image comparisons at multiple resolutions. Finally, the use of edge maps computed from the images has been proposed to enable the user to query the database using hand-drawn sketches. The sketch and the image edge map can then be compared by simple correlation methods [4].

Most approaches described above have been successfully applied on databases containing several thousands images. However, all of them represent images based on their visual appearance. For this reason, they are very sensitive to viewpoint changes, which can dramatic alter the object appearances. In this paper, we propose an alternative approach to image representation that is invariant to affine and projective transformations, and can thus be used when the query image representing a target 3D object is taken from a different viewpoint than in the archived images. In particular, we propose invariant descriptions that apply to 3D objects containing planar surfaces. Examples of objects, whose planar surfaces can be easily discriminated, are commercial packages containing distinguishable trade logos.

For this class of objects, we propose a shape representation using parametric curves. Such curves are defined over an object-centered reference frame, which also serves as a canonical coordinate system, common for all shapes in the database. Using this representation, shape similarity can be estimated and neighbourhood relationships can be established for subsequent search. The contributions of this work are the following. The construction of reference frames is proposed by combining different types of local invariant properties of the curves. In the context of search operations, a two-step process is introduced to achieve fast retrieval. The first step consists of a rough candidate selection, using moment-based indexing. The second step performs accurate shape comparison on the most likely candidates. These strategies are tested on a database of trademarks, obtained through snapshots of supermarket box packages taken from varying viewpoints.

2. Viewpoint Invariant Similarity of Shapes

In this section, the comparison of two shapes seen from two different viewpoints is considered, where each viewpoint transformation corresponds to either an affine or projective transformation of the image. For shapes that can be characterized in terms of points, lines or higher-order algebraic curves, comparison can be done using algebraic invariants for both affine and projective camera transformations [11, 8, 14]. For a broader class of shapes, general non-closed-form invariants can be obtained by exploiting local, differential properties of the shape [7, 12, 16]. In this latter situation, the approach consists of constructing a reference frame based on local invariant properties of the shape itself, and in studying the representation of the shape with respect to this frame. The selected frame becomes a canonical or unit coordinate system, in which the shape becomes an invariant signature.

2.1 Curve Representations for Invariant Shape Representation

For image database retrieval, shape comparison requires intensive geometric transformations of the curve representation. A parametric representation of curves should thus be chosen so as to guarantee the lowest possible cost at this step. This has restrained our attention to the class of parametric curves $p(t) = \sum_{i=1}^{N} C_i g_i(t)$, where C_i are the control points and $g_i(t)$ are the base functions [1, 7]. In this case, only the control points are affected by geometric transformations, under the condition that the relation between the curve and the control points is invariant to the applied transformation. In the case of projective transformation this nice property is available only for *rational* curves, i.e. those for which the base functions are of the form $g_i(t) = f_i(t)/\sum_{j=1}^{N} f_j(t)$. Another useful property of rational curves is their ability to model almost polygonal objects while preserving differentiability at "corners". Two families of rational curves were selected and compared in this work: NURBS [13] and RaG [3], respectively defined with polynomial and exponential base functions.

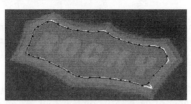

Fig. 1. Example of Rocky logo shape with fitted NURBS.

In both cases, curves are fitted using constrained minimization with the Levenberg-Marquardt method and uniform placement of initial knots. In the case of NURBS a constraint was set on second derivative between conic spans [13] to assure C^2-continuity along the whole curve. The side-effect of this constraint is that only a limited set of *points* of the fitted curve can contain inflections and cusps which is an additional simplification of their search. For example, under the constraint, the highest curvature can be produced only at peak point of the span so only these peaks are capable to approximate cusps of the curve. Conversely, inflections can be approximated only by a span joint with its continuity property. Their presence can be detected by comparing the respective orientation of adjacent spans. In order to search for bitangent, two constraints are applied: a bitangent cannot join two adjacent NURBS spans and neither of its contact points can lay on a part of the curve already covered by a line. Example of curve fitting is given in figure 1. The advantages of RaGs include easy multiscale analysis, control of smoothness, infinite differentiability and simplified fitting (minimization is global); NURBS, however, allow fast matching operations. After extensive tests, NURBS have been preferred for efficiency considerations; RaGs will, however, be kept as a possible alternative.

2.2 Invariant Reference Frames

Given a parametric curve representation, we now concentrate on the construction of a reference frame for this representation, based on projectively invariant properties of a shape. Example of such invariant properties are straight and bitangent lines, cusp and inflection points [11, 8, 16]. In general, lines lead to more stable invariants. For this reason, we replace cusps and inflections by their tangent lines (in the case of cusps the number of tangents is two), which yields four types of lines that can be extracted from the shape. Whenever each of these lines intersect one another or a shape, the intersection point gives a stable invariant reference point (cf. figure 2).

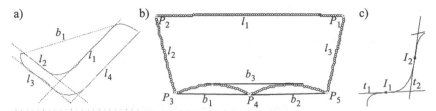

Fig. 2. Finding invariant lines associated with the curve. (a) Four straight lines $l_1, ..., l_4$ and one bitangent b_1 were found for the L-shape curve. (b) Straight lines $l_1, ..., l_3$, bitangents $b_1, ..., b_3$ and cusps $P_1, ..., P_5$ were detected for the Levis' logo. (c) Example of inflection points I_1, I_2 with their corresponding tangent lines.

To compensate for affine transformations, three reference points suffice, while for the projective case, the number of necessary points is four. As an example, let us consider the affine projection case. The selection of triples of points amongst n invariant points of the curve gives C_n^3 possible combinations. By associating each invariant point with an "anchor" point on the curve, their order with respect to the curve is established; by only selecting successive triples of points, the number of possible coordinate frames thus reduces to n. As our invariant points are constructed from the intersection of invariant lines, their anchor position should be deduced from the anchor positions of those lines. Lines obtained as tangents at inflection points and cusps, both already have a point on the curve as a part of their definition and thus possess such anchors upon construction. Straight lines and bitangents have two points of contact with the curve. For example, the straight part of a curve which can be approximated by a line is delimited by two points which can be considered as anchors for this line. Using the anchor positions of all invariant lines, an adjacency relation can be imposed on them. The intersection points of any two consecutive lines is thus also invariant. By taking triples of such consecutive intersection points, one can define an invariant reference frame.

There are a few cases when intersections of *two* pairs of lines of different types produce points that are infinitely close to each other (cf. figure 3). Selecting them as two different points and using then in a reference frame construction would lead to a serious instability in shape signature matching. Therefore, this multiplicity has to be removed. In a), the point P_1 can be detected twice as the intersection of line l_1 and either bitangent b_1 or cusp tangent t_1. Selection of either case will not influence the precision of signature, so in this case the bitangent-related invariant point was removed.

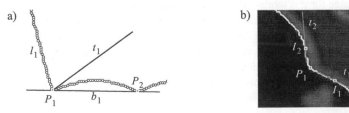

Fig. 3. Removing multiplicity of points (see text).

Another special case of multiplicity depends on the extraction of curve properties. If the shape is tilted enough, two inflection points I_1 and I_2 (cf. figure 3.b) may be detected simultaneously with a cusp point P_1 in their proximity. In this case, one must use either tangents t_1 and t_2 at the inflection points or two tangents at the cusp point (not shown in the figure).

3. Searching the Shape Database

In this section, a method for comparing images of the database with a query image is proposed. In order to speed up the search operation, a moment-based indexing technique is then introduced for selecting a small number of likely candidates from the database.

3.1 Computing Shape Similarity

Two curves are considered similar if in *one* of their n invariant reference frames they perfectly match, where n is the number of their invariant points. In one frame, e.g. given two triples of points, the measure of match is defined as the sum of closest distances from a number of sampled points on the first curve to the other curve (cf. figure 4).

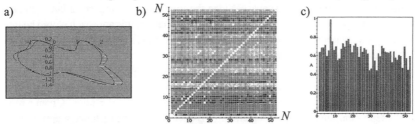

Fig. 4. Distance measures between curves in invariant reference frames. (a) Direct comparison between two curves that have been affinely transformed. (b) Distance matrix between any two curves in the database of 52 shapes (lighter gray levels correspond to small distances). (c) Distance between an affinely transformed version of the Levi's shape and all other shapes in the database.

The use of the closest distance provides this similarity measure with the useful property of being independent of curve parametrization. Moreover, even if the query curve is partially occluded, but corresponds to a subset of the target curve, the measure of distance will remain small. The overall similarity measure between two curves Γ_1 and Γ_2 with n and m invariant points respectively is the maximum of $mn/2$ curve matches in all combinations of their invariant reference frames i and j: $\sup_{ij}\{M_{ij}(\Gamma_1,\Gamma_2)\}$, where M_{ij} is the match using reference frames i, j. This requires n signatures of the first curve in its n frames to be compared to the m signatures of the second curve in its m frames, leading to $m + n$ transformations of original curves and $mn/2$ comparisons. The cost of each transformation and comparison is heavily dependent on the curve representation that will be adopted. For the case of NURBS used in the present paper, this cost is only linear in m and n .

In order to assess the discriminative power of the retrieval, experiments were performed with a database of $N = 50$ shapes, with the query shapes obtained after affine transformations of the original shapes. Figure 4.b describes the results of a first experiment, where a pairwise distance comparison was done between all shapes in the database according to the similarity measure defined above. All distances are depicted in the distance matrix. It can be seen that the values of diagonal elements are significantly higher that the others by at least one order of magnitude. This demonstrates strong discrimination capability as well as high precision of comparison. The asymmetry of the distance matrix originates from the use of the closest distance in shape comparison. Figure 4.c describes the results of a second experiment, where a shape already stored in the database was subject to an affine transformation (random rotations in $[0, \pi]$, random scaling in $[0.4, 1.3]$), and then used as a query. The original shape was still recovered as the most similar one, with a value of match 1.3 times higher than the other shapes.

3.2 Moment-Based Indexing

Given an input shape containing n invariant points, the search in a database of N shapes will require $O(n\bar{n}N)$ comparisons, where $\bar{n}$ is the average number of invariant points for each shape in the database. Since the time for the comparison between any two curves is approximately 0.2s on a Sparc 10 workstation, this approach would be unfeasible for very large databases. In order to speed-up of the search operation, an indexing mechanism is employed to reduce the subset of shapes to compare. As signatures are represented in invariant frames, all Euclidean measures performed in this frame are also invariant. For instance, first-order moments (which can easily be computed from the curves' control points) can be used as a first, rough shape description. Given a moment vector computed from the signature of a query shape, the distance measure with any other vector in the database can be obtained in about 0.01s. In order to reduce the overall complexity of the search, we thus propose to select the k nearest neighbours to the query vector, and then to compute a detailed measure of match only on the corresponding curves. An appropriate value of k must be estimated, ensuring with a certain probability that the target shape is among the k nearest neighbours to the query. The value of k can be estimated empirically by analysing the distribution of shape moments for a given database. Experiments with our database of 52 logo shapes show that noise, produced by viewpoint changes, entail variations in the vector of the first-order moments equivalent to 4.5% in orientation and 0.01% in magnitude. Using these values we can construct a ring-sector neighbourhood, which always guarantees the retrieval of the correct shape (cf. figure 5). For our database, this neighbourhood contains an average of $k = 7$ other vectors, which yields a total computing time of $52 \times 0.01s + 7 \times 0.2s = 1.92s$, compared with approximately $10s$ of the direct approach. This reduction becomes even more relevant, as the number of shapes in the database increases.

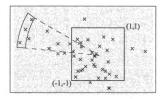

Fig. 5. Shape indexing by searching for the k-nearest neighbors in the moment vector space.

3.3 Experimental Results

To describe the behaviour of the system, we present the results of four queries, over the database of 52 trademark patterns. The first experiment, described in the top row of figure 6, shows the query image on the left, and the four most similar shapes retrieved from the database, in decreasing order of similarity. This shows that the target shape is correctly recognized, and that the other ones are indeed perceptually similar to the query. The second and third rows show two query images that have been subject to an affine transformation with respect to the stored images. Still, the results are exactly the same of the untransformed queries, confirming the viewpoint invariance capability of the proposed representation. Finally, the fourth row describes the results of a query image that does not exist in the database. In this case, images of the database are still ranked by similarity. In particular, the most similar one is selected due to the similarity between the query image and the "H" part of the HM logo.

Fig. 6. Experimental results. The left column contains four query images; the other images in the corresponding rows are the most similar ones retrieved from the database.

4. Conclusions

In this paper, we presented a method for representing shapes which enables viewpoint-independent content-based image retrieval. Shapes are first approximated using NURBS parametric curves, which present various advantages: they provide a compact representation, they enable very efficient geometric transformations, and they can be defined over a set of invariant points of the original shape. For each shape, a set of object-centered, invariant reference frames is then identified to represent the curve. These multiple reference frames are canonical, and thus provide two advantages: they enable curve representation by parts (which guarantees robustness to partial occlusion), and they enable comparisons between different shapes. A shape comparison technique, employing the Euclidean distance between two curves in the canonical reference frame has been proposed. In order to speed up the search process, a technique which allows the selection of a small number of likely candidates is proposed, using moment-based indexing. Experimental results using affine-transformed images over a database of 52 trademark shapes confirm the validity of the proposed approach.

5. References

[1]   F. S. Cohen, J.-Y. Wang, "Part I: Modeling image curves using invariant 3-D object curve models - a path to 3-D recognition and shape estimation from image contours", IEEE Trans. Patt. Anal. Mach. Intell., 1994, vol. 16, No. 1, p. 1-12.

[2]   M. Flickner, H. Sawhney, W. Niblack, J. Ashley, Q. Huang, B. Dom, M. Gorkani, J. Hafner, D. Lee, D. Petkovic, D. Steele, and P. Yanker (1995). Query by image and video content: the QBIC system. *IEEE Computer*, September, 23-32.

[3]   A. Goshtasby, "Design and Recovery of 2-D and 3-D shapes using rational gaussian curves and surfaces", Intern. J. Comput. Vis. 10:3, 1993, pp. 233-256.

[4]   K. Hirata and T. Kato, *Query by Visual Example: Content-Based Image Retrieval*. A. Pirotte, C. Delobel and Gottlob (Eds.), Proc. E. D. B. T.'92 Conf. on Advances in Database Technology. Lecture Notes in Computer Science Vol. 580, Springer-Verlag, 1994, 56-71.

[5]   C.E. Jacobs, A. Finkelstein, and D.H. Salesin, *Fast Multiresolution Image Querying*. Proc. SIGGRAPH 95, ACM, New York, 1995.

[6]   R. Milanese, D. Squire and T. Pun, *Correspondence analysis and hierarchical indexing for content-based image retrieval*. IEEE Intl. Conference on Image Processing, Lausanne, Switzerland, Sept 16-19, 1996.

[7]   T.Moons, E.J. Pauwels, L.J. Van Gool, A. Oosterlinck, "Foundations of semi-differential invariants", Intern. J. Comput. Vis. 14, 1995, p. 25-47.

[8]   J.L. Mundy and A. Zisserman (editors), "Geometric Invariance in Computer Vision", MIT Press, Cambridge Ma, 1992.

[9]   E.J. Pauwels, T.Moons, L.J. Van Gool, P. Kempenaers, A. Oosterlinck, "Recognition of planar shapes under affine distortion", Intern. J. Comput. Vis. 14, 1995, p. 49-65.

[10]   A. Pentland, R.W. Picard, and S. Sclaroff (1994). Photobook: tools for content-based manipulation of image databases. (Storage and Retrieval for Image and Video Databases II, San Jose, CA, USA, 7-8 Feb. 1994). *Proceedings of the SPIE - The International Society for Optical Engineering*, 2185, 34-47.

[11]   T. H. Reiss, "Recognizing planar objects using invariant image features", Lecture Notes in Computer Science, 676, 1993.

[12]   E. Rivlin, I. Weiss, "Local invariants for recognition", IEEE Trans. Patt. Anal. Mach. Intell., 1995, vol. 17, No. 3.

[13]   Rogers D.F., Adams J.A., "Mathematical elements for computer graphics",McGraw-Hill, New York, NY, 1990, p. 371-375.

[14]   S. Startchik, C. Rauber, T. Pun, "Recognition of planar objects over complex backgrounds using line invariants and relevance measures", Workshop on Geometric Moaeling & Invariants for Computer Vision, Xian, China , 1995, p. 301-307.

[15]   VIRAGE web site, http://www.virage.com.

[16]   A. Zissermann, D.A. Forsyth, J.L. Mundy, C.A. Rothwell, "Recognizing general curved objects efficiently", In [56], p. 228-251. [8]

Database Support for Image Retrieval Using Spatial-Color Features

Niels Nes, Carel van den Berg, Martin Kersten

University of Amsterdam
{niels,carel,mk}@wins.uva.nl

Abstract

Quality, efficiency, and scalability are the key issues in the design of image retrieval systems for large image databases. Although the quality of image retrieval
methods still depends strongly on the application domain, color-based retrieval
techniques have been shown to be competitive and generally applicable. In this
paper we describe several algorithms to improve the retrieval process by combining spatial information with color features. The algorithms are embedded in
an extensible database system, which provides for the efficiency and scalability
towards tens of thousand images required in practice.

1 Introduction

Quality, efficiency and scalability are key issues in the design of image retrieval
systems for large image databases. This is exemplified by the growth of multimedia information on the Web. The Web already provides access to collections
up to several thousands of images and a growth towards 1M images is foreseen.

It has been repeatedly shown that image retrieval techniques based on image understanding is very application dependent. A more generic and re-usable
technique is in high demand.

Retrieval methods based on color features are a promising track [5, 4] to
provide for the required functionality. However, the retrieval algorithms based
on color histograms largely ignore spatial information in the matching process.
At best a query can be specified in terms of color percentages or the user has
to outline objects as part of entering the image into the database. Then color
histograms for the (sub-) objects can be used in the retrieval process. In both
cases this leads to a high percentage of false hits.

In this paper we address the problem to find a best match for a complete
image using both color and spatial information. The input to the query engine
is a representative sample of the desired answer set. The system extracts color
and spatial information from this example and returns a list of matching images
sorted by similarity.

The approach taken is based on extensible database technology provided by
the Monet database system [2]. It enables us to include at the system level functionality to store and manipulate large numbers of images, to enhance the system

with image analysis modules, and to use a high-level query language to express the queries. In particular, we use a relational algebra query language featuring image analysis operations and a hierarchical indexing scheme is provided for spatial-color features.

In particular, the indexing scheme for the spatial-color features is based on a recursive splitting of the image. The information stored for an image will be called its *multi-level signature*, as it characterizes the image at various levels of detail.

The relational model enables us to express the image retrieval problem using the standard set-oriented relational operations like SELECT (σ) and INTERSECT ($\cap$). In [9] we have shown that this approach applied to a line-clustering in utility maps resulted in a factor of 100 performance improvement over the non-database solution.

The main component of the content-based query, i.e. which sub-images have the same color and spatial properties as the quety image *example*, can then be expressed as: $\sigma_{spatial(example)} spatial \cap \sigma_{color(example)} color$

Using a relational algebra language to express the image retrieval problem introduces flexibility and scalability in the number and size of the image database. The operations work on sets and are distributive over the set union operation. The effect is that, the operation can be performed in parallel by the underlying database management system.

The Monet database management system [2] has been extended with search accelerators for user-defined abstract data types to speed up the SELECT and JOIN operations over image features. Furthermore, the database management system can optimize these queries based on selectivity and the cost of the operations. The current experimentation platform supports both hashing and R-tree accelerators.

The search accelerators have been extended with a the multi-level signature built through a split and calculate algorithm. The image is split recursively into adjacent parts and an average color signature is calculated for each part. It has been shown in [12] that a quadratic form distance function on the average color provides a lower bound on the distance function on color histograms. In other words, the matching on average color will allow some false hits but no false dismissals. We will validate this result in our approach by comparing our method with signatures based directly on color histograms.

Two different algorithms for image splitting have been designed *quad-tree*, and *prime-factor*. The quad-tree algorithm builds the SPATIAL relation of the multi-level signature using a method much like the quad tree index structure in spatial information systems. Since the quad-tree rectangles usually do not agree with image object boundaries its accuracy is often poor. Better splitting methods commonly used in image analysis, like the triangulation algorithms, are too complex, too space consumptive and too computationally intensive to consider for the moment in a 1M image database. Therefore, we designed the *prime-factor* algorithm for spatial indexing. The prime-factor algorithm splits the original image in p^2 parts, where p is a prime factor, so that parts at all different levels overlap. Splitting occurs as long as the color signature differences encountered are beyond a given threshold. In other words the color signature is discriminating up to a-priori set limits. A low threshold leads to a deep indexing tree for cluttered images.

The remainder of this paper is organized as follows. Section 2 describes the approaches recently taken in literature to tackle this problem. In section 3 the Monet database system is introduced. Section 4 explains the data model for the different split- and calculate- algorithms. In Section 5 the prototype image retrieval system is explained and experimental results are given. Section 6 provides a summary and outlook of future research.

2   Related Research

Several image database retrieval projects are underway. A few snapshot descriptions are illustrative for the approaches taken.

The QBIC project [4] studies methods to query image databases based on the image content. The content features used include color distribution, texture, and position and shape of edges. Similarity is based on the Euclidean distance between two feature vectors. The use of color is limited to the global color histogram.

To improve efficiency, the search space is reduced using a lower bound metric on the color histogram distance. It is proven that the average color is a lower bound of the color histogram distance [12]. Therefore, using the average color does not result in missing actual hits, though extra false hits will be found.

The Photobook [11] system uses semantics preserving image compression, which reduces images to a small set of perceptually-significant coefficients. Using a training set of images, the "eigenimage" vectors are computed. These vectors are used to compress the image content information. The similarity between two images is computed using the distance in this compressed "eigenimage" space.

The approach taken by [5] is to build histograms of the local hue, the dominant hue edges and hue corners. The hue color component is chosen since it is invariant to surface specularities like shadow and highlights. The similarity measure used is the color histogram intersection [14], which is less variant to occlusion and less dependent on the view point. Histograms are invariant under a number of transformations.

The VISUALSeek image retrieval system [13] segments the image into objects which have equal binary color content. The spatial information about these objects is stored. Using both the spatial and color properties the user can query this database.

3   Architecture of Monet

Monet is a novel database kernel under development at the CWI and UvA since 1994. Its development is based on both our experience gained in building PRISMA, a full-fledged parallel main-memory RDBMS running on a 100-node multi-processor, and on current market trends in database server technology.

Developments in personal workstation hardware are at a high and continuing pace. Main memories of 128 MB are now affordable and custom CPUs currently can perform over 50 MIPS. They rely more and more on efficient use of registers and cache, to tackle the ever-increasing disparity[1] between processor power and main memory bus speed. These hardware trends pose new rules to computer software – and to database systems – as to what algorithms are efficient. Another trend has been the evolution of operating system functionality towards micro-kernels, i.e. those that make part of the Operating System functionality accessible to customized applications. Prominent research prototypes are Mach, Chorus and Amoeba, but also commercial systems like Silicon Graphics' Irix and Sun's Solaris increasingly provide hooks for better memory and process management.

Given this background, we applied the following ideas in the design of Monet:

- *binary relation model.* Monet vertically partitions all multi-attribute relation-ships in Binary Association Tables (BATs), consisting of [OID,attribute] pairs.
  This Decomposed Storage Model (DSM) [3] facilitates table evolution, since the attributes of a relation are not stored in one fixed-width relation.
- *perform all operations in main memory.* Monet makes aggressive use of main memory by assuming that the database hot-set fits into main memory. All its primitive database operations work on this assumption, no hybrid algorithms are used. For large databases, Monet relies on virtual memory by mapping large files into it. In this way, Monet avoids introducing code to 'improve' or 'replace' the operating system facilities for memory/buffer management. Instead, it gives advice to the lower level OS-primitives on the intended behavior[2] and lets the MMU do the job in hardware.
- *extensible algebra.* As has been shown in the Gral system [7], many-sorted algebras have many advantages in database extensibility. Their open nature allows for easy addition of new atomic types, functions on (sets of) those types. Also, an SQL query calculus-to-algebra transformation provides a systematic framework where query optimization and parallelization of even user-extended primitives becomes manageable. Monet's Interface Language (MIL) interpreted language with a C-like syntax, where sets are manipulated using a *BAT-algebra.*
  The MIL has a sister language called MEL (Monet Extension Language), which allows you to specify extension modules. These modules can contain specifications of new atomic types, new instance- or set-primitives and new search accelerators. Implementations have to be supplied in C/C++ compli-ant object code.
- coarse grained *shared-memory parallelism.* Parallelism is incorporated us-ing parallel blocks and parallel cursors (called "iterators") in the MIL. Un-like mainstream parallel database servers, like PRISMA [1] and Volcano [6],

---

[1] In recent years this disparity has been growing with 40% each year

[2] This functionality is achieved with the `mmap()`, `madvise()`,and `mlock()` Unix system calls.

Monet does not use tuple- or segment-pipelining. Instead, the algebraic operators are the units for parallel execution. Their result is completely materialized before being used in the next phase of the query plan. This approach benefits throughput at a slight expense of response time and memory resources.

4 Data Model for Image Database

In this we will explain the data model for the Monet Image Retrieval (**MIR**) system.

The *quad* and *prime* factor algorithms both split the image in equal sized blocks before the indexing features are calculated. The quad split algorithm recursively cuts the image into four parts. The prime factor algorithm cuts the original image into p^2 parts (p should be a prime factor).

The data produced in the splitting process is stored in BATs managed by Monet. This required extension of the system with an atomic type **Image**. Its implementation provides all the operational primitives to handle image processing in a structured way and orthogonal to the other data types.

The BATs needed for our retrieval system (MIR) are *MIR_source*, *MIR_color*, *MIR_spatial* and *MIR_image*. The *MIR_image* BAT contains an icon of the actual image data. The *MIR_source* BAT contains the relationship between sub-images and their original image.

The *MIR_color* BAT contains the color part of the signature. The color feature can be represented in several ways, e.g. as an average color, dominant color or color histogram. Another possibility is to use a color set representation, expressing the colors present in an image.

In our implementation we use the hue component of the HSV-color model[8], because it is the prime color component. Moreover, the hue is invariant to specularities and light reflections. Furthermore the hue closely resembles the human perception of related colors, which improves image retrieval from an ergonomic perspective.

The spatial component describes the spatial information obtained by the splitting process. A simple spatial representation is a rectangle or box. The scale of this rectangle is relative to a virtual bounding box. That way the description is invariant to the size and scale of the image.

Monet is also extended with search accelerators for the multi-level signature. There are search accelerators for both the color and spatial properties. The color property uses the Monet built-in hash and B-tree index structures. For the spatial property the R-tree index structure was chosen.

4.1 Stop Condition

Image splitting continues up to the point that further splitting does not produce significant new information about the spatial color distribution. This requires a flexible and user-controlled stop condition. For example, spitting should stop when one of the following conditions are met:

- Stop when the split level equals some predefined α.
- Stop when the average color of corresponding parts on level n and n+1 differs less than some β.
- Stop when there are less than γ colors remaining in a sub image.
- Stop when the image index entry occupies too much space.

The first is independent of the image content. The second condition is intended to signal smoothness, but it suffers from large outlayers. The last variant would be of use if the image contains a large number of small details with different color distributions. In the worst case the index becomes larger than the image itself. We chose the third option, since it is less sensitive to outlayers.

4.2   Querying the image database

The selection process is initiated when the user specifies a query image. This input to the query engine should be a representative sample of the desired answer set. The process will split the query image recursively and uses the signatures obtained to exploit the index. The spatial information is used to assure that candidate images in the database have the same spatial relationships amongst them as the query image.

Lets look at the selection process of quad split and calculate algorithm in detail. The user first supplies the query image, QI. The system will then calculate the average color and bounding box of the whole QI. From the image database the candidate (sub) images CIs, are selected based on an equal bounding box. From this set of candidate (sub) images those images are selected which have an average color within a given range from QIs average color. Using the source relation the original images belonging to the selected (sub) images are found.

QI is then split in 4 parts as described before. For all parts again the average color and bounding box are calculated. These are used to reduce the candidate image set. Again the (sub) images with equal bounding boxes are selected from the set of candidate images. Only those images which have for all parts about the same average color as QIs parts are selected. For each of the parts the process repeats.

The selection process continues until a small enough set is selected. The selected images are than ranked, based on a similarity measure which takes both spatial and color properties into account. The similarity measures known from literature, Histogram intersection[14] and Histogram distance [4] do not use spatial information, which makes them inappropriate.

So we use a similarity measure, which we call the *Multi-level signature simularity measure*. This measure is computed using the weighted distance between the signatures of the query image and the selected images on the split level on which the images where retrieved. The similarity measure requires a non-expensive computation. Formally, at each level λ the similarity between the QI and CI is calculated as

$$\delta(QI, CI) = 1 - \left(\sum_i \left(\frac{C_{QI_i} - C_{CI_i}}{cb}\right)^2\right)^{-n}$$

Where C_i is the average color of the sub image with i as its spatial representation. The n is the number of spatial descriptions at level λ. The function is normalized using the given color bound cb.

5 Prototype and Experiment

A prototype image retrieval system has been implemented. It uses the Monet database kernel and the image extension built. A graphical user interface is build using Tcl/Tk[10]. Queries are specified by selecting an example image form a set of randomly taken images from the image database. The result of this query are images ordered on their similarity measure.

The image database of this retrieval system is filled using the frames of multiple video sequences to test the similarity measure. It turns out that our approach returns all the consecutive fames of the same scene followed by other images that have a significant less similarity measure.

We performed experiments with different number of images in the database to show the scalability of the system. The results can be seen in Figure 1.

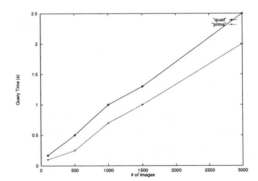

Fig. 1. The results of the Scalability Experiment.

The figure shows that the processing time is linearin the number of images. Detailed analysis of the quad and prime split algorithms make clear that the prime split algorithm has a better selectivity. The Images can be selected on a lower level and with less parts. So the calculations for the prime split are less which explains the slightly better performance.

6 Conclusions and Future work

In this paper we presented an image retrieval system based on spatial and color properties. The multi-level signature approach proofs to be scalable and flexible as the similarity measure can be defined at varias levels of detail. We described two splitting algorithms. Both result in high quality image retrieval from a large image database. The prime-factor split has a higher selectivity because of the overlapping sub-images.

In the future we will look at content based splitting methods to base the signature more on the object boundaries. Futhermore, we will extend the algorithms to allow search on objects contained in the image by building the multi-level signature for the image without the background or for a segmented image. Also the system will be extended with an interface for sketch based image retrieval.

References

1. P. M. G. Apers, C. A. van den Berg, J. Flokstra, P. W. P. J. Grefen, M. L. Kersten, and A. N. Wilschut. PRISMA/DB: A parallel main memory relational DBMS. *IEEE Trans. on Knowledge and Data Eng.*, 4(6):541, December 1992.
2. P. A. Boncz and M. L. Kersten. Monet: An impressionist sketch of an advanced database system. In *Proc. IEEE BIWIT workshop, San Sebastian (Spain)*, july 1995.
3. G. Copeland and S. Khoshafian. A decomposed storage model. In *Proc. ACM SIGMOD Conf.*, page 268, Austin, TX, May 1985.
4. C. Faloutsos, R. Barber, M. Flickner, J. Hafner, W. Niblack, D. Petkovic, and W. Equitz. Efficient and effective querying by image content. *Intelligent Information Systems 3*, pages 231–262, 1994.
5. T. Gevers and A. W. M. Smeulders. Evaluating color and shape invariant image indexing for consumer photography. In *Proc. of the First International Conference on Visual Information Systems*, pages 293–302, 1996.
6. G. Graefe. Encapsulation of parallelism in the volcano query processing system. In *19 ACM SIGMOD Conf. on the Management of Data, Atlantic City*, May 1990.
7. R. H. Güting. Gral: An extensible relational database system for geometric applications". In *Proceedings of the 15th Conference on Very Large Databases, Morgan Kaufman pubs. (Los Altos CA), Amsterdam*, August 1989.
8. J. Kender. Saturation, hue and normalized color: calculation digitization, and use. *Computer science technical report, Carnegie-Mellon University*, 1976.
9. N.J. Nes, M.L. Kersten, and A. Jonk. Database support for line clustering, June 1996. ASCI conferentie, Vosse-Meren.
10. J. K. Ousterhout. *Tcl and the Tk Toolkit*. Addison Wesley, Reading, 1994.
11. A. Pentland, R. W. Picard, and S. Sclaroff. Photobook: Content-based manipulation of image databases. In *SPIE Storage and Retrieval for Image and Video Databases II, No. 2185*, 1994.
12. H. S. Sawhney and J. L. Hafner. Efficient color histogram indexing for quadratic form distance functions. *IBM report*, 1993.
13. John R. Smith and Shih-Fu Chang. Tools and techniques for color image retrieval. In *SPIE Storage and Retrieval for Image and Video Databases IV, No 2670*, 1996.
14. Swain and Ballard. Color indexing. *International Journal of Computer Vision*, 7, 1991.

Domain Concept to Feature Mapping for a Plant Variety Image Database

Gerie van der Heijden[1] and Marcel Worring[2]

[1] CPRO-DLO
Wageningen, The Netherlands
g.w.a.m.vanderheijden@cpro.dlo.nl
[2] Department of Computer Science
University of Amsterdam, The Netherlands
worring@wins.uva.nl

Abstract. The most intuitive way of retrieving images is on the basis of domain concepts. However, this requires a mapping between the concepts and the content of the image. Such a mapping should be based on a proper visual guideline. We illustrate this with plant variety testing as an application for which such guidelines are available. The methods seem to have general applicability for every application domain where such guidelines can be made.

1 Introduction

Before we consider domain concept to feature mapping we first give an introduction to the application for which the techniques have been developed.

Plant Breeders' Rights (PBR) are a means to reward plant breeders for their breeding efforts. They are special type of patents granted for plant varieties. To obtain PBR, a variety has to fulfill a number of criteria, most importantly it should be distinct from established varieties worldwide. Hence, given new variety application a set of similar established varieties should be selected for comparison with the application. This selection is currently based on the expertise of the crop-expert, on variety descriptions containing the physiological and morphological properties of each variety, and on pictures stored in picture books. As an indication of the size of the latter: for the flower Gerbera, hundreds of different varieties exist and the picture book consists of three large volumes for the yellow flowers alone.

The selection of reference material based on morphological properties and pictures lends itself for an image database approach. Preferably this should be done using a generic content based image retrieval engine (CBRE) like QBIC [1]. A problem with such engines is that they are based on generic i.e. low level image and object features. These do often not correspond to the domain concepts of the user. To enhance acceptance, the system should interact with the user in terms of specific domain concepts. Since in plant variety testing these domain concepts have evolved over many years they can be expected to yield much higher accuracy in matching and retrieving images then generic features of image details. To bridge the gap between the two, the specific domain concepts should be mapped to generic features via possibly complicated classification algorithms.

The Chabot system [2] was one of the first CBRE providing the user with the possibility to define domain concepts. In their system this is limited to concepts describing the color distribution in the image which are then mapped to low level color histogram features. In this paper we follow a similar approach for morphological properties in the domain concepts of plant variety testing.

2   Domain concepts in plant variety testing

To standardize the plant variety testing the International Union for the Protection of New Varieties of Plants (UPOV) introduced a set of guidelines. These guidelines form the domain concepts in our application.

A guideline contains for each crop a set of about 40 (on average) variety characteristics related to morphological and physiological aspects. Over 90% of the characteristics are morphological i.e. relate to size, shape, and color of specific parts of the plants. They are defined on an ordinal or nominal scale. In figure 1-3 examples of guidelines for various characteristics are shown.

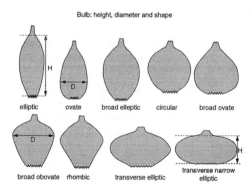

Fig. 1. *Bulb of onions: height (H), diameter (D) and shape. (after UPOV, 1976 [3]).*

3   Concept mapping

To allow the user to interact with the system in terms of domain concepts i.e. the guideline, requires that each characteristic is mapped to a (set of) generic feature(s). The possible outcomes of the features have to be mapped to the ordinal or nominal scale of the characteristic.

Seed: shape of median longitudinal section

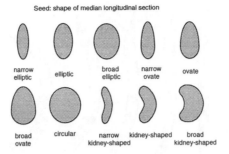

Fig. 2. *Seed of French bean: shape of the median longitudinal section at dry stage. (after UPOV, 1982 [4]).*

Since a characteristic may be defined for a specific subpart of the image object, the object first has to be decomposed into its constituent parts. As this is steered by the domain concept, each of the derived parts can automatically be given a semantic label (bulb, beak, pod, leaves etc.).

In practice, for each incoming image, the relevant domain concept has to selected and the following processing steps are performed to instantiate the domain concepts with the proper values:

1. segment the object from the background
2. decompose the object into its constituent parts
3. measure features for each part
4. classify the variety into the ordinal or nominal class using a set of one or more generic features

The different steps will be explained in the following sections and are illustrated in figure 4.

3.1 Segmentation

A proper segmentation of the object is very important and should preferably be done by controlling the circumstances under which the image acquisition takes place. As in our application the image recording is fully controlled, a simple automatic thresholding algorithm suffices.

3.2 Object decomposition

Decomposition of the object is facilitated by a good description of the object. For symmetrical natural objects, one useful description is based on its axis of symmetry.

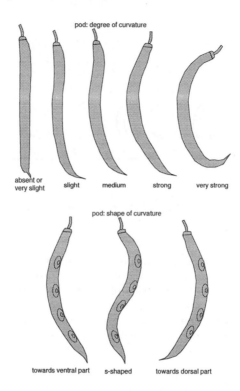

Fig. 3. *Pod of French bean: degree and shape of curvature. (after UPOV, 1982 [4]).*

For objects with an approximately straight symmetry axis the easiest way to find the axis is by aligning the objects during recording in such a way that a Cartesian axis of the image can be used as symmetry axis. Another approach is to use one of the axes of the best fitting ellipse. For curved objects the symmetry axis often coincides with the medial axis or skeleton of the binary object. Note that in this case, the symmetry axis is also curved.

By storing the width for each point of the symmetry-axis, a one-dimensional description of the object is obtained. If the symmetry axis is based on the distance transform, the distance values on the axis provide direct estimates for the local width.

Inflection points of the width distribution are often the transition points between specific parts of the object. They can be found as the local extrema of the first order derivative of the width function which can be derived by convolution with a differentiated Gaussian kernel.

Another useful technique to decompose objects is by using dominant contour

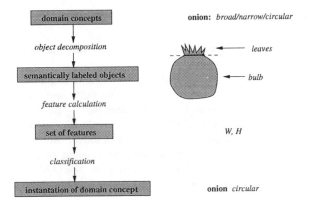

Fig. 4. *Overview of the different steps required for the instantiation of a domain concept by mapping the concept to generic features.*

points defined as local extrema of the curvature function of the contour.

3.3   Feature measurement

For each of the semantically labeled subparts found in the previous step generic size and shape features can be measured.

Common size features derived from the contour are area and perimeter, Feret-diameters (especially the height and width of the bounding box) and the length, width and area of the Minimum Area Enclosing Rectangle (MER). Size features based on the axis of symmetry are for example the length of the axis, and the maximum or average width along the axis. An overview of these and other size features is given in [6].

Many useful global shape features are based on ratios of the above derived size features e.g. the shapefactor defined as the ratio of area and perimeter squared, or the length/width ratio. Another shape feature is the ratio of the area of the object, and the area of its convex hull. This so called convex hull area deficiency is 1 for convex objects and between 0 and 1 for concave objects.

3.4   Classification

The classification of the objects on the basis of the derived features is basically a statistical problem and is performed in a supervised way by having domain experts label the different images and use these to optimize the division of the possible feature outcomes into the proper classes.

Often several different generic features can be used as suitable estimators for a characteristic. The best choice has to be made based on the classification results. For ordinal characteristics this can furthermore be tested by studying the correlation between manually derived and computed measures.

4   Results

Now we will describe some examples of the concept mapping for the previously introduced example guidelines.

Three characteristics for the bulb of onion are shown in figure 1. Two are size characteristics namely height and diameter of the bulb, and one is the shape of the bulb. The object is composed of leaves and bulb. The decomposition was done using the inflection point of the width distribution along the symmetry axis which is positioned during recording. The diameter and height of the bulb were calculated as the generic features width and height of the bounding box. The shape of the bulb was derived by combining the height/diameter ratio with the relative position of maximum width along the height-axis of the bulb. This is shown in figure 5.

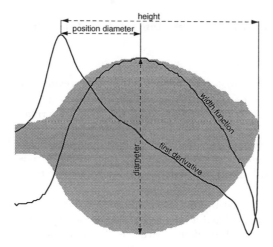

Fig. 5. *The width of the bulb $f(i)$ and its first order Gaussian smoothed derivative are shown as overlay over a bulb. From these functions, the features height, diameter and position of the diameter are extracted.*

Another example is the shape of a seed of French Bean (median longitudinal section), where the different classes as described in the UPOV-guideline are shown in figure 2. For these type of objects no decomposition is required. The classes of the shape of seeds of French bean can be derived from the combination of the following three generic features:

1. convex hull area deficiency, to assess the kidney-shape of a bean,

2. the ratio of the length and width or the MER to assess the broadness of the bean

3. the position of the largest diameter along the length axis of the MER to assess the ovateness of the bean.

For French bean, 17 characteristics are defined for the pod. These include the length of the pod, the median width of the pod, the size of the beak (tip) of the pod, the degree of curvature of the pod and the shape of curvature (figure 3). Note that this is another example of a misfit between domain concepts and generic features as curvature here relates to the global shape of the object and not to its contour.

A bean is composed of pod, beak, and stalk. Decomposition was based on the inflection points in the distance skeleton.

Length of the pod was measured as the length of the medial axis (skeleton) of the pod. The median width was calculated as the ratio of area and length of the pod. For the degree of curvature a specific feature was needed. It was measured by connecting the end points of the skeleton by a straight line and calculating the distance between skeleton and line halfway the skeleton. The direction of the vector connecting line and skeleton combined with the number of cross points gave the shape of curvature.

The mapping has been statistically validated for size characteristics of onion and French bean. It was shown that the correlation between manually and computer assessed features is very high [5].

5 Conclusions

For a good interaction between user and database system, we believe that it is necessary that the system can communicate in the domain concepts of the user, in our case in plant variety concepts. Furthermore, domain concepts have evolved over many years and have proven their success in determining differences between varieties. To be able to communicate in terms of domain concepts, mapping between the domain concept and low level image features is required. We have shown several mappings using a rather general approach, consisting of four steps. The first two steps are the segmentation of the image into objects and the decomposition of the objects into semantically meaningful parts. The next step is the measurements of generic features and the final step involves the classification of the outcome-space into the scale of the domain concept.

The examples given have proven to be in accordance with the domain concepts for plant variety testing. The domain concepts are however extensive and many more mappings have to be defined. We believe that most of the mappings for size and shape characteristics can be done using the algorithms for decomposition and feature measurement already available. A major step is the extension with the mapping of color and texture characteristics for which at the moment mappings are studied.

Although the mappings are illustrated with plant variety testing as an application we feel it has more general applicability. Consider for example the fish database used as illustration of the capabilities of QBIC [1]. Retrieval quality can be expected to be much better if the fishes are first decomposed in body, fins, and tails before shape computation is performed. A query for a shark could than be : "find a fish with a slim body and a large fin". Of course it does require to establish domain concepts related to fishes.

As concerns the database it should be noted that after computation of features and performing the required mappings the results can be stored in any relational database with standard SQL interface. However, full integration of the decomposition and feature computation with content based retrieval requires a more elaborate engine. Due to the hierarchy in the guidelines and hence in the decomposition and feature computation algorithms, ranging from generic to very specific an object oriented approach seems the obvious choice. Our next step is therefore to use the object-relational Content Based Retrieval Engine Horus [7] as the basis for the plant variety testing database system.

References

1. M. Flickner, H. Sawhney, W. Niblack, J. Ashley, Q. Huang, B. Dom M. Gorkani, J. Hafner, D. Lee, D. Petkovic, D. Steele, and P. Yanker. Query by image and video content: the QBIC system. *IEEE Computer*, 28(9), 1995.
2. V.E. Ogle and M. Stonebraker. Chabot: retrieval from a relational database of images. *IEEE Computer*, 28(9), 1995.
3. UPOV. Tg/46/3, guidelines for the conduct of tests for distinctness, homogeneity and stability. onion (allium cepa l.), 1976.
4. UPOV. Tg/12/4, guidelines for the conduct of tests for distinctness, homogeneity and stability. french bean (phaseolus vulgaris l.), 1982.
5. G.W.A.M. van der Heijden. *Applications of image analysis in plant variety testing.* PhD thesis, Technical University Delft, 1995.
6. G.W.A.M. van der Heijden and A.M. Vossepoel. On defining length and width for botanical object discrimination. In *Aspects of visual form processing, Capri*, pages 562–573, 1994.
7. C. v.d. Berg, R. van den Boomgaard, M. Worring, D.C. Koelma, and A.W.M. Smeulders. Horus: towards integration of image processing and databases. In *Proceedings of the First international workshop on image databases and multimedia search, Amsterdam*, 1996.

Horus: Integration of Image Processing and Database Paradigms

Carel van den Berg
Rein van den Boomgaard
Marcel Worring
Dennis Koelma
Arnold Smeulders

ISIS,University of Amsterdam, Amsterdam, The Netherlands

Abstract. This article describes a software architecture for building image retrieval applications. Its primary objective is to facilitate application development through the use of detector based image processing and integration of image processing and database technology.

An application is built by combining detector objects from a standard set of low-level detectors, which use the database for efficient storage and retrieval of the images and the spatial and photometric properties of elements detected in the image.

Furthermore, the use of a database facilitates data sharing and data reuse by different applications.

1 Introduction

The amount of pictorial information in business applications has increased considerably in the last decade. Effective use and reuse of information requires content-based methods for storage and retrieval. Ideally, similar to text retrieval systems, an image information system can retrieve visual information that "looks like" a given picture or that satisfies a certain semantic or symbolic description.

Advances in image processing technology show that content based retrieval on exterior features becomes feasible. A large collection of low-level image processing algorithms are available to extract features like color histograms, texture information and edges. Whereas in the past the emphasis was on computable features, nowadays the attention shifts towards features which portray some invariant property of the object making the information more valuable. In addition, application specific algorithms use domain knowledge and a combination of these features to arrive at a similarity measure.

From the database point of view, relational database systems provide an efficient and scalable solution to the management of textual information. However, they can not be used to build efficient image information systems, because they can not handle the complex data structures used in image processing applications and therefore typically store images as uninterpreted byte sequences.

It is our opinion that content-based image retrieval requires an integration of image processing technology and data base technology. Several projects already use a combination of image processing and database technology [6]. We take the level of integration a step further through standardization of the data structures produced by the image processing routines for feature data and storing them in the database so that applications can reuse the feature data derived by other applications.

This article is organized as follows. First we present an evolutionary view of image processing applications. Then we will introduce the detector model, which represents the image processing component in the Horus architecture. Following, we give a short description of the database component. Then, we show how these two components are integrated in the Horus architecture, providing a framework for image processing application development in Horus.

2   The evolution path

The software architecture for image processing applications in general and image retrieval systems in particular has changed from the early stand-alone applications, lacking portability and did not use standard data structures to the future systems based on the elaborate code base for image processing and vision applications, i.e. IUE [4].

In the following overview (See Figure 1) we distinguish four generations in this evolution path in software development to motivate the Horus architecture. The distinction between each generation is based on reuse of data, data structure, and software.

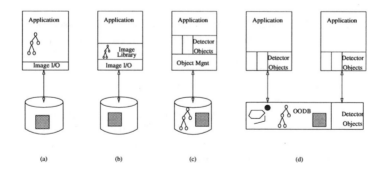

Fig. 1. The four generations in image processing application development

(a) The first image processing applications were developed independently. For each prototype the (low-level) data structures were designed and implemented specifically for that application and are part of the application code. The algorithms, using these data structures are consequently not portable and therefore implemented repeatedly for each new application.

Finally, the only data that is shared between applications are images, provided that the same file format and compression technique is used.

(b) Image processing libraries such as provided by Khoros, ScilImage and VisiLog [3] alleviated the portability problem. The library offers support for storage and retrieval of images in (standard) file formats and offers a large collection of functions to manipulate images.

However, a file format for representing feature data and spatial data is not available. The data stored by an image database application can not be shared or reused by another application.

(c) The portability issue is relieved by the development of an extensive object oriented library which provides an extensive library of standard data structures and algorithms for image processing and understanding (IUE [4]).

The use of this library will enable researchers to exchange algorithms and increases the portability to different platforms.

In this framework the input and output data structures of algorithms and operations are made explicit, so that the algorithms can be grouped into *detector* modules. The developer can now design a new algorithm using more abstract, application oriented, modules. Algorithms and data structures can be reused. The need for such an abstraction is also recognized by IUE. The IUE sensor object allows the design of such abstract detectors.

However, because the meta-data is not stored on the file system and access methods are still implemented in the application, data sharing and reuse is practically infeasible.

(d) Assuming that the image data will be used for more applications, it becomes necessary to maintain some of the derived features in the database for future use, because collecting this data and building an index structure for a large image database is a time consuming operation. Therefore, in this approach the extracted feature data and index structures are stored and maintained by the database. The database schema contains a description of the images, the derived features and available indices.

The database is manipulated by detector modules that store, retrieve and search for spatial objects and features of images. The database system has a basic knowledge about the primitive data types such as points, lines, polygons, edges and color histograms, so that high level detectors can be formulated in terms of predicates on these objects and their spatial relationships. This architecture allows reuse of data, software and data structure through the use of a database, a limited set of data structures and a modular design of the software.

The Horus system is an example of a software architecture from the last category software architecture. It goes beyond the IUE standard. The requirement to handle complex data structures such as spatial objects, edges or histograms has lead to the use of an Object Oriented Database System. Detectors are defined by their input and output data types and are separated from the objects themselves to facilitate extensibility and software reuse.

Figure 2 illustrates the spatial object hierarchy. Spatial objects are used to store the geometrical properties of the items detected in an image. As we intend to offer fast access to the data through the use of an index on the spatial representation, we require that each spatial object can produce a polygonal approximation of itself. This enables the database management system to maintain an index on for instance `spline2D` objects.

Next to the spatial representation information on the photometric properties are maintained for each detected item. This can range from average color and color histograms to other types of measured data.

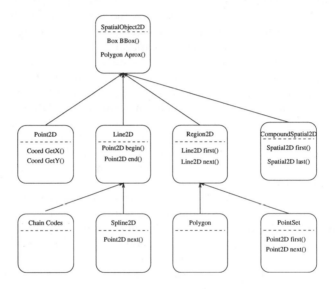

Fig. 2. The Spatial Object hierarchy

In the following two sections we discuss the detector model and the integration layer in more detail.

3   The detector model

3.1   Motivation

We like to motivate the detector model by comparing image analysis to the parsing of natural language. Our ideal is to find an image alphabet that can form the basis for all image analysis tasks. Low-level detectors produce elements from this alphabet, such as corners or edges. Medium-level detectors use rules to detect words composed of the letters from the image alphabet. An example could be an arrow head, composed of edges and corners in a certain spatial relationship. This interpretation of the image data is still only syntactical. High-level detectors use semantics from the application domain to further classify the words to arrive at information.

As an example, for the stamp collector willing to classify unknown stamps, a meticulous search through a pile of catalogs is the common possibility. Instead, an image database could provide the means to compare an unknown stamp with all stamps stored in the database, thereby classifying the unknown stamp.

The standard approach to reduce the computational complexity of retrieval by image contents is not only to store the image itself but also a pre-computed image signature facilitating faster comparison. In order to lower the linear order complexity in the number of stored images the signature should also be such that indexing techniques can be applied.

Given this approach the search for the stamp similar to the unknown one looks something like: first compute the signature of the unknown stamp image and retrieve the image from the database whose signature most closely resembles the given one.

3.2 Statement of the problem

The problem thus boils down to the choice of an image signature, allowing efficient querying of the image database. Unfortunately image processing theory is not yet capable of providing an all powerful signature independent of the type of query (find a "near" copy of this image, or find an image containing a specific 3D object, or find the image of a car with a sunset as background in a tropical environment) and independent of the specific application domain (finding near copies in a database of stamps is likely to be based on different techniques than finding near copies in a database of medical images, the most obvious reason is that stamps are likely to be color image whereas medical images are most often black-and-white).

To facilitate the definition and development of image signatures for a specific application domain and specific queries, the application programmer is to be equipped with the tools to address the information contents of the images on a high level without the need to get into the pixel details. Traditional image processing development tools like ScilImage, Khoros and Visilog [3] are focussed on the low and intermediate level image processing tasks. The image-to-image type of processing is paramount in these systems.

The application programmer accesses the information contents of the image in terms of the collection of image detectors that are defined in Horus. Figure 3 shows the software architecture used for retrieving stamps form the stamp image database. The image processing methodology itself is a near copy of the methodology developed by Gevers [2] to query a database of color images of 3D objects. The attractivity of the methods laid out in the reference is that the features have viewpoint and illumination invariances, of great importance in the recognition of industrial objects.

A simple signature is the histogram of abrupt color changes (i.e. color edges). For the stamps database this will probably eliminate almost all stamps from the collection as possible near copies. Instead of working with the color image itself (i.e. the three components: red, green and blue) only the HUE component (representing the color itself and not the intensity and saturation of the color) is used. An adopted version of the Canny edge detector is used to find the most prominent edge points in the image. This detector thus results in a list of edge points with associated edge direction. Then the mean hue values (h_1 and h_2) on both sides of the edge are measured. These hue values, for all prominent edge points, are collected in a two dimensional histogram $H(h_1, h_2)$ representing the percentage of edge points with color changing from h_1 to h_2.

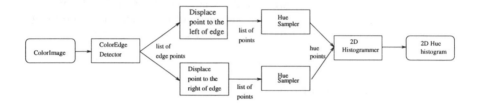

Fig. 3. Calculating the Color Signature

In order to ensure re-usability of software components the development of image signatures is based on a common model. Within this model an image feature is defined as the combination of a spatial primitive (a point, line, curve, region etc.) as found in an image and the associated photometric properties (like the principal color within a region) and/or the associated shape properties. For the stamp database the spatial primitives are simple (directed) points and the associated photometric properties are the two colors on both sides of the edge.

The data produced by each detector can be stored in the database for future use. For another application one might be interested in sampling light intensity instead of hue. The database supports this kind of reuse.

4   The Horus OODB

The Object Oriented Database in Horus is based on Monet [1], a small and powerful database micro kernel, which offers a set of algebraic operations that can be extended to offer efficient kernel support for special purpose data types like images and histogram data.

In the Horus architecture the Monet database is extended with data types for the representation of spatial objects and photometric properties. Operations and indexing on these types is supported. For instance, operations for comparing color histograms and intersecting line objects are built-in.

The Monet database provides persistency, concurrent access to its data and a small API to build client-server applications. Through this interface (different) applications can share and query the image data on their features, spatial - and photometric properties.

All the operations can be executed by the database server. The advantage of this approach is that the database server can reduce the amount of information returned to the client and reduce the I/O cost. Furthermore, it can use efficient set-oriented operations. In an early experiment, this approach applied to a line clustering problem used in automatic map recognition showed a performance increase by a factor of 100 [5] over a standard implementation where the derived data was stored in memory and the program used pointer traversing and indexes to solve the problem.

5   The integration layer

From a system developers point of view an application consists of three software layers: application specific code, a set of standard detector objects and an object-oriented database for storing the spatial data and features extracted from the image data.

Integration is based on the use of a common data model and control mechanism. Because of the complexity of the data structures, multi-dimensional data is not uncommon, we have opted for an object oriented data model.

From a system integration point of view its is advisable to provide interfaces to more application languages. For instance, the user interface could be programmed in Java, while the detector modules are implemented in C++. Therefore, we choose an language independent specification language, based on the OODB standard ODMG as a common data model. A schematic overview of the system architecture can be found in Figure 4.

The control mechanism is based on remote procedure calls (RPC) and the client-server model. The client is the application program, which initiates all actions. The server is composed of the detector modules and the OODB.

In the ODMG standard objects (data structures and operations) are defined in an application language independent specification language called ODL. From this specification the schema, storage structures and access methods for the database are derived. Furthermore, compilers are provided that can generate stub objects which include the access methods and operations for specific application languages. Currently, language bindings for C++, C and Java are implemented. This approach allows us to build a distributed application that can transparently share and access the database objects between for instance a graphical user interface implemented in Java and the detector objects implemented in C++.

The run-time system provided by the OODB implements the location transparency and ensures the consistency and persistence of the database objects. For

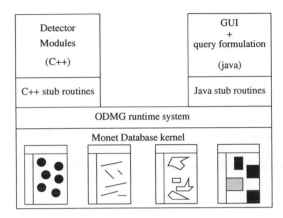

Fig. 4. The Horus system architecture

efficiency, the run time system can decide whether the objects are copied to the application process or whether the operation is executed remotely.

In principle all the operations defined in the ODL specification can also be executed by the database server. The advantage of this approach is that the database server can optimize the operations using bulk operations.

Finally, the ODMG standard provides OQL, a declarative query language. Because all the operations defined for the basic objects can be used in a query predicate, part of the image matching can be expressed in OQL.

6   Conclusion

The Horus architecture distinguishes itself from other image application architectures in that it offers a fully integrated system providing both database functionality and image analysis support.

The basis for application development is formed by the detector model. Low-level and medium level detectors aim to be application independent and will be standardized as much as possible to provide a solid basis for application development.

The integration of database and detector objects is based on the object-oriented model and includes both the data structure and operations. This makes it possible to implement the high level detectors in terms of operations on the spatial - and feature data stored in the database. In fact it is possible to express semantic constraints from the application domain into queries on the database, thereby exploiting the access methods and optimization techniques provided by the OODB for spatial and multi-dimensional data.

Currently, the ODMG interface is implemented and the database is extended with a few image types, spatial data structures like polygon, point and line, and histograms. Furthermore, we are working on an example application to prove the validity of this approach.

References

1. C.A. van den Berg and A. van der Hoeven. Monet meets 007. In *Object-Oriented Database Systems Symposium*, july 1996.
2. T. Gevers and A.W.M. Smeulders. Color and shape invariant image indexing of consumer photography. In *Proceedings of Visual96, Melbourne*, 1996.
3. Special issue on image databases. *IEEE computer*, 28(9), 1995.
4. J.L. Mundy. The image understanding environment program. *IEEE EXPERT*, 10(6):64–73, December 1995.
5. N Nes, M.L. Kersten, and A Jonk. Database support for line clustering, June 1996. ASCI conferentie, Vosse-Meren.
6. V.E. Ogle and M. Stonebraker. Chabot: retrieval from a relational database of images. *IEEE Computer*, 28(9), 1995.